Mixing
Memory
& Desire

Why Literature Can't
Forget the Great War

Brian Kennedy, PhD

FOLK
LORE
PUBLISHING

The Publisher: Folklore Publishing
Website: www.folklorepublishing.com

Library and Archives Canada Cataloguing in Publication

Kennedy, Brian, 1962–, author
Mixing memory & desire : why literature can't forget the Great War
/ Brian Kennedy, PhD.

Includes bibliographical references.
Issued in print and electronic formats.
ISBN 978-1-926677-26-2 (softcover).—ISBN 978-1-926677-28-6 (EPUB)

1. English fiction—21st century—History and criticism. 2. Canadian fiction (English)—21st century—History and criticism. 3. World War, 1914–1918—Literature and the war. 4. War in literature. I. Title.

PR890.W65K46 2017   823'.92093581   C2017-903065-5
                                                  C2017-903066-3

Project Director: Faye Boer
Project Editor: Dr. Robert Oventile
Cover Image: Havana1234/Thinkstock
Photos: Gabriela Moya Huerta

We acknowledge the financial support of the Government of Canada.

Funded by the Government of Canada
Financé par le gouvernement du Canada | Canadä

Produced with the assistance of the Government of
Alberta, Alberta Media Fund.

Alberta
Government

PC: 32

Contents

For my grandfather,

A. Philip Kennedy (1896–1967),

a soldier of the Great War

Acknowledgments

This book is the product of many years' research and writing. All through the process, I have had the encouragement of my great love, Gabriela Moya, who has sacrificed as much as I have in completing this project. My promise to her is simple: with this done, I will return to living in the present.

I also owe thanks to many friends and colleagues. My academic interest in the Great War was sparked by conversations I had with Dr. Kathleen Green. Dr. Robert Oventile was key to my getting this manuscript into publishable condition. In addition, he gave a good deal of his time performing committee work that should have been mine so that I could have time to do the research for this book. My dean, Amy Ulmer, has encouraged me as I have focused my research on the Great War and integrated many of the books I've studied into my courses. Colleagues like Dr. Martha Bonilla, Professor Beverly Tate, Dr. Michelle Banks, Dr. Jill O'Hora, and Dr. Derek Milne have pushed and prodded me as I have wound my way toward the finish line of this project.

My dad has always been my biggest cheerleader, and he has kept tabs on my work on this book all along and has bought me many books that have helped in my research.

Pasadena City College has been gracious in granting me regular sabbaticals, and I hope that the completion of this book repays them by enhancing the reputation of our academic programs.

Finally I must thank my students, who have embraced study of the war just as I have. Each one has been an amazing inspiration!

Introduction

Mixing Memory and Desire:
The anxiety of remembering
what can't be recalled

By the late 1930s, Europe was replete with memorials to fallen Great War soldiers. There were plaques in almost every church in England, as well as the rest of the UK and in much of the Commonwealth. Most towns had a physical memorial of one of two types: a building, such as a town hall which could be used for the public good, or a monument, whether that be statuary or some version of a cenotaph. And the grand monuments—the Menin Gate, Thiepval Monument, and their like—were capped off by the unveiling of the Vimy Memorial in 1936. The north of France and Flanders were covered with beautifully designed and tended graveyards holding the bodies of hundreds of thousands of soldiers. Looking back two decades from the point of view of 1939, one might reasonably say that the work of commemoration that started with the Cenotaph in Whitehall was finished.

But in 1939, the possibility of a second world war consumed Western Europe, and when World War II became an actuality, any thoughts of the glorious dead of the prior conflict were put on hold. Six years of fighting, a time-and-a-half the length of the First World War, and several years of deprivation to follow, further distanced the dead of the Great War from the public imagination.

By the 1960s, when most of the combatants who survived the Great War were retired, and many were dying, even the grand public ceremony of Armistice Day had been transformed into Remembrance Sunday, and that was losing its teeth. Peter Parker traces the change in focus that this commemorative day was undergoing in the shadow of the nuclear threat of that decade, saying that by this time, people were questioning whether the day should be observed at all (cf. 153, 157, 163). The sacredness of "The Silence" was under siege as early as the 1930s, as "by 1938, 20 percent of the population no longer observed the two minutes' silence but simply carried on with work" (129).

So one might say that, as the 1970s rolled around and the Great War became an event as far in the past as World War II

Menin Gate Memorial to the Missing, Ypres

is in our day, the Great War was well and truly beyond commemoration, having become a fragment of the past. Further,
every day that passed took more people with firsthand memories of its existence to the grave themselves.

What replaced this oral testimony is what Randall
Stevenson, following Samuel Hynes' diagnosis, calls "a settled
set of assumptions about 'what the war was about and what it
meant,'" an agreed-upon narrative constituting "an imaginative or simplified version of the war," which might be summarized as "envisaging a generation of idealistic young men
disillusioned and betrayed by their elders—by stupid generals,
cynical politicians, and profiteering businessmen, who
ensured they were slaughtered needlessly, in vast numbers, for
no valid purpose" (195). But this version of "collective narrative" has been challenged even as it has persisted (Hynes, qtd.
in Stevenson 195).

Since the mid-1970s, fiction concerning the Great War has
exploded, with books of all types—from popular fiction to literary, serials to children's stories—focusing on the events of
1914–18 and their aftermath. This fiction has used a set
of familiar tropes, but it has gone well past what the texts of
an earlier generation did, delving into new subject areas and
taking on new forms. The irony, of course, is that any new
work centered on World War I now is received into a context
devoid of witnesses to the war. Memory thus takes on a curious quality in that it cannot be anything but invented from
traces of the past.

In the 1920s, it is commonly said, there was so much
mourning done, and so much focus on commemoration, that
there was no time, nor appetite, for fiction or memoir about
the war, though writers were not entirely silent. Monumental
works such as Ford Madox Ford's *Parade's End* tetralogy came

out during this time, not to mention other, less literary, novels. Yet as Jonathan Vance explains, the "conventional wisdom" says that 1920s were "a decade of reflection" after which followed "what came to be known collectively as the war book boom" that began in 1928 with the publication of "ten war novels…in Britain and dozens elsewhere" (186).[1] The late 1920s and 1930s brought about a critical viewpoint in such enduring texts as Robert Graves' *Goodbye to All That* and Erich Maria Remarque's *All Quiet on the Western Front*, both of which debuted in 1929. One critic says of Remarque's work that with its commercial success, the "impulse to commemorate transformed memory [memory rendered aesthetic] into the form of war memoirs and novels became ubiquitous" (Wurtz 212). The flood of publication that followed was interrupted only by the paper rationing and consequent publication restrictions in effect during the second world war.

One explanation for the delay, which saw relatively little published until late in the 1920s, was offered by Vera Brittain in a piece originally published in 1968: "The significance of these events did not become clear until those who had suffered them began to write about them—which meant that they had time to think about them. In some cases, as in my own, the thinking process lasted for years before it was decanted into words" (204). How tempting it would be to say that this decanting process has continued into the present, since there has been a spate of novels about the Great War published in the past few decades. Any such claim, however, would be negated by the fact that the present crop of writers has no direct access to memory, because the original experiences are not theirs (except as collective cultural memory, an argument which will shortly follow here).

---

1 Vance calls the point into question, at least as far as war protest literature is concerned (186).

Yet one might say that for each succeeding generation, a renewed significance is established as they write about these same events, spurred on by an impulse not to forget. It is not enough, in this equation, to assume that readers will consume what others, prior, have written. The present generation must itself write, or the events will become lost. That is not to say that they will be forgotten entirely, but lost in the sense that they are no longer tangible—firsthand in the sense not that the writers write about their own experiences, for none now can do that about World War I, but firsthand in that their stories are new to them and to their audience.

Odd, then, that a survey of British and English-language fiction from the 1950s through the 1970s yields comparatively few fictional titles devoted to the Great War, with some notable exceptions such as Irish writer Iris Murdoch's 1965 *The Red and the Green*.[2] Though there was a small boom in 1964, surrounding the 50th anniversary of the war's outbreak, a good deal of that, as Randall Stevenson discusses, was in poetry and memoir rather than fiction (194). It was into this cultural moment, that is to say, right about the time that the Great War seemed to be fading irretrievably into the past, that Paul Fussell inserted his seminal book about the war and its influence on the modern consciousness, *The Great War and Modern Memory* (1975). He asserts that "the dynamics and iconography of the Great War have proved crucial political, rhetorical, and artistic determinants on subsequent life" (xv). His study uses literature produced about the war to categorize the many ways in which the war shaped the modern mind, from its tropes of violence to its tendency to see the world as

---

2 Note that while some American fiction of this period concerns itself with the Great War, my interests exclude U.S.-based writers. My concern is with the cultural memory of the war in the constellation of countries in Britain's orbit at the time of the conflict, primarily England, Ireland, Canada, New Zealand, and Australia. In the U.S., both the Civil War and World War II are much more front-of-mind in the figuration of cultural identity.

a series of binaries. The irony about this book, which leans so heavily on diagnosing irony in others, is that, as it turned out, Fussell was not describing a phenomenon, literary treatments of the war, that had passed, but one that was about to be renewed. Note in this regard Neta Gordon's comment while discussing critics' take on Timothy Findley's *The Wars* (1977), which I figure as the start of this recent phenomenon of fiction about the Great War: "Findley's novel represents a mature stage of Canadian First World War writing and not just because it was, at the time, one of the only contemporary works to take up the subject" (86).

Forty years later, Fussell's study is still read, having been issued in a commemorative anniversary edition in 2000 and with an illustrated version coming out in 2009. What he could not know, however, was that fiction centered on the Great War was not at an end as he wrote. In fact, as time went on, its production would increase, taking on new forms for a new generation, one, ironically enough, which was living in a time after direct memory of the war was possible. The uptick in interest, one must note, came alive mostly in schools, but not where one might first assume it to have, in the history department. Citing Gary Sheffield, author of the 2002 volume, *Forgotten Victory: The First World War, Myths and Realities*, Stevenson says, "[I]t has generally been 'teachers of English, not history, who have had the greatest impact on the shaping of views on the First World War'" (195). My argument in what follows will be that the literary production reflecting this interest does more than preserve memory. It signals a cultural need to mourn that has not been satisfied. This is especially interesting as a feature of the past ten years (approximately), when the remaining combatants—those with firsthand memory—have died.

Why is the common cultural heritage of the British constellation of nations suffused with the need to remember this war? What fictional forms does that memory take now, given that all of those with firsthand memories are gone, and what does that tell us about the construction of cultural memory? These are the questions informing *Mixing Memory and Desire: Why Literature Can't Forget the Great War*. Focusing particularly on fiction of the period from about the mid-1970s to the present, this study explores the compulsion to tell stories about this war, even though these are now others' stories, entirely beyond the scope of firsthand memory.

In fact, the resurgence in Great War fiction coincides with the rise of "memory studies" over the past twenty years in fields such as anthropology and history. David Berliner offers an anthropological definition of cultural transmission useful for my purposes: Cultural memory transmission occurs via "practices [that] re-enact, modify, and conserve 'pastness' through time" (204). And those practices are sustained by memory, Berliner argues (204). Functionally, along with culture, "memory helps us to think through the continuity and persistence of representations, practices, emotions, and institutions" (205). As such, and this is Berliner's point, anthropology, when using the idea of memory, is really studying what it always has: cultural practices as carried down through time.[3]

In critiquing memory studies from a standpoint ten years past Jan Assmann's seminal work in the field (Berliner acknowledges Assmann's influence[4]), Berliner actually offers a description of memory quite resonant with the context I am discussing:

---

3   Berliner is anxious to separate history and anthropology from the snares
    of postmodernity, as he says in his piece, though he does not see the rise
    in interest in memory as exclusively a product of that focus (203).

4   An extended discussion of Assmann's notion of cultural memory appears
    in Chapter 4.

> [E]*very little trace of the "past in the present" is designated as*
> *memory. Here, there is neither perception nor remembering.*
> *Memory is not seen as a set of representations of events and*
> *experiences that are shared, but as the way lasting traces of*
> *the past persist within us, as the transmission and persistence*
> *of cultural elements through the generations. Memory is not*
> *these series of recalled mental images, but a synonym for cul-*
> *tural storage of the past: it is the reproduction of the past in*
> *the present, this accumulated past which acts on us and*
> *makes us act.* (Berliner 201)

While Berliner's quarrel with the current memory craze (he wrote in 2005) is evident in, for instance, the tone of his first sentence, the idea that "lasting traces of the past persist within us" strikes me as an interesting way to describe memory as it relates to this war, since, as I will discuss, the fact that the war is so long over that none of us can remember it firsthand yet we quest to remember it anyway is worthy of rumination. Further, since no one alive is capable of firsthand recollection, it is also true that memory of the war cannot be "a series of recalled mental images" except if those be images of images. However, if we let go of the demand for these images to be firsthand, then our memory (of memories) in fact is exactly "a synonym for cultural storage of the past" and "reproduction of the past in the present." What this means, how it works, and how "real" such memories can be is the subject I am interested in pursuing here.[5]

Witness these words, written about Lieutenant Stephen C. Norris, a member of the Newfoundland (later "Royal" Newfoundland) Regiment, killed October 11, 1916 when a shell blast caved in his dugout in France. Eight men died with him, and his body was never recovered: "[T]he memory

---

5 Berliner's quarrel, in addition, is with the foregoing of study on how
   perception works, a process which he thinks anthropology leaves behind
   to its peril (201).

Menin Gate Memorial to the Missing, Ypres

of his valor will endure as long as there is one of his platoon to tell of the heroic action in which he took such a prominent and honoured part" (Sullivan 70).

Schoolboy prose at its finest, forgivable because it is in fact the death notice inserted into the *Adelphian*, the newspaper of the St. Bonaventure School, of which Norris was a graduate. At the moment of writing, the scribe, presumably a teenager himself, might have imagined that those fellow soldiers who survived Lt. Norris would have lives that would stretch an almost infinite number of years into the future. Youth sees life like that. But even with the best of luck, the longest-lived of these men, who were mostly born nearer the beginning of the 1890s than the end of that decade, would be dead by now. And so the words of the eulogist suggest something other than memory—they suggest forgetting. When nobody is left to speak for Norris, or any of the other 1300 Newfoundlanders who died in the War (Sullivan 64), memory no longer exists (it seems).

In fact, it doesn't take one of Norris' platoon to keep him alive, but contemporary journalist Joan Sullivan, whose *In the Field* tells the story of Norris' regiment in spare and yet precisely detailed prose, quoting the transcripts of letters that notify his parents of his death, including one which comes a few weeks after the first with the message that the army regrets to inform the family that Stephen died not on October 12th, but on the 11th, as if having this exactly right would form any consolation to them (64–65). Sullivan stands in here for the many writers who, far after the fact, keep memory alive, and it is not just documentarians writing the stories of real (historical) people, but fiction writers also who vivify soldiers like Norris, whether real or imaginary. Collectively, this effort takes up the challenge unknowingly posed by Norris' eulogist to speak for the men who never came back. Memory thus exists in multiple ways. It begins in recollection, moves on to documentation, and, if we take fiction into account, can continue to live in narration, even by those who don't have living memory of the events.

In that vein, the present book argues that the legacy of the Great War burdens us with a desire not to forget mixed with the anxiety that there is no living memory left. Stevenson characterizes this balance between remembering and forgetting as it trails down to the present when he answers his own question, "What then can Great War writing still offer its readers?" In context, he is speaking about literature written contemporary to the war, but his answer speaks to our historical moment:

> [T]*he Great War's continuing presence, in the twenty-first century, perhaps [is] not even a matter of choice. Like the troubled mind of a trauma patient, the conscience of later ages continues to turn repeatedly to the Great War, simply because its events were too deranged and desolate—too far*

*beyond the destructiveness of earlier conflicts—ever to have
been fully contained in mind or conscience.* (224)

This residue in the contemporary consciousness is what
produces contemporary (to us) World War I fiction, but, as
I will discuss, with this engine of cultural production comes
fear that these memories are merely invented, created post-
facto, and hence not genuine, being beyond verification by living witnesses. Thus if the Great War invented modern
memory, as has become a cultural commonplace after Fussell,
getting beyond the reach of the modern involves rethinking
memory's connection to experience, especially since the war
still forms a key part of the contemporary worldview.

The title of this book, as is obvious, comes from TS Eliot's
seminal Modernist poem *The Waste Land*, a piece that owes its
originating contexts to the shattering impact of the Great War.
The poem may be read in its fragmentary form as describing
accurately the cultural legacy of the war as it created modern
memory. In fact, however, I propose to invert Eliot's formulation, arguing that current efforts to represent the war in fiction might be better described as a process of "mixing desire
and memory." While there is a compelling desire to keep the
war alive as seen in the books under consideration, this effort
takes on new forms of late, and it betrays the anxiety that
comes from loss of memory due to a very Modernist problem—belatedness.

How can one remember what can't be recalled through
experience? What is memory when there's nobody left to
remember, that is, to witness to the truth of what is recalled?
Harry Patch, the last living British combat veteran, died
in 2009. We thus find ourselves in an interesting position
vis-à-vis this war post-Patch and after Fussell.[6] As a culture,

---

6   Again, my "we" references those descendants of the British tradition whose
     heritage roots in the constellation of countries in Britain's orbit at the time of
     the war, primarily Great Britain/the UK, Ireland, Canada, New Zealand, and
     Australia.

we still remember, and the flow of memories seems, if anything, to be increasing. At the same time, we can't remember firsthand, and this leaves a gap—a desire—at the heart of the culture that we seek to fill with story. Said in another way, because we collectively experience a fear of forgetting, we create and consume fiction as a way to prove that we remember. Yet we are always beset by the anxiety that our memories are merely secondhand.

To account for this, it is useful to follow the recent work of scholars in the field of traumatic memory. Much of this work has come out of focus on the Holocaust, which, obviously, is still a present memory for many people, both victims and others.[7] A similar set of work comes from women's novels about Indian partition. But note the claim that "these novels function...as testimonial narratives do for survivors of the Holocaust: they provide a means for the narrative integration of traumatic memory, thereby opening up possibilities for mourning and reconciliation" (Kabir 178). The emphasis again is on writers integrating their firsthand experience. None of the writers of the novels I'm considering here can claim firsthand experience. What, then, is the nature of their coding the war experience into words?

The following claim might serve as a definition for traumatic memory: "Traumatic experiences of individuals and groups, whether physical or psychological, leave deep scars and have long-lasting social, psychological, political, and material effects" (Saunders and Aghaie 16). Certainly we could affirm this with respect to the Great War. One aspect that we could cite is the need to memorialize that ran unabated

---

7 Scholar Andreas Huyssen points out the recent interest in memory and its origin in concern with the Holocaust in his article "Present Pasts: Media, Politics, Amnesia." He says that this "turning toward the past...stands in stark contrast to the privileging of the future so characteristic of earlier decades of twentieth-century modernity" (21).

through the 1920s and 30s, which I began by referencing, and another would be the loss of many young men of marriageable age, which left social scars and the material effect of rearranging the lives of the women they left behind. My grandmother, born in 1899, always said that she had lost a fiancé in the war. She was rather young for that, but two facts remain: I have a photo album with a number of pictures of unidentified soldiers in it, one of whom might have been that young man, and she did not end up marrying until 1928, late for that day, except for the fact that the war reordered social relations. In fact, there is a third material consequence of the war: the man she did marry was a friend of a cousin of hers. Rather more than a friend, he was someone who had served with her cousin in the Canadian Expeditionary Force in France.

But if this suggests that there is a material remainder of the war that comes to me, is that the same thing as citing a traumatic effect of the war that has transferred to me, leaping past the generational- and time-divides that separate me from that war? That's the very problem I seek to solve with respect to the novels I study, with the question being this: Do they transmit traumatic memory, or does the fact that they are written by people and for people for whom no firsthand experience of the war is possible mean that they cannot transmit trauma, because the *record* of trauma is at arm's length from trauma itself?

There might be an answer in U.S. slavery studies, described by Ron Eyerman by saying, "[T]here is a difference between trauma as it effects individuals and as a cultural process.... [A]s a cultural process, trauma is mediated through various forms of representation and linked to the reformation of collective identity" (qtd. in Saunders and Aghaie 17). Cultural trauma in this definition occurs "when members of a collectivity feel they have been subjected to a horrendous event that leaves indelible marks upon their group consciousness, marking their memories forever and changing their future identity in fundamental and irrevocable ways" (Alexander et al, qtd. in Saunders and Aghaie 17–18). According to Saunders and Aghaie, "Alexander contends that trauma is a social construction, that it is humans' reactions to events (rather than events themselves) that are traumatic" (18). This is then transmitted through a number of means including mass media and, as one might guess, literature, if "aesthetic…institutions" can be taken to mean that (18).

This might establish room for traumatic memory to have transcended down the generations from the Great War to now. The problem we might encounter with this claim, however, is that as time goes on, trauma must inevitably lose its force. The effects might persist, but how drastically?[8]

In fact, the common cultural heritage of the war in the contemporary moment is not the "Modern" consciousness Fussell describes. The time for that has passed. Rather, it is a nostalgia (desire) for a time long enough left behind that its horrors have been absorbed and recoded into myth in the collective memory, combined with a worry that invoking myth will make truth unrecoverable. In saying that, however, it must be recognized that with that distance comes freedom—both freedom to reinvent the war in ever-new literary forms, and liberty to tell what could not be told when there were living witnesses to bear testimony otherwise, or to bear the shame of the truth, for instance, of the violence of the war.

Surely, no need to commemorate remains? Surely, no strategy to do so has been left untouched? The cultural logic that lives in the fiction of the past forty years reveals that neither of these questions can be answered with a "yes" and yet also suggests that the Great War will remain at the center of our cultural imagination.

---

8 This is not, in the least, to impugn studies of traumatic memory which focus on slavery.

Deferred Collective Memory

The fact is that memory (of a sort) does persist from the Great War until now. Call it deferred collective memory, or collective memory delayed, and it comes from one of two related impulses—willing suspension of disbelief, and the desire to mourn or to commemorate. With respect to the first, consider this: when, in the early 1920s, the French spread the news of an unidentified amnesiac veteran (given the name Mangin) who came to be known as the "living unknown soldier" and publicized his photograph and description, hundreds of families stepped forward to claim him as a lost son, brother, or husband. Relatively quickly, most of their claims were dismissed because of obvious discrepancies in the physique of their lost soldier compared to that of the unidentified man. But nine cases were sufficiently similar, and the families sufficiently interested in pursuing them, that they had to be investigated (and litigated).

When the evidence was further weighed, most of these were likewise dismissed, and no claim was seen as nearly conclusive enough to declare that the amnesiac soldier's family had been found. Still, several families persisted in the belief that the man was their relation, two women old enough to be his mother so convinced that each moved to the town where he was resident in an asylum so that, in the words of Jean-Yves Le Naour, who tells the story, "[f]rom then on, Mangin had two mothers in Rodez" (139). The director of the institution, who took charge of the amnesiac's care, a M. Fenayrou, who also approved and supervised the man's visits with these strangers-cum-families, was never convinced that any one of the claimants was his blood relative. But even his belief and the fact that one of the "mothers" must, by definition, have been wrong did not dissuade the two women from altering their lives and living as if he were their lost son.

They remembered, in other words, what logic said they should not. As Le Naour says, there is "a madness that self-persuasion [can] nourish" (142). This is a situation analogous to our own when it comes to the war. We know that we cannot remember, and yet the details are so familiar as to feel first-hand, and this is aided by fiction, which has the capacity to do what written history is not free to do: present compelling and absorbing detail in narrative form which can exist without fact-checking, that is, without anchoring to any particular individual's experience. There is no demand that the literary narrative be "true." In fact, all it has to do is to *seem* true, and somewhere in the transformative engine that is the brain, it can become so, so that many readers of World War I fiction can give what seems at least to be a compelling picture of trench life, for instance. How close they are to accuracy about a particular trench is no longer the point.

The question is *why* we need to do this, and the answer may be in the collective cultural and also radically individual need to commemorate. Jay Winter discusses this impulse in *Sites of Memory, Sites of Mourning*, where he defines what he calls the newly emerged genre of war literature after 1918 by saying, "Much of this prose was in itself a kind of war memorial, a ritual entombment of and separation from those who had fallen by those who had survived" (73). In reading this material down to the present, but especially by writing new versions of it, we actually participate in an ongoing project of collective mourning, which forges tangible links back to the real people and moments of the past before the war receded irretrievably from living memory.

Again, Winter: "War memorials were places where people grieved, both individually and collectively" (79). The fact that all the memorials that could be built had been by World War II closed that chapter of commemoration. Because no space remains to build memorials in France, Gallipoli, and the other sites where the Great War was contested (and since the need to build physical monuments has been exhausted—Gavin Stamp says that Thiepval, dedicated in 1932, perhaps "had nothing new to say while being embarrassingly monumental" 157), then perhaps fiction that showcases the war is the contemporary generation's attempt at memorializing.

Not bricks and stone, not standing on hilltops the way Thiepval and Vimy do, fiction nonetheless has substance. It becomes three-dimensional, in a sense, as it is experienced by readers and shared amongst them. It has enduring qualities, not the least because it sits on shelves and gets carried around in backpacks and forgotten on coffee shop tables (leaving ebooks out, of course). It can be stumbled upon, the way a tourist stumbles upon graveyard after graveyard following the lanes of Flanders in a rental car. Whatever the intention of the writer, the result is the same—a living, moving, tangible memorial to the war. The fact that fiction is not mortar and stone, then, might be taken not as a sign that we don't have the intention to memorialize, but that, in the face of the saturation of memorials in the geographic spaces of the war, the impulse has moved somewhere else.

Fiction as commemoration provides an antidote to the deadness presumed to have overtaken architectural memorials with the passing of time. Concerning memorials made of stone (etc.), Winter claims that over the years, their purpose shifted. At first, they were sites of mourning, where the bereaved could go to vent their grief. However, "Once the moment of initial bereavement had passed, once the widows had remarried, once the orphans had grown up and moved away…then the meaning of war memorials was bound to change" (98). He indicates that "they could have had no fixed meaning, immutable over time" (98). Once people's grief came to be assuaged, the wounds healing, "then the objects invested with meaning related to loss of life in wartime became something else. Other meanings derived from other needs or events may be attached to them, or no meaning at all" (98). Fiction-as-memorial provides a corrective to Winter's claim that over time, significance may fade or disappear. As a living, contemporary form, fiction can be argued to create new worlds in which to experience the war, and, perhaps, to grieve for its losses in the contemporary moment. Grieving, while it may have become non-specific because living memory of dead soldiers has been erased by time, gains renewed power. The continued production of these novels indicates this to be true while also showing that grief has transferred from individual mourning to an amorphous cultural melancholy.

The latter claim might be urged along by referencing Freud, his 1917 essay "Mourning and Melancholia" interjecting itself to explain the hinge point where the former term turns into the latter and becomes prolonged past the point of having a source in or attachment to memory. He argues that for a person (not a culture, which creates a gap that it will be necessary to bridge momentarily), normal mourning is a process which runs from remembering and grieving a loss (say, of a loved one) to "being [able to] overcome [it] after a certain lapse of time" (244). Melancholia is much more severe in its manifestation. Like mourning, it involves "profoundly painful dejection, cessation of interest in the outside world, loss of the capacity to love" and more (244). But melancholia distinguishes itself by adding a defining feature: "[t]he disturbance of self-regard" (244). This leads to "self-reproaches and self-revilings, and culminates in delusional expectation of punishment" (244). Mourning may take quite some time, says Freud, because "all libido must be withdrawn from its attachment to that object," a process which doesn't come without "opposition" from within (244). Sometimes, this leads to clinging to

the lost object, "through the medium of a hallucinatory wish-
ful psychosis" (244). Eventually, however, the process concludes, and "the ego becomes free and uninhibited once again"
(245). Melancholia, however, persists, because it "borrows
some of its features from mourning, and the others from the
process of regression from narcissistic object-choice to narcissism" (250).[9]

Freud's description of melancholia leaves room to push his
definition from the individual to the social level. Melancholia
looks like it is a more profound case of mourning, Freud
indicates, but in fact melancholia happens when the patient
"knows *whom* he has lost but not *what* he has lost in
him" (245). As a result, melancholia may be "related to an
object-loss which is withdrawn from consciousness," which
Freud also labels an "unknown loss" (245). The realization of
the specificity of loss that would allow for the healthy
completion of the mourning process is just past arm's length.

The distance Freud poses—losing something but not
knowing quite what, the sense of loss withdrawing from
consciousness, which is both a spatial and time-oriented
metaphor—allows us to account for mourning-turned-
melancholic at a communal level as a way to read the extended
time from the Great War to the end of the 1930s in terms of
monument-building, and to the present in terms of writing
fiction about the conflict, as an enactment of melancholia.

Freud describes melancholia by saying that the patient will
view himself as "petty, egoistic, dishonest, lacking in
independence, one whose sole aim has been to hide the
weaknesses of his own nature," but then he says that in fact,
this is a mask (246). It is not the patient him/herself who is all
of these things, but the lost loved object. These "self-
reproaches are reproaches against a loved object which have
been shifted away from it on to the patient's own ego" (248).

---

9   When this occurs at a cultural level, it is possible to overlook narcissism as an
    outcome. See what follows.

At one time, there was an attachment to what Freud calls "this loved person," but "owing to a real slight or disappointment coming from this loved person, the object-relationship was shattered" (249). Rather than displacing the libido onto a new object, it was "withdrawn into the ego," and this withdrawl "served to establish an *identification* of the ego with the abandoned object" (249, emphasis original).

Raised to the level of culture and speaking particularly of Britain in the aftermath of the Great War, this idea might aid in a diagnosis of melancholia, particularly if we keep in mind Tom Lawson's claims about the connection of mourning to British fears over its lost Empire. Lawson reads the extended period of cultural mourning post-World War I in two ways: as indicating Britain's shift to a more inclusive, Eurocentric mode of being, or, the entire opposite, as a way of reinforcing Englishness and thus enhancing Empire though it was arguably in its initial decline (103). Perhaps the need to continue memorializing after what might be viewed as a normal period of loss-processing suggests the self-loathing of melancholy expressed as fear of losing the Empire or, in the latter (Commonwealth) days, the sense of the Empire which once was. If the latter is too strong a claim, how about this: contemporary Commonwealth fiction about the Great War signals a sense of mourning whose cause has receded out of reach, and this distance, combined with the fact that mourning has not concluded in the normal course of time, indicates a melancholic state that stems from a now-unshakable sense of object-loss.

And out of melancholia, at the cultural level, comes the desire I urge into the forefront of this discussion with my title. Given the distance of time that separates us from the Great War, writing about the war, reading about it, or pondering its many after-words in the form of memorials is not performed in an attempt to heal. Indeed, melancholy has gone past the efficacious healing of mourning, leaving its subjects with a vague and unfulfillable desire perhaps indicated in Freud's phrase "lacking in independence" (246).

Since this is a book about literature, it's appropriate to illustrate this point from fiction. At the end of Tom Phelan's *The Canal Bridge*, it is 1970, and of two men and one woman who went off to World War I, and one who waited for them to return, but one is left. Kitty Wrenn is the widow of Matthias, who left to see the world in 1913, served in the trenches as a medic, and died defending his employer's property from a band of local thugs who wanted to burn the house down in the name of Irish Freedom just after Matthias returned from the war. Kitty walks across a bridge spanning the now dried-up canal which held her, Matthias', and the other two young people's hopes when they were young. And she considers the matter of war and remembering.

> *When I die, gone forever will be the pain created by the loss of Lionel and Con and Matt, and now Sarah and her husband, Phillip. There will only be knowledge. History books cannot pass on the pain endured, the anguish, the terror of the times. I suppose it's good that they can't. Even a headstone in a cemetery, leaned on and wept at for years, becomes just one more piece of cold granite when the final rememberer dies.*

> *The War and all the lads who died in it, who were crippled in it, will only be knowledge soon. There will be no one left to lean on the headstones and cry in sorrow.* (278)

It sounds like Kitty Wrenn rightly diagnoses our moment in the hundredth anniversary time of the Great War. Now, there is no one left who remembers the war firsthand, and only a handful who remember the times. But there's more than knowledge left, especially when one considers fiction as a repository of human experience. Novels (and poems and plays, but those are only in very minor ways considered here) are not just fact, if they are fact at all. History books can pass on the broad scope, and they can argue about who was responsible for what. But once events are concluded, only fiction can hold onto anguish. And the fact that so much of it (fiction, and hence anguish) emerges now points to something larger: a shared sense of what needs to be retained about the Great War. This is not fact, in the cold, analytical, "historical" (a problematic term of course) sense, but grief.

Thus while prolonged and unfinalized mourning may, in the Freudian economy of the individual, point to narcissism or other signs of an unhealthy mental state, when it comes to the collective culture, it might also be read as a sign of value for actions and losses now in one sense beyond memory but having sedimented themselves into a desire deep enough to sustain fictional output over time, even after those who write the stories down are generations removed from the events that prompted the writing. Freud comments that "the exciting causes of melancholia have a much wider range than those of mourning, which is for the most part occasioned only by a real loss of the object, by its death" (256). Not being able to pinpoint cause now that the loss is too old for us to remember is not, as it might seem, a reason for us not to mourn. Rather, it is the enabling condition of melancholy, and the desire to act that this prompts expresses itself in contemporary texts of lives that should have by now been transformed from grief to knowledge, to use Kitty's terms, but which are kept alive exactly because they exist as fiction.

Jay Winter is correct when he claims in *Sites of Memory, Sites of Mourning* that "the backward gaze of so many writers, artists, politicians, soldiers, and everyday families in this period [1914–18] reflected the universality of grief and mourning in Europe from 1914" (223). From that developed a "vocabulary of mourning," traditional and "derived from classical, romantic, or religious forms," which had as its purpose an attempt to "mediate bereavement" (223). Grief and bereavement were "mediated by mourning, a set of acts and gestures through which survivors express grief and pass through stages of bereavement" (224). As Winter points out, "Commemoration was a universal preoccupation after the 1914–18 war" (28). "Each nation developed its own language of commemoration, but some features were universal" (82). War literature "was in itself a kind of war memorial, a ritual entombment of and separation from those who had fallen by those who had survived" (73). Yet Winter misses something when he claims that things changed post-1945.

His reasoning may be sound, namely that "[a]fter the Second World War, the same flaring up of older languages appropriate to a period of mass mourning did not take place" (228). Further, "older forms of the language of the sacred faded," as did the ability for humane compassion, which now seemed "strangely out of place" (228, 229). Winter claims that when, for most people, healing began to take place, the meaning of the objects used to focus their mourning, like memorials, shifted. They took on other meanings, or none at all, so that "now, seventy-five years after the armistice [as he writes], war memorials have become the artefacts of a vanished age, remnants of the unlucky generation that had to endure the carnage of the Great War" (98). Maybe so, though I'm skeptical that no one grieves at these monuments any more, having observed the reactions people have experienced in commemorating the war's centenary. But if the point is that memorial building, once ceased, gave way to mourning and then to forgetting, then I would suggest that fiction still does what it did a hundred years ago: it draws its reader in and prompts her or him to grieve for what was lost. It is thus both a sign of continued processing of the loss—i.e. melancholia—and a place to do that.

Contemporary Fictional Remembering and Forgetting

Frances Itani, author of *Deafening*, offers a quite practical answer to explain the impulse to write Great War novels today: "[T]his was our grandfathers' war. And we [writers like herself, Cumyn, Hodgins, and Urquhart, all studied here] are of an age to write about it. All of us who have done so have been writing for a number of years, and we seem to be ready and willing to tackle the material. It is pretty difficult material to deal with..." (qtd. in Fisher, "Hear, Overhear," 53–54). At what point will this cultural production finally fade? Thus far, it shows no signs of doing so, because it continues to have cultural work to accomplish. Fiction allows us to extend into the present Winter's claim about the interwar years: "The dead were there, in one way or another, living among the living. In their public ceremonies on Armistice Day and in their private thoughts and dreams, the survivors had to live with the fallen" (144). Anthropologist Johannes Fabian is helpful in understanding the delicate balance of remembering and forgetting. His area of study, at least as he draws upon his fieldwork for *Memory Against Culture*, is Africa, both as a place and as a set of events or histories. He comments, "Reflecting on forgetting Africa means of course not to forget Africa," and we might easily substitute "the war" for "Africa" in that sentence (65). His contexts, of course, take into account the political-social realities that Africa as a colonial (i.e. subjugated) site entails, and hence he can define remembering

Sheffield War Memorial, England

and forgetting, respectively, as "recognizing and denying its [Africa's] presence," something that might happen even while Africa exists right in front of the observer (66). He glosses the idea by citing "[Leo] Frobenius's exhortation 'never [to] forget'" in a way that helps me make my point (69). This means, Fabian claims, "[N]ever to let what we think we know be overcome by remembering what we know better" (69).

The formulation Fabian offers suggests that in retaining the knowledge we have at the margins of our minds—"what we think we know," in his parlance—we resist the temptation to know only what is commonplace—"what we know better," to cite his words. As David Williams says when talking about the way that a renewed oral culture can shape memory, "shared memories and common bonds...are the basis of a living community" (*Media, Memory* 279). Andreas Huyssen says something similar when he claims the following:

> *Memory is always transitory, notoriously unreliable, and haunted by forgetting—in short, human and social. As public memory it is subject to change: political, generational, individual. It cannot be stored forever, nor can it be secured by monuments; nor, for that matter, can we rely on digital retrieval systems to guarantee coherence and continuity.* (38)

For the fiction writers I am describing here, this suggests that their attempts to build on what is known about the war, the commonplaces that fill every book of history and pop up in every Great War photograph—topoi that are easily or commonly remembered—offer truths that, though at times perhaps not knowable in the sense that they may be verified, are nonetheless valuable, contributing to the cultural memory of the war. Is that the war itself? No, but as I have been arguing, the war is too far behind to be apprehended in its reality anymore.[10] We must thus make do with remembering of another sort.

Theorists of traumatic memory have identified "the pattern of giving meaning to a traumatic event by emplotting it within a broader theoretical, contextual, or thematic framework. Often this entails constructing a narrative with a beginning, middle, and an end and, most importantly, with a specific purpose and meaning (Saunders and Aghaie 20). Cultural memory, in fact, is often the product of

---

10 This is neither to denigrate written history's ability to vivify the past, though history as a discipline is not my interest here, nor to suggest that any version of the past represents its phenomenal reality, which is always gone in the instant it is experienced.

this conversion process. Kabir describes this: "To convert traumatic (non)memory into narrative memory, the traumatic event itself has to be integrated into a story, which in turn must be addressed to someone," she explains, adding that this process is often individual, but that scholars take the notion and extend it to "groups and communities, often by using the term *cultural memory*" (182, italics original).[11] Rigney says something similar when she claims that "cultural memory is collective activity and not a thing: it involves the ongoing production, reproduction, and dissemination of narratives with a capacity to reconfigure social relations and to constitute publics" (618–19).

The novels I study here, thus, are imagined as being read in community. The question I pursue is not, "Why write about the war?" The answer to that might be curt and dismissive, as simple as saying, "The war has been written about." Rather, the question is, "What particular forms does the cultural memory of the war take as readers share it?" Nor is it presumed that the canon of contemporary Great War literature is closed. That people of England, Canada, and beyond will continue to write about the war into the foreseeable future is, to me, unquestionable, because each new book is a way of remembering.

Contemporary Great War fiction goes past the familiar forms that its predecessors took in the years immediately following the war and ranges to what could never have been imagined before. This is so because of the curious irony of the contemporary moment, when those whose heritage this canon of literature represents share a collective cultural desire to remember the war but also a collective cultural anxiety that they are on the verge of forgetting. The problem is

---

11 Many scholars, including Greenberg, discuss how cultural memory is used as a tool of states to control people. See for instance his discussion of Israeli narratives (98).

unresolvable, but each new attempt to recall the war through representing it in fiction creates a further part of the contemporary consciousness.

In contemporary fiction, the Great War continues to evolve new ways of being and to offer new truths both about its events and about the details of human experience and suffering that are its cultural heritage.

SECTION 1

MEMORIES FAMILIAR, RENEWED, AND PASSED DOWN

CHAPTER 1

Familiar Tropes Renewed:
Visions of violence

Writing in the 1920s, Vera Brittain pinpointed a fear that many in that decade must have had as she talked about a day a decade or so after the war when she looked at her brother's picture on her mantle. He was killed in Italy in 1918.[12] She says that he is still real to her, but points out that to her children, "[H]e will be but a name, a legend, scarcely distinguishable...from Kingsley's fabulous heroes" (134). And her claim is strikingly appropriate in the present context: "[M]emorial celebrations are not enough. Time has a deceptive habit of blurring our pain while preserving the glamour of our larger-scale tragedies. Our tears and our anguish fade into oblivion, but the thrill of catastrophic events...[lets them] keep the same peculiar vividness that they wore in the yesterday in which they belong" (134–35). The tone of the question she follows up with is demanding, as she asks, "By what means shall we recall to life our grief and our terror, in order that posterity may recognize them for what they were?" (135).

---

12 Edward's death might have been a suicide, though the version Vera Brittain propagated was a battle wound suffered while leading his men on attack. See http://www.dailymail.co.uk/news/article-2881799/Testament-tortured-youth-Vera-Brittain-s-heartbreaking-WWI-memoir-love-loss-major-movie-s-WON-T-hero-brother-s-suicide-dash-guns-gay-affair-secret.html

She is speaking of events of less than two decades prior, saying that since the war, she and others have done much to make up for the time it cost them, but the result is that "the war has come to appear to us as an event that happened long ago in the lifetime of somebody else" (135).

For us, it does not simply *appear* that way; it *is* that way, and with the loss of firsthand witnesses to recall it, irretrievably so. Brittain goes on to postulate the need for a method that would allow people of her time "to preserve the memory of our suffering in such a way that our successors may understand it and refrain from the temptations offered by glamour and glory" (136). She offers a clue as to what that might be even as she reiterates her fears: "[A] mass of literature has already grown up around the war [yet] it is still—despite the fact that the immense civilian armies were more articulate than actual fighters have ever been before—inadequate to save from self-destruction a new generation…" (135).

The concern of *Mixing Memory and Desire*, as was made plain in the Introduction, is not with the war stories of the combatant generation, no matter how vivid they might have been or may remain to a contemporary reader. My point, rather, is to think through why, despite the passage of time and the intervening trauma of World War II and other conflicts, writers keep going back to the experience of the Great War, and how writers with no firsthand memory are able to connect back to the time in a way that combines authenticity to events with contemporary sensibilities and thus answers a continued need to remember the war. One way, as I will discuss while considering Timothy Findley's *The Wars*, Alan Cumyn's *The Sojourn*, and Joseph Boyden's *Three Day Road*, is to use and extend the trope of violence, offering a vivid portrayal that confronts the reader with the horrors that happened during the war but that might have been lost to time through the frailty of memory, the death of those who lived it during the war, or the timidity of (other) writers who suggest violence without portraying it fully.

Common sense tells us that when a soldier dies, be that during battle or decades afterwards, he (or she) takes his bodily memory with him, erasing it from view, rendering it healed, in a sense, because no longer on display. However, this presumes a division between the individual body and memory at the collective level, a notion that might be ascribed to western modernity's focus on the bourgeois individual subject. Seeing individual experience/memory as being continuous with cultural memory, by contrast, would allow for the possibility of a continuity between the bodies, say, of Great War soldiers and our own bodies (or those of later subjects), a continuum formed and reinforced by narratives that invoke injury to the body as a trope. Exposure to violence via fiction, then, would be tantamount, psychologically, to exposure to injury in the war itself, allowing for memory of the traumas of the war to live on into the present.

Johannes Fabian helps with the following definition: "As a cognitive faculty memory can only be attributed to individual minds (or brains); in that sense collectivities cannot remember. As a social practice, memory is a communicative practice; all narrative memory is in that sense collective" (93). He further describes the mechanism by which memories are retained. "Remembering, especially in the hortative sense of commemoration, that is, something that is to be done, performed, or fulfilled, calls for stories to be told" (99–100). With this is mind, one might say that the war exists contemporaneous to now, not just as memory, but in the sense that the stories told of it mark themselves upon the bodies of later subjects.

Canadian National Vimy Memorial, France

Saunders and Aghaie, writing on the topic of trauma and memory, say this: "Traumatic experiences of individuals and groups, whether physical or psychological, leave deep scars and have long-lasting social, psychological, political, and material effects" (16). They go on to ask a further important question: "[D]oes traumatic memory operate in the same way in communities as it does in individuals?" (16). Their answer, which they put in the context of studies on Post Traumatic Stress Disorder (PTSD), makes the following claim:

> *While this clinical paradigm is focused on the individual psyche, Kai Erikson's work on disaster argues that "sometimes the tissues of community can be damaged in much the same way as the tissues of mind and body" and that the term trauma can thus "serve as a broad social concept as well as a more narrowly clinical one." (17)*

While Saunders and Aghaie are suspicious of how well the clinical metaphor of individual trauma as codified in PTSD transfers to the collective, they do offer a gloss from the work of Dominick LaCapra:

> *In* Writing History, Writing Trauma, *for example,* [LaCapra]
> *employs the psychoanalytic categories of "acting out" (Freud's*
> *term for the behavior of a subject who is controlled by*
> *repetitive, unconscious wishes and fantasies) and "working*
> *through" (Freud's term for a repetition modified by*
> *interpretation, capable of arresting unconscious repetitions*
> *by integration of a traumatic event into the subject's psyche)*
> *to analyze collective responses to historical events such as the*
> *Holocaust.* (17)

These formulations could be taken to describe the process whereby those in the contemporary English-speaking world continue to relive the Great War via the cultural practice of writing fiction. Because this production continues, the trauma can be understood as continuing to be acted out.

The writers also caution that "Ron Eyerman, in his study of slavery and the formation of African American identity, insists that 'there is a difference between trauma as it affects individuals and as a cultural process' and, specifically, that 'as cultural process, trauma is mediated through various forms of representation and linked to the reformation of collective identity'" (17), which seems precisely to leave open the possibility that a discursive field such as the contemporary Great War novel could pass the wounds of war from one generation to another in a process which might, someday, result in the trauma having been worked through.

Further necessity that fiction serve as a catalyst for bodily memory comes because the actual sites of the war were relatively quickly erased of their specific reminders of the conflict, though the battlefields became important sites of memory for families and for the soldiers who had survived the war, with the numbers of people who participated in battlefield tourism ranging from 5,000 in the time up to June 1919 to as many as 60,000 taken by the YMCA alone in the early 1920s (van Emden 287). Perhaps the most poignant description of this phenomenon is given by Adam Hochschild in his cultural history, *To End All Wars*:

> *Thousands of British, French, American, and Canadian widows and mothers roamed the former war zone. Hotels were filled with the grieving, and former Red Cross hospital trains had to be pressed into service to house the overflow. Shattered tanks dotted meadows, and everything from cathedrals to farmhouses lay in ruins. Along hundreds of country roads, lined in European style with rows of plane or poplar trees, all that remained were bare trunks, the limbs victim to shrapnel.* (356)

Yet so many visited that one former combatant was led to say, "'Our war, the war that seemed the special possession of those of us who are growing middle-aged, is being turned by time and change into something fabulous, misunderstood and made romantic by distance'" (qtd. in Mosse 155).

The crucial difference between tourism and pilgrimage is explored in George L. Mosse's study of how both world wars are remembered, *Fallen Soldiers*. He explains that the latter had a sacred quality to it, while the former did not, and that this difference was remarked upon by soldiers with resentment (153–54). The fact that what he labels "the process of trivialization" won out meant that "[t]he reality of the war was transcended once more, not by absorbing war into a civic religion, but by making it mundane and reducing it to artifacts used or admired in daily life and co-opted by those who wanted to satisfy their curiosity about the fighting" (155, 156).

For those currently seeking an understanding of the Great War, the ability to visit the battlefields remains. Now dotted with the neatly arranged graves tended by the Commonwealth War Graves Commission and sprinkled with monuments as stupendous as Lutyens' Thiepval and as unassuming as the

Newfoundland Park Memorial in Beaumont Hamel, the north of France and Flanders will never, in the memory of anyone alive today, be other than a former battlefield. Yet what the image of a memorial does, in effect, is stop one's vision. Rather than looking beyond the scene it depicts to the (horrid) details it suggests, the viewer settles for what she sees.

These places of battle, former sites of death, retain none of their horror, having been completely domesticated both purposely—by the building of graveyards and memorials—and naturally, by the return of the land to its prewar state (which also, of course, involves the human agency of farming). Those who observe such spaces know that what they see is not the war itself, but a cleaned-up post-trauma version of the catastrophe, a lie, or at the very least a lack, because it cannot correspond to the specific trauma that cultural memory says must have existed at one time. Likewise in Great War fiction that employs the trope of violence, certain passages seem to depict the entirety of the truth they are based on, but in fact, guide the reader's eye subtly away from the truth and horror of what must have happened. Take for instance this passage, in Ben Elton's *The First Casualty*, which depicts a trench attack:

> [T]*wenty Britons rose up and hurled themselves over* [*the lip of the German trench*] *and down on to the heads of the soldiers chatting within. Kingsley followed as the first thuds and screams began, peering over the parapet into the darkness below where the crunch of metal on bone punctuated German cries of panic and blood-curdling yells of pain.* (326)

It is perhaps significant that, like we do, the character observes from a distant, at this point neutral, position. This distance further signifies that his description of the violence engaged in stays at arm's length from showing the reader what happened. What were those cries? And what damage, in specific, does a bludgeon inflict on the head? What does it feel like to deliver that blow? These aren't questions that the reader wants answered, in many respects, but in not having them answered, he or she loses contact with the war as it was fought, and hence loses the capacity to remember its vivid and shocking aspects.

It might be surprising to read a World War I novel that did not have the familiar half-dozen elements of machine guns, trenches, gas, No Man's Land, barbed wire, and shrapnel/artillery attacks, all constituent elements of battle and, hence, death and dismemberment. However, it could be our familiarity with these tropes as readers that renders fictional violence ineffectual. By now, we've read so much about the war that its violence feels familiar, and its power to stun us has been lost— the grotesque having been domesticated by constant repetition. The work that shrapnel could do, such as slicing an arm clean off without the victim even realizing, for a moment, what had happened to him, or creating jagged holes in the trunk out of which leaked intestines while the stunned man tried to bundle them back in, remains un-scriven. Yet certain novels in the canon of recent Great War fiction push their scenes of violence to an unfamiliar and graphic brutality. I would like to argue that we read them not as outliers, too frightful in their portrayal of the grotesque, but rather as indicators of truth that might be lost by either the elision of violent detail or its coding in familiar tropes.

Saunders and Aghaie, following the work of Jeffrey Alexander et al on trauma, indicate that the following is true:

> The cultural construction of trauma…begins with a claim to some fundamental injury that is then transmitted through influential cultural agents such as the mass media and religious, aesthetic, legal, scientific, and state institutions, which define the nature of the trauma and the victim, establish the relation of the trauma to those who experience it only indirectly, and assign responsibility. (18)

Literature is not mentioned, though the use of the word "aesthetic" implies it. Thus I would argue that certain contemporary Great War novels help form a "cultural construction of trauma" by pushing the trope of violence into new and increasingly explicit representations of what might have happened in battle, and in doing so, they ensure that the war is remembered vividly and dramatically.

Of course contemporary writers of Great War fiction are not inventing violence. Great War literature from the time of the poets (Wilfred Owen's "Dulce et Decorum Est" comes immediately to mind) has featured graphic detail. Perhaps the word is not "invent" so much as "remind," in the sense that they are recovering details that challenge the reader to deal with both the horror and the shame of violence, renewing memories that, oddly enough, might not have been possible to voice while those who had been involved in the conflict were alive due to willful forgetting by former combatants or an unwillingness on the part of the writer to step in and speak about events without having firsthand experience.

Sometimes, the levels of violence that a given novel reaches take the reader almost by surprise. Such is the case with Timothy Findley's *The Wars*, in which passages depicting the days prior to protagonist Robert Ross' direct involvement in conflict never indicate any real sense of dread, because he has no idea how horrible things will be once he is in action. One such instance is a description of Ross' meeting with Eugene Taffler, a character who, when Ross encounters him on the Canadian Prairies during his training, has already gone to France, been wounded, and returned to Canada to recuperate. When Ross comes upon him, Taffler is throwing stones at bottles, hitting and breaking every one. He says, "The distance...between our lines and theirs is often no more than a hundred yards. Did you know that?" (17). Robert replies "No, sir" (17). The narrator reports that the encounter makes him wonder what Taffler wants out of the war—a chance to go up against a Goliath? (18). But never does Ross think about the possibility that he, too, could come home hurt, or indeed, what Taffler's future might be.

The naiveté of Ross pre-combat is a mirror of the now-clichéd claim of summer 1914, "We'll be home by Christmas"[13] and the hopes of soldiers and their loved ones for an experience of heightened emotion. Vera Brittain in her letters to her fiancé Roland Leighton indicates as much. Exulting in the possibility that Leighton will soon be in trench combat, she exclaims, "After all no experience however terrible can be counted as loss, if one is not overcome by the experience but is stronger than it, as I know you will be" (Bishop and Bostridge 72). Her romanticized tone indicates that she does not read the upcoming events as real—i.e. likely to kill Leighton. She can say this because she does not know what will happen.

In fact, the volume from which this is taken, letters between her and four men, including her brother, her fiancé, and two more, all of whom ended up dead in the war, is replete in its early pages with the hope for glory and the men's desperation to move to the Front as quickly as possible. When death is discussed at all, it is only as glory. Leighton says in a letter of September 29, 1914, that war is "something... horrible, yet very ennobling and very beautiful, something whose elemental reality raises it above the reach of all cold theorising" (30). He would be dead three months later, having suffered a horrid wound. At the time that this becomes apparent to the family, war loses all its glory, as described by

---

13 There is no shortage of commentary which has attempted to debunk commonplace understandings of the war, not the least something so easily mythologized as a battle cry. (Cf. here Gordon Corrigan's *Mud, Blood and Poppycock* for instance). But in fact, documentary evidence abounds that this is exactly what the soldiers themselves, and their loved ones, were thinking and saying in the days prior to their deployment. See for instance Richard Holmes, *Tommy*, 140+.

Brittain when she looks at Leighton's uniform, returned from the Front complete with holes indicating both entry point and exit point of the bullet that killed him: She felt "overwhelmed by the horror of war without its glory.... [T]he smell of those clothes was the smell of graveyards & the Dead [sic]" (Bishop and Bostridge 211).

Exposing the body in ways not typical of everyday life, war renders bodies grotesque. War novels, thus, should talk about the distortions suffered in the bodies of soldiers, no matter how awful, if they are to participate actively in the production of cultural memory. In *The Wars*, Findley gradually reveals this strategy as the narrative moves along. The most vivid of these passages tells the story of the aforementioned Taffler, who returns from the Front a second time to recuperate at the private hospital run by the d'Orsey family.

This time, he was not so lucky as when he had returned to Canada and encountered Ross, for now Taffler has lost both arms. One afternoon, he is glimpsed in his room, lying there "with his forehead touching the stones. The end of the bandage was in his teeth. One of the walls was covered with great wide swipes of red at shoulder height where he must have been rubbing his wounds to make them bleed. The stumps where his arms had been were raw and one of them was pumping blood in spurts across the floor" (173).

The scene, the most vivid in the novel, is remarkable for other reasons: it happens far from the fighting, and it is first seen by the unlikely eyes of a twelve year-old girl. By portraying this event from this point of view, Findley forces the scene into the reader's memory, because we, too, are distant observers of the war, or at least we believed ourselves to be such before picking up *The Wars*. Tom Hastings comments that as "a novel about the Great War, *The Wars* devotes surprisingly little time to the actual historical people and events of the war and even less time to describing the conditions of battle…" [EP5] He goes on: "Although a gas attack against the Allied forces at Ypres is described in *The Wars*, a battle scene of any significant detail it is not" (EP5).

For Findley's Robert Ross, the war proceeds exactly like it did for many: he experienced the mud of the Western Front, he was gassed, and he learned how to dive into shell craters to save himself. As in many World War I novels, these events occur essentially in summary form. Findley saves portrayal of Ross' most vivid experiences of violence for less-familiar horrors, including a brutal assault at the hands of his fellow soldiers and a final breakdown as he witnesses the potential that a barn full of horses might be incinerated. As such, Findley is able to highlight the violence through defamiliarizing a common fictional trope.

For instance, when leading his men out of a shell crater under the eye of a German sniper, Ross proceeds almost ploddingly, knowing by instinct what his risks are and what he ought to do. And when he does take action and shoot the enemy, he barely knows what happens:

> What happened next was all so jumbled and fast that Robert was never able to sort it out. He fell. He turned. He saw the German reaching over the lip of the crater. Something exploded. The German gave a startled cry and was suddenly dead.…(145)

Ross and Findley both here follow the script—in Ross' head, of the typical war novel—retaining emotional distance from what is happening and allowing for the reader to do so as well. Ross is not reluctant to participate in what is happening, but neither can he think within the moment. Instead, he codes what happens as a distant experience, and the narrator relates it as a third-person version of Ross' point of view.

Ross' real experience of violence begins with his assault by fellow soldiers in a scene where Findley goes beyond the stock moments of World War I fiction to show the brutality of men to men of their own side. Robert, having taken a bath, is set upon and raped by a group, the scene described by the narrator in the most vivid language of the book:

> His throat was constricted and his mouth had gone completely dry. He could barely breathe. The dark was terrible and seemed to invade his brain....His mind went stumbling over a beach of words and picked them up like stones and threw them around inside his head. (192)

The physical details of the attack are even more graphic, "They pulled at his lips until he thought his jaw was going to snap...," being just a sampling of them (192).

Findley faced a good deal of pressure about the depiction of the rape scene after the book was published. Tom Hastings quotes Findley in an interview about the scene:

> "Tell me why it has to be there," she [Margaret Laurence] said.

> "It has to be there because it is my belief that Robert Ross and his generation of young men were raped, in effect, by the people who made the war. Basically, their fathers did it to them."

> Margaret said: "Yes, I agree with you. But surely that's implicit in the book already. You don't have to say so."

> "But I [Findley] cannot remove it. As a scene, it is intrinsic—deeply meshed in the fabric of the book as I first conceived it. I cannot cut away its arms and legs—no matter how convinced other people are that the book will stand and function without them." (qtd. in Hastings 85 EP1)

It is after this event (rather than following the traditional war scenes cited earlier) that Ross starts to remove himself mentally from the scene of the war—thinking in fragments

Thiepval Memorial to the Missing of the Somme, France

and burning the picture of his deceased sister, Rowena, in the middle of the floor of his billet (Findley 195).

Ross' transformation into someone who can no longer deal with the war's violence becomes complete when he himself perpetuates an act of violence after willingly disobeying a direct order from his superior officer in order to save a group of animals in proximity to the battlefield from burning alive. The scene reads like this:

> He got out the Webley [revolver], *meaning to shoot the animals not yet dead, but he paused for the barest moment looking at the whole scene laid out before him and his anger rose to such a pitch that he feared he was going to go over into madness....*[H]*e thought, "If an animal had done this—we would call it mad and shoot it," and at that precise moment Captain Leather rose to his knees and began to struggle to his feet. Robert shot him between the eyes.* (203)

Ross, rather than participate on the higher-ups' terms, decides to play by his own rules. So he shoots his commanding officer and then escapes. Shortly thereafter, he frees a trainload of horses and wanders with them until he is arrested. He is tried, but he is too injured and brain-addled to be imprisoned. He dies in hospital in 1922.

Donna Palmateer Penee claims that, at least as it concerns Canadian identity as formed by the Great War, what makes Findley somewhat exceptional is that he sets his novel prior to the moment when popular belief has it that that the nation's identity was formed through war, at the battle of Vimy Ridge in 1917.[14] Hastings explains the following: "Ross's exit on that date [June 1916]…means that he would not have participated in Canada's greatest military moment of the First World War, the Battle of Vimy Ridge in April 1917, or the historic Battle of the Somme on 1 July 1916, which so devastated both the Allied and German-Austrian forces" (EP6).

Findley thus rewrites Canada's received notions about itself as formed by World War I by invoking the war and yet eliding the experience most commonly claimed as the war's contribution to national identity. In place of this experience, he inserts scenes more graphic and violent than in almost any other contemporary Great War fiction.

At this point it might be worth asking, why Findley? Susan Fisher says in "War of Words" that there is "plenty of evidence that war, which is destructive of so much else, is strangely fertile for literature" (EP 4). Speaking of another World

---

14 Though this perception has existed since 1917 and has been reinforced in the Canadian consciousness by the building of the Canadian National Vimy Memorial (dedicated 1936) and its restoration (completed 2007), it has been reinforced for the current generation by late popular historian Pierre Burton in his bestselling 1986 book, *Vimy*. Even more recently, Vimy's centrality in Canadian myth is reflected and reinforced in the following statement from the website of the Canadian War Museum: "Many historians and writers consider the Canadian victory at Vimy a defining moment for Canada, when the country emerged from under the shadow of Britain and felt capable of greatness.… But it was a victory at a terrible cost, with more than 10,000 killed and wounded" (warmuseum.ca). This obviously, once more, points to the horrors of the violence that had to take place for the victory to happen.

War I-inspired text, Fisher explains the pull of these narratives:

> *So why then should we read war literature? For me, the best answer appears in Pat Barker's* Another World *(1998), her fourth and presumably final novel about World War I: 'you should go to the past, looking not for messages or warnings, but simply to be humbled by the weight of human experience that has preceded the brief flicker of your own few days…'*
> (Fisher EP11),

by which we might once more see an arrow pointing to the horrors Findley's text contains. By advancing the trope of violence and confronting the reader with it in horrible and direct ways, Findley pushes the Great War novel in a direction few are willing to by surfacing detail that most writers do not have the interest in surfacing, or the courage to portray. By doing so in 1977—in the shadow of Fussell's publication of *The Great War and Modern Memory* (1975) which, as I discuss elsewhere in this book, seems to indicate the closing of an era—and winning the Governor General's award for his work, Findley inaugurates an era of cultural memory production which continues unabated to the present.

Findley further sets his novel apart from the run of war narratives by the choice of form in which he presents Robert Ross' story. This has been discussed often since the book's publication, most recently by David Williams, who argues that its fragmented form is an instance of the writer deploying photographic technique as a visualized textual metaphor. He says, "Closing the book on an epistolary narrative that might have recounted events in the first person, Findley eschews the conventions of Great War combatant narratives" (Williams, "A Force" EP7).

Williams intercuts the words of Eduardo Cadava with his own to make a claim which explains Findley's technique:

> *By separating the moment from itself, the photographic event*
> *actually atomizes time, making it possible to "see" time as*
> *a conglomerate of particles. The result is a phenomenology*
> *that differs from older conceptions of time as "eternal return"*
> *or as linear flow. And since the photographic event "marks*
> *a division within the present"* (Cadava 61), *it "names a pro-*
> *cess that, seizing and tearing an image from its context,*
> *works to immobilize the flow of history" (xx).* (Williams
> "A Force" EP7)

"Separating the moment from itself" in this case could also indicate the way in which the shocking depictions of violence in *The Wars* form tableaux—images frozen in time that assault the reader, leaving her or him with no choice but to absorb into memory the scenes they depict.

Moving from Findley to Alan Cumyn's *The Sojourn*, it should first be noted that, as was discussed earlier, the Great War novel often appears to follow a checklist of tropes—miss one, and the reader will feel the lack almost by instinct. Gas, machine guns, barbed wire, rats, lice, and other familiar elements are what soldiers experienced, of course. Because of this, it might be possible, theoretically, to line up "lice"

Canadian National Vimy Memorial

passages from any number of these novels and find that they greatly resemble one another. Some writers, however, take the strategy of adding to the list of tropes by introducing new ones, and others find themselves pushing familiar tropes into unseen territory. Often this means more extreme detail, presenting the outcomes of, for example, rat infestation in ways that go well past the commonplace into the graphic or grotesque. So, for example, Cumyn confronts the reader of *The Sojourn* with a horrific moment almost as soon as events begin. Ramsay Crome is doing trench duty, trying to move about in particularly muddy and wet conditions. The narrator tells us, "The ground is slime and shattered wood and strange, destroyed artifacts of war: wagon wheels, planks, odd bits of iron, unexploded shells, shrapnel, parts of corpses" (9), a list detailed enough to prompt the imagination to draw a vivid picture of the scene. Then he pushes it: "A severed hand on a mess tin, and a soft blur in the muck underfoot that could be a dead rat or a bit of internal organ or even an abandoned pair of boots" (9). The "soft bit" goes from rat to body part and back down to possibly some boots, but readers' nerves jangle at the idea that it's not just a leg or arm, familiar pieces of wartime detritus due to shelling.

It might seem from the placement of this moment at the beginning of the narrative that Cumyn's purpose will be to transgress the boundary that normally keeps writers from shocking their readers with the grotesque, but in fact, his book marches along with quite a familiar set of tropes offered: rats (25), a body on the wire (29), greasy tea (because the water was carried up in old petrol tins) (34). Ramsay even comments on the familiar at one point. "So I say what we all still know," he begins before reciting to his friends the things that soldiers are taught to believe about the German enemy— "Fritz won't back down until we've fed him enough iron. It's all the Germans believe in, and if we don't give it to them, they'll give it to us" (36). In this way, the novel dances between pushing the trope of the grotesque violence of the war into new areas and retreating into the comforts of convention.

As the novel's title suggests, the plot is mostly consumed with Crome's leave time in London anyway, so much of the truth it tells is a personal glimpse into wartime in the capital. There are moments of flashback, perhaps predictable (and offered to the reader of British fiction in the 1920s by Virginia Woolf, who in her novel *Mrs. Dalloway* has Septimus Warren Smith glimpse his dead friend, Evans, coming out of a stand of bushes in Regent's Park years after he was killed in the trenches). Thus there is a moment in *The Sojourn* when Ramsay suddenly sees his army buddy, nicknamed "Snug," "slumped across the floor in front of him, his chest blown open by the sniper's bullet" (94). He comments, "He *couldn't* be here, of course not, and yet the stench of the body rises up" (94, italics original). He jumps up, so shocked is he that his cousins will see this fright in their living room, and exclaims something that, he recognizes in the moment after, makes him look to them like a madman. They calmly offer him some tea.

Later, out for a walk around London, he looks down the road they have just come from and "see[s] for a moment instead the Menin Road—the corpse-filled mud, the shell-holes brimmed with poisoned water, the ambulances forever stuck to the axles, horses bleeding…" (124). He makes a point to say—to the reader, who hears his reported internal dialogue—how remarkable it is that this world and the one he's enjoying on a sunny weekday in London are only a day's journey apart (124). If he later admits to his cousin, Margaret, that, "It's like nothing, really—I mean nothing can prepare you for it.…When shells are falling one on top of the other, and it's so loud your brain is scrambled, and the boundaries between bodies—I mean, you see things you never would, and that you'll never, ever forget" (224), even that is a confession *that* things are shocking more than about *what*.

Nevertheless, Cumyn does tread into the graphic in places where he talks about trench warfare, particularly the results of shelling. For instance, he has Crome, having left London and returned to the trenches, glimpse his comrade's severed head:

> [T]*here's Lives beside me. Lives! With a silly grin and a bad scar...and no body. I move in a sudden spasm of panic, grab the thing by the hair and hurl it down the side of the shell-hole. It bounces and rolls like a rock and skids to the bottom, where water is already starting to collect.* (296)

French Memorial at Feigères

In one moment late in Cumyn's narrative, Crome approaches telling some truth to Margaret about what he's experiencing, writing a letter that details how he uncovered the decomposing body of one of his teachers early in the war. But he goes on to claim that he could contextualize that into the course of events, because all of them had a story like that. What now affects him the most horribly is "*being granted a reprieve, a temporary glimpse at life as it ought to be*" (282, italics original). He reprises that claim as he closes the letter: "*[T]he worst of it, as far as I can tell, is that I was freed for a time*" (283). The reader must fill in the gap left by this claim, imagining how horrible life must be as compared to the carefully detailed world of upper middle class propriety that Cumyn has drawn as the surroundings for Crome's leave in London. Cumyn thus dances around the idea of the violence trope as the novel ends. He has invoked it (early), suggested it (in the living room scene) and avoided it (in the late going).[15]

---

15 This discussion leaves aside his portrayal of the effects of sniping, discussed just below in context of Boyden's *Three Day Road*.

Over against Cumyn's toe-in-the-water, toe-out-of-the-water approach, Joseph Boyden's *Three Day Road* pushes the reader to the limits of toleration by offering hideous, graphic violence as it intimately and horribly depicts the life of the sniper and what he does through telling the story of two Canadian First Nations soldiers, Elijah Whiskeyjack and Xavier Bird. So graphic is the detail, in fact, that its presence threatens to steal the focus from the intricate narrative point of view which Boyden offers.

Boyden's risk-taking with regards to the level of violence his text reaches might best be interrogated if it is set up in context of *The Sojourn*. Above, I described that novel by claiming that Cumyn largely sticks to the commonplace other than in a few exceptional, and notable, scenes, and that is so. But the opening (trench) scenes do offer one compelling element that stretches beyond the familiar, because they focus on a realistic depiction of the other side of sniping—those on the receiving end. Cumyn's depictions in this brief stretch of plot register as particularly violent, but Boyden takes this two steps further in that he is even more graphic in his detail about the work of the sniper and that he spreads that detail over the entire scope of his text, rather than limiting it to a single scene, as does Cumyn.

Witness for instance, this scene from *The Sojourn*: "I see Gryphon slumped over, his chest ripped open. I push his body back, straighten him up in a stupid fit of inquiry, and a bullet smashes against my helmet, knocks me back against the wall. Then I'm down on my face and belly, my helmet spinning like a drunken saucer before it comes to rest on my hand" (Cumyn 40). Their lieutenant stupidly and madly tells them to go get the sniper, in broad daylight. He and Snug head out to find the man, probably behind a farmhouse wall, but certainly with an elevated position from which to peer down into the Canadian trench. Snug is hit, and Crome tries to fire back, "but my own head snaps and the world spins. I'm slammed back and fall, bounce off something, feel my face in muck with my brains ringing" (44). Sure that he's dying, he looks at the sky as his friend, Ferguson, comes over and shakes him. The only effect is that Crome sees him shouting but can't hear him well: "[H]e sounds like he's at the other end of a corridor" (45).

The scene becomes yet more graphic when Snug is hit and Ferguson too, in an attempt at rescue: "For the rest of the day we listen to Ferguson's wailing blasphemies, to Snug's rattling moans, to the cold rasp of death breathing down our necks" (48). The sniper leaves them there "as bait," and the men go about their day, "left with an agony of time, slower than mud, than life leaking out of a wounded body" (48). Crome says that they "listen and do nothing," and that "It's enough to stop the blood in the heart, to freeze the breath," but adds that "it doesn't. This is the horrible thing: the blood and breath continue. We cling to our fragments of life and let our friends fail, do nothing to help" (48). This is the horror on the other side of the scope Xavier and Elijah see the world through—not once, but every day they are in combat.

The day progresses with Snug talking to Crome, asking him to write a letter home with the usual platitudes about death. They joke, and Snug dies. Crome and Reese are ordered to bring in the two bodies, and this prompts machine gun fire in which Reese is hit (51). Crome rescues Reese but is forced over the top again to get the two bodies. He almost refuses the order, willing to be shot for it, but he goes. As he slumps back into the trench, he asks, "Where are the bullets now? I expect to be cut in two at any moment. But nothing" (53). Such is the reality of sniping and its aftermath, the effects of the work that Boyden's characters Bird and Whiskeyjack become so proficient at performing.

Boyden pushes his sniping scenes several steps further into the grotesque than Cumyn or any other Great War novel does that uses this same motif. The risk in being offensively graphic is that this element might overshadow or steal the subtlety from an otherwise cleverly constructed and nuanced novel, but to critics, who don't seem particularly concerned with measuring the level of graphic detail offered in the text, the violence of the novel smacks of stereotyping of First Nations men. This point of view comes from their concern with the novel as a part of a larger discourse on First Nations issues. Sophie McCall, for instance, sums up critical work done on Boyden's novel with the following statement:

> [C]*riticism on* Three Day Road *has been…influenced by debates concerning Indigenous literary nationalism following the novel's publication in 2005, leading to a general acceptance of the notion that Xavier and Niska, both of whom are more firmly Cree-identified than the culturally hybrid character of Elijah, define the moral center of the text.* (71)[16]

Another critic sums up the novel this way: "*Three Day Road* by Joseph Boyden is the deeply moving account of an Anishinaabe woman's search for her boy lost in World War I" (Weaver 247). The novel is also remarked upon as a Great War text, but this is much less common. Harting and Kamboureli suggest the following:

> [T]*he book might be read as a narrative that interrupts the patriotic fictionalization of the Canadian nation-state, so vividly dramatized in [the 2008 film]* Passchendaele. *Not merely a counter-narrative to patriotic reminiscences of Canada's participation in the First World War,* Three Day Road *unsettles dominant legitimizing discourses of security. It alerts us to the complex relationship between land claims, narrative, and security, and ultimately calls for a renewal of the bonds of indigenous land, life, and community.* (676)

---

16 The controversy over Boyden himself as a representative of First Nations voices, and his pledge not to act as such, is aside from my concerns here.

Robert Talbot calls Boyden's novel the best known of the recent novels and historical texts that highlight the combat experience of First Nations soldiers (91–92). His concerns, however, are not with literature, but rather with archival evidence as to the nature of First Nations' participation in the war, including donating money and enlisting.

What these readings leave aside is consideration of the novel's fit in the orbit of Great War fiction. Renate Eigenbrod describes the commercial placement of the text as a way to answer this question: "The enthusiastic reception of Joseph Boyden's *Three Day Road*, for example, [saw the book] very quickly catalogued and shelved in bookstores as 'literature' and not under 'Aboriginal Issues'...," but then she returns to the matter of First Nations violence: "Although the novel is very well written, its theme of 'savage' Windigo killings may indeed appeal to archaic racial stereotypes and account at least as much for the book's success in mainstream reception as its literary qualities" (12).[17]

Neta Gordon manages a more appropriate balance as she discusses this novel in a chapter of *Catching the Torch* called "Other Canadians: The Representation of Alternative Versions of the Canadian War [in three novels]." As she describes her intention in the chapter, she says, "The point...is not to collapse the particularities of experience of all those participants in the First World War who were not part of the Central Anglo-Canadian community" but to note how "texts explore the myth of the homogenizing Canadian collective" because "[t]he discursive work of imagining a common national cause pervades contemporary Canadian literature about the First World War" (119, 120). She then reads *Three Day Road* as, in part, "a celebratory novel, whereby First

---

17 These killings were of people turned Windigo, explained in Boyden's narrative as "people who eat other people's flesh and grow into wild beasts twenty feet tall whose hunger can be satisfied only by more human flesh" (49).

Nations contributions to Canada's First World War effort are commemorated and given constructive meaning as part of a living community's narrative" (140). Her reading, which analyzes the novel's construction "via structural and figurative doubles," shows how "Boyden makes visible the mythmaking process that romanticizes both Canada's participation in the First World War and stereotypical representations of First Nations representatives that reduce the Other to a type" (143).

Early in her discussion, Gordon says that Boyden's intention is the "defamiliarizing of tropes associated with the First War" (140). She later comments on the novel's violence by saying, "Though the Cree community that *Three Day Road* depicts is often under physical and psychic attack by encroaching *wemistikoshiw* culture, the violence included in this narrative is not strictly oppositional; more important, it is not depicted in the elegiac terms of a 'last stand' " (149). It is here that I would like to insert my argument about *Three Day Road*.

Newfoundland Memorial, Beaumont-Hamel, France

My question is whether the novel's violent elements, stereo-typing aside, might *be* (to return to Eigenbrod) the book's lit-erary qualities, but my emphasis is not exclusively on the novel's Windigo killings—that of Niska's father of Micah's wife, and that of Xavier Bird of his companion Elijah Whiskeyjack. Rather, I want to recontextualize Boyden's wide-spread and explicit use of combat violence in order under-stand the novel's contribution to the canon of contemporary World War I literature. The novel's violence, in this argument, serves as an intensification of a common trope, confronting the reader and demanding that he or she experience the war in a way that is uncomfortable. As such, it is a marker for the need not to erase the horrific heritage of the war from (cul-tural) memory.

The first violent encounter Boyden offers is frightful but takes place offstage. A sentry has fallen asleep on post. The narrative of Xavier reports, "There are rumours about that Gerald, a young one in our company, was found sleeping at his sentry post last night. Some say that he has been taken a few hundred yards behind the lines and shot already" (70). The truth confronting us here is shielded, described as rumor, as said rather than as factual, and already accomplished, and thus almost not real. The same is true of the next killing detail. Xavier is out in the trenches, and he and another man each throw a Mills bomb, after which he hears screaming. All night long, he replays the moment of pulling the pin, the sound he hears. His conclusion: "I have killed someone now" (84).

In complex and shifting narration that moves between Xavier's recounting of his wartime experience while on a jour-ney back home through the bush with Niska and various other past time frames reflecting Niska's life events and those of Xavier and Elijah as boys, early on we learn of the magnitude of death in France. Xavier tells Niska, for instance, that "So many dead lay buried over there that if the bush grows back the trees will hold skulls in their branches.... We once left a place covered in our dead. When we came back a few months later flowers redder than blood grew everywhere.... They even grew out of rotting corpses" (85). But this description is no different than that in other similar novels, except perhaps in being more poetic. Where Boyden turns up the wick on the violence is in his accounts of the men's sniping.

They take to the task right away, Xavier reporting, "I am made for this" (97). Early on, they lie out in their nest for hours. Later it will be days. Xavier describes the synchronicity of their spirits with the job by saying, "A spell descends on us and makes us a part of the earth" (97). Shortly, they record their first kill, with Xavier spotting and Elijah shooting: "The young soldier's face is a red smearing explosion that exits the back of his head in a spray before he crumples from sight" (99).

The discussion of this plot element—sniping and its aftermath—amongst Boyden's academic readers takes offense at the fact that picturing the two young men as natural to this kind of killing creates an unfair equation of who they are with what they do, arguing that Boyden takes a stereotypical viewpoint on the First Nations man and his training and proclivity for killing, as was indicated. However, read carefully, the novel in fact offers a rebuttal of this claim. This is suggested when, for instance, a white man, Thompson, comments through the narrative of Xavier on what they do: "He says he is amazed by how long we can lie still despite the lice and without falling asleep, how we can spot movement that he is not able to see," and it is the answer that rankles readers: "Elijah explains to him that it is hunting, and hunting is what we have done all our lives" (107).[18] But it only makes sense that someone who grew up hunting might be good at sniping of men.

---

18 Pegler indicates that few snipers in the early going had specific training in the discipline, but that "telescopic-sighted rifles and their knowledge of hunting provided them with a positive advantage" (62).

Canadian National Vimy Memorial

In explaining away their exceptionalism, Xavier offers an apology that allows Boyden space to work his violent plot. He speaks not for First Nations men, but for *these* First Nations men, and Xavier corrects the white man's misperception, though only to himself, as he says, "There is no point in telling Thompson that I am the only one of the two of us really from the bush, the only one who has truly hunted for a lifetime" (107–08). In other words, the outsider may read the events as totalizing of First Nations experience, but those in the know will realize that this is reductive. This claim for specificity rather than stereotype might also be extended to Boyden's novel as critics view it. Accepting that this applies to the text as a whole frees us to look at the violence, and the psychological aftermath of it, which fills this novel, not as an indictment of or unfair characterization of a people group—i.e. as a "race" given to violence, or a certain kind of violence—but as representative of a new level of detail in a novel treating a familiar topic. These snipers, in this view, could be anyone.

The process begins with Xavier describing what they do as "the art of the sniper" and with his amazement at the power of the scope which Thompson attaches to the rifle they train with, seeing the innovation as a white man's invention: "These *wemistikoshiw* amaze me sometimes," he marvels (95, 96). Xavier describes their building of nests as just like what's done at home in hunting goose, and he says that their bodies must be tuned for the job. ("A spell descends on us and makes us a part of the earth"). But that's not about their being of a certain ethnic identity. After all, their trainer is a white man. And, it must be noted, the Germans were excellent snipers as well, as Bird observes (98).[19] The Germans kill character Sean Patrick at one point in a spree that has them shooting by sniping quite a few of the Canadian and British side. Xavier's description of the effects maybe tells a great deal about how he and Elijah feel about what they are doing: "[T]he snipers eat away at morale like a fast disease" (126).

The history of sniping in the Great War, in fact, is not a history of First Nations participation. Amongst those who practiced this occupation, the overwhelming majority were not from those groups. No matter who was doing the shooting, the results, and the emotional-psychological aftermath, were the same, or one would think so, though Martin Pegler points Canadian snipers out for particular praise, saying that they were "the most aggressive and successful of the early part of the war" (44). The effects are psychological, but they have distinct physical manifestations: "Few soldiers were used to the power of these high velocity bullets and the appalling effect they had on the human body" (Pegler 48). Yet those doing the shooting also came to suffer. For Elijah Whiskeyjack the cost is a morphine addiction that grows worse as the war goes on.

---

19 Pegler traces out the history: "From the eighteenth century the creed of the *Jäger*, or hunter, had been deeply embedded in the German psyche. These men—stalkers, hunters, and gamekeepers—learned their craft in vast forests and private estates and thus, for many German youths, the mastery of hunting skills was almost a rite of passage" (25).

The reader learns of it through Xavier's observation: "[Elijah] awoke from sweet dreams to find me sticking a syringe in his arm. He accused me of taking the medicine too, but Elijah knows that I don't. I fight my own struggles just as Elijah does, and every other man.... We all fight on two fronts, the one facing the enemy, the one facing what we do to the enemy" (369).

This belies what he had earlier said when assessing the effects on his friend. "Elijah has killed more men already than I can count on both hands. It doesn't seem to bother him" (110). But by the time he has at least 356 kills, he is heavily addicted, and either that or his principles or the strain of the war has caused him to kill in other circumstances as well. He puts a German in a shell crater out of his misery (111). He kills a gravely wounded soldier on a stretcher in order to get morphine (382). And he violently kills men on trench raids. He tells his friend about his actions: "I slit the throats of three of them so quickly that I surprised even myself!" (260). Xavier looks at his hands, black in the darkness, and realizes that blood covers them. The war has Xavier in its grip, indifferent to his ethnic identity.

For Xavier Bird, also addicted to morphine by the latter stages of the conflict, the results of the violence he experiences, and perpetrates, are mostly psychological. At first, he is the spotter, Elijah the shooter. But he knows the day is coming when he will be shooting. "Easier for me to picture soldiers with antlers on their heads, I tell Elijah. It will make it all the easier when the time comes to shoot one" (128–29). This happens when he dispatches a German sniper who has been victimizing their line for a long time. It's not the kill that startles, though, but the conditions. The German had been lying beneath a rotting corpse in and among other dead bodies as cover (146). Elijah marvels that "[h]e could lie there for hours among the dead and the rotting. He lay there in that stink of death like death itself" (146). The informed reader encounters this scene with the grim realization that Boyden has surfaced or invented details that appear nowhere else in the canon of contemporary literature of this war.

For Elijah, the effects of violence are different than for Xavier. "[He] has learned to take pleasure in killing," Xavier reports, and Elijah warns Xavier that "the freedom of this place will not present itself again" (231). The "freedom he talks about [is] the freedom to kill," something that Xavier has grown weary of (321). But not Elijah. They kill yet another sniper hiding in a nearly destroyed building, and then in clearing the building, they come upon a mother and child. Xavier shoots the woman before he realizes it is not a soldier confronting him, then holds his fire, but Elijah doesn't. Xavier witnesses this: "A rifle shot explodes and the child goes still, a red hole punched in her chest by the bullet" (347). The woman dies also, "each breath gurgling red spittle…. A large red bubble forms at her mouth," and she stares at him (347). Her death is not recorded, but the detail offered to this point is enough. He later reports the death to another soldier, in a blankly unemotional confession. "There is a dead woman and child in Passchendaele," he says, and walks away (351).

At this point near the end of the war (it is 1918), Elijah is acting foolishly, taking chances. Xavier realizes that "Elijah is mad. The acts he does will bring bad luck onto all of us" (356). When the two men and two others, Lt. Breech and a soldier called "Grey Eyes," suffer a mortar explosion, Elijah kills them, not out of mercy due to wounds, but to stop them from revealing the atrocities he and Xavier have committed on the battlefield (384).[20] This is the point where Xavier gives up on the other man's humanity. Even Elijah recognizes that

---

20 Rather like the Biblical prophet Elijah, who ordered the murder of the prophets of Baal.

he is beyond help. "He's fighting what's become of him, he tells me," Xavier reports (386). He wishes that his friend would be killed in battle, so that Xavier himself would be free of the guilt of knowing what he has done. "To me he is mad. I am the only one now to know Elijah's secrets, and Elijah has turned himself into something invincible, something inhuman" (395). He shortly proves it with another horrifically rendered scene. On a trench raid, Xavier comes on him kneeling in tall grass, "a young German pinned below him. The German is bleeding but still alive," and just as Xavier gets there, "Elijah cuts hard into the soldier's solar plexus with a knife" (395–96). The man "writhes and screams," and "Elijah plunges his knife once again into the man" (395–96). The aftermath is almost worse, and he smears his own face in the man's blood in trying to clean himself (396). It's a scene from a slaughterhouse, and it puts a wedge between the two Cree soldiers which cannot be bridged. In the course of this, Boyden in *Three Day Road* manages to depict detail that pushes well past familiar depictions of violence and death.

Understanding why he does this is perhaps as simple as dislocating the violence enacted by these soldiers into the present day, as David Williams does when he speaks of Timothy Findley's Robert Ross as being as much a soldier of the Vietnam war, which had ended just two years before *The Wars* was published, as a Great War soldier. Williams sees Ross as "a soldier whose conformity with his era is kept at a distance, but whose contemporary pacifism is portrayed in extreme close-up" (*Media, Memory* 170).[21] By this measure, Xavier, and more particularly Elijah, are recognizable as characters out of something like *Call of Duty: Advanced Warfare*, which gamers have embraced and that is not shy about rendering violent detail to those who play.

---

21 James F. Wurtz makes a similar argument for the *Charley's War* comic strip (discussed in Chapter 6), which he says was set in World War I but at times "reflected the fears and concerns of the time which produced it," such as during the Battle of the Falklands (207).

Contemporizing these two characters is tempting and perhaps not illogical, since the audience for Boyden's novel could be the same college student who spends his or her time on the PlayStation or Xbox before going to class. However, doing so takes something away from Boyden's contribution to the Great War canon, because what he offers is not an updating to contemporary standards of violence so much as a way of seeing back into a war that has become for most of us a black-and-white or sepia-toned conflict, with the redness of the blood spilled having lost its shock value. Consider Geoff Dyer's claim, which looks compelling but that actually reduces violence to an imprecise image of itself: "[T]he photographs of men queuing up to enlist seem wounded by the experience that is still to come: they are *tinted* by the trenches, by Flanders mud. The recruits of 1914 have the look of ghosts. They are queuing up to be slaughtered: they are already dead" (37, emphasis original). What Boyden (not to mention Cumyn and Findley) does is show us the detail about how they died rather than mute this into sepia, as the photographs, Dyer's description, and many recent Great War novels do. Thus in the end, Boyden, Cumyn, Findley, and any future novelist who takes on the violence of the war and pushes the familiar trope to gruesome new levels of detail, should be viewed not as exploiting an underserved figuration so much as giving another reason the war is written about at all—to preserve a sense that this was the war to end all wars, no matter how miserably that ambition failed.

These novelists see things clearly; they depict violence honestly. Perhaps they even tell the truth in detail for the first time. It is commonly said and believed that people did not know the truth of the trenches, not during the war, not in the decade or so after, not in the ten years after that when fiction and memoir on the war were coming out with regularity. And not, certainly, in the 1940s, taken up as they were with another

war. But now, distance and the exhaustion of familiarity con-
spire together to inspire a generation of writers to reach into
the recesses of their unconscious to recover detail—truthful,
invented, or perhaps on the border between invention and
verification—that offers their readers the chance to understand the war as it really presented itself to its combatants.
And perhaps those who read these books can speak using the
voice of Julian Barnes' narrator Tony Webster in *The Sense of
An Ending,* in asking the question, "What did I know of life, I
who had lived so carefully? Who had neither won nor lost, but
just let life happen to him? Who had the usual ambitions and
settled all too quickly for them not being realized? Who
avoided being hurt and called it a capacity for survival?"
(155). Now, because of the vivid detail that writers like those
discussed in this chapter portray, knowing is possible in ways
that it hasn't been since the moments of the war themselves
were transpiring.

CHAPTER 2

The War for Children: Offering cultural memory to new generations

The recruiting poster from the Great War that has a child asking her father, "Daddy, what did you do in the Great War?" might indicate the limit of knowledge that a youngster would have had of the war in that time. The conflict was a reality, but its details remained at the distant edges of a child's mind. It is interesting to note that in the background of this image is a boy playing with toy soldiers, which critic Margaret Higonnet points out reveals that "mimicry works in more than one direction" as the boy serves as a father model to the man (117). One hundred years and several global or near-global conflicts later, children would be right not to have any idea that World War I existed, and yet it is used as the setting for books that both entertain and give children without even a distant connection to the war a cultural inheritance of knowledge. Such texts can thus be read as addressing implicitly the memory problem posed by the passing of time, their existence as cultural products created by adults for children betraying the "desire" that I use in the title of this book to indicate a cultural need to keep memory of the war alive. To say it another way, the fact that adults choose to publish these works and that parents and libraries make them available to children to read indicates the collision of memory and desire that is at the core of the contemporary mind with respect to the Great War.

Turner and Falgout make the point that "[c]ultural memories must be purposefully constructed…. [B]ut since cultural memory only persists through time if each new generation renews the effort of construction, it is inherently fragile in the way that personal memory [of what one actually experienced] of the past is not" (108). This, perhaps, is the challenge that people who write war books for children are responding to as they make a conscious attempt to create and pass down memory.

Certainly it is not an uncomplicated pursuit. Scholar Esther MacCallum-Stewart bluntly declares, "The First World War has haunted literature, including writing for children, throughout the twentieth and twenty-first centuries" (176).[22] She indicates that such writing has come to use the "parable" method of depicting the war, "an emotive, literary retelling of the war based on a series of texts and cultural shifts rather than on historical perspectives" (176). This has come about because the ideological demands of fiction force a choice on the writer—what to portray and how. Adult readers, she indicates, are seen as having the ability to choose to focus on action or moral outcomes when reading, whereas for children, such a choice is not a feature of their reading experience. Hence writers tend to use a parable form when writing about the war for a young audience (176).

MacCallum-Stewart discusses the debate surrounding writing about World War II, and particularly the Holocaust, indicating that while no absolute standard exists as to what is

---

22 For an account of the literary output aimed at children in the first twenty years after the war, see Flothow, who claims, for instance, "the numerous narratives written for children after the conflict had ended were used to remind their readers of the importance of this historical event and to shape their attitude toward it" (147).

the correct or incorrect method, many scholars have decided
opinions about what should be presented and how. This body
of literature, for example, sometimes sanitizes events, a practice many find irresponsible (177). She adds that Great War
texts written for children tend to follow the lead of those written about World War II, with the result being that they focus
on both moral instruction and on portraying commendable
actions to make the point that war is never positive (177). The
problem, as MacCallum-Stewart sees it, is that this approach
limits World War I children's fiction by disenfranchising ideas
from the time contemporary to the war itself and affecting
"the historicity of the text," focusing on a familiar set of
"events and actions" at the expense of "alternate views of war"
(177). Such literature "privileges more recent political and ideological beliefs rather than the actual events. This erases subtleties of distinction and contrasts in behavior and/or belief
that occurred during the war" (178). This makes such literature reductive, valorizing certain (contemporary) notions of
historical "fact" and creating didactic writing, a criticism ironically leveled at prior iterations of children's war literature,
which tended earlier in the 20th century to "be overly propa-
gandistic or...[reflect] old value systems" (178). Her claim
is that "contemporary children's literature about the war is
just as—if not more—didactic" as what was written in the
past (178).

In fact, the specific problem of children's literature about
this war reflects the more general question/problem of memory I am setting forth: What is remembered, why, and how,
especially now in the long aftermath of the war? MacCallum-
Stewart says that "since 1919, the war has been primarily
remembered through literary, rather than historical, accounts"
with the favored themes being redemption of the individual
through sacrifice or the loss of a friend, a focus on the pity

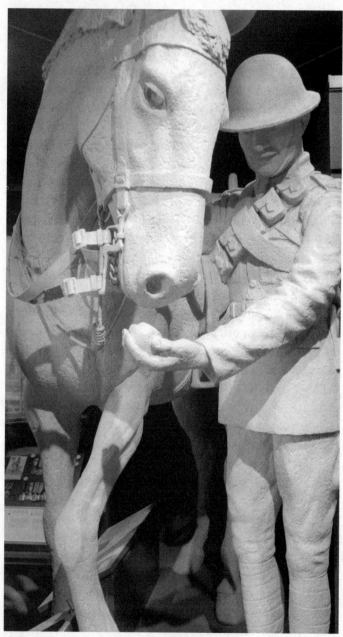

National War Museum, Edinburgh

of war, and war as the vehicle of instruction in moral truth, a reductive set of outcomes (178, 179).

In Britain, MacCallum-Stewart says, the war works its way into the school curriculum almost inevitably. Mentioning specifically Michael Morpurgo's *Private Peaceful* and *War Horse* (the former considered in the present chapter along with Sonya Hartnett's *The Silver Donkey* and Iain Lawrence's *Lord of the Nutcracker Men*), she claims that their canonization in school curriculum "implicitly endorse[s] each text as both well-written *and* accurate and implies that the war is a subject for *serious* children's writers" (180, emphasis original) but only those, she later adds, who are willing to use it to make a moral point, a fact which holds it back (186). Her claim that, "Overall...children's literature is far more stymied than its adult counterparts" is paid off in her summary statement about the topic of Great War literature written with a youthful audience in mind (186):

> While children's literature has expanded greatly in recent years and often found new modes of expression, First World War literature is largely held back by exterior moral concerns, including the need to educate children about the history of the British Isles in certain ways and the paramount desire to present war as always negative. (186)

The question of whether a book ought to be characterized as children's literature has its own complicated history, with more recent scholars making the appeal to abandon the effort to circumscribe particular categories for texts. As Marah Gubar points out, anything read by children is in one sense children's literature, while on the contrary, texts written with children or mixed audiences in mind often become standards which adults read as well. *Huckleberry Finn* provides a ready example, as does *The Little Prince* (209).

In fact, Gubar starts her article by citing Roger Sale, who said, " 'Everyone knows what children's literature is until asked to define it' " (qtd. in Gubar 209). Problems include defining based on perceived authorial intention, defining based on reader perception, or defining based on publisher preference (209). And, the thinking goes, spending time arguing about such matters is neither particularly productive nor an activity which preoccupies most scholars in the field (210). John Rowe Townsend makes an interesting claim in this regard when he says, "[J]ust as 'children are not a separate form of life from people,' children's books are not a discrete and distinctive type of literature" (qtd. in Gubar 210). They might not be a distinct type, but the first thing that strikes the reader of some of these books is the thinness of development, perhaps a necessity of their abbreviated length but also, perhaps, based on the (adult) perception of audience demands. Children's books at times allow for weak, overgeneralized, or highly (but ineffectively) symbolized narrative that would not stand scrutiny were the presumed text intended for a more "sophisticated" audience.

In such novels, war is often a distant shadow, a feature of someone's experience in another place or another time with only a reflection occurring in the visible surface of the text. It's almost as if the child audience is a collection of Plato's cave-dwellers, mutely observing the shadows thrown on the wall by the events of a war out of their view. What wartime action exists is often told in a catalogue-like way, even at times as a reporting of past events. In this respect, these novels recycle common tropes, and as such they arrive at their moral points perhaps too easily. That said, there are exceptions, like the beautifully rendered text by Iain Lawrence considered below.

Hartnett's *The Silver Donkey* has large gaps in terms of the verisimilitude of the war. The action takes place a mile from the seacoast of France, with the battle having been left behind by the lieutenant who has deserted. Because the novel features the conversations he holds with two little girls and their 13 year-old brother, it couldn't help but be set well away from the Front. Battles go on out of sight, and men are lost, with the reporting of that being, again, at a remove: "[I]n war it is impossible to keep every soldier alive. For every man that was lost, the soldier grieved as if for a brother" (79). But there is no indication how they were lost, and no portrayal of the substance of this grief. Reportage takes place at arm's length, with the conclusion equally so: "[H]e hated the war and could never shake from his mind the memory of the dreadful things he had seen," though the reader does not know what these are (79).

The war comes slightly closer when the brother of the two girls, Pascal, comes into the scene, about halfway through the girls' interaction with the soldier. He is interested in knowing what any boy of that age and moment might want to know: "What did you see there? What did you do? Have you fired a machine gun?…Do you have any medals? Have you thrown a grenade?" (179). Leaving aside for a moment that a child that age in a time when press censorship of the war ruled might not have had any idea what a grenade was, the questions seem obvious enough, especially if Pascal (who is French) was like most British boys of the time, an avid consumer of boys' adventure stories. But his sister immediately shuts his line of inquiry down. "Pascal…don't ask him those things," says Marcelle (129). Ignoring Marcelle, Pascal presses on to ask whether it is true that the enemy is going to win the war. The soldier says, "I don't know, Pascal. I only know that the fighting is dreadful" (129). The dual resonance might escape Pascal, and indeed, the intended young reader of this book. "Dreadful" can be used in the military sense to mean closely engaged, a fierce battle. The statement then would replicate what a newspaper might say by way of eliding the details of what "dreadful" really suggests. Or the lieutenant might be speaking in a personal voice, explaining why he fled—because to be involved in these experiences is more than his psyche could handle.

Pascal's response is to say that nobody in the village knows anything about the war, even their teacher, and that he is anxious for details. But Marcelle quiets him, citing their father, who has told them that "[t]he war is awful" (130). Little sister Coco chimes in to say that "[e]verything is spoiled now" because, in effect, the war has been brought to this placid village not by the soldier's presence, but by Pascal's questions (130).

The war is thus simultaneously at the center of *The Silver Donkey* and quite distant from it. When it is present, it is in the form of common tropes and abstract, romanticized language. Witness the second time it is invoked by Lieutenant Shepard. He lists the elements soldiers experience including trenches, hard biscuits, foot problems, getting packages and then shrapnel, snipers, and shells (137–39, 142). He uses completely skewed syntax to depict his experience: "And fight they did; and die" (140). Even the detail is high-flown in its diction: "[T]he soldiers bravely obeyed, plunging across the quagmire earth in a fraught attempt to claw from the enemy a handful of ground. In the stinking expanse of no man's land, only the color of their uniforms stood between a soldier and his enemy" (142).

This diction is reprised by Hartnett when she offers this sentiment through her narrator: "Lieutenant Shepard's men were tough, smart, fast, and brave, too good to waste: but wasted they were, as the lieutenant knew they would be, for war is only waste" (143). Didactic, obvious, and in a voice altogether unnatural, this is lesson-making at the most apparent level. It has none of the emotional resonance that it might given the circumstances: he has fled the Front and thus could be subject to the same punishment Charlie Peaceful is at the end of Morpurgo's *Private Peaceful*.[23]

In *Private Peaceful*, even an attack is described in distant, clinical terms. A two-day bombardment is "the longest two days of my life," says character Tommo: "I cower there, we all do, each of us alone in our own private misery" (144). Ironically, the deaths of German soldiers are portrayed in a more realistic manner (145), because as Morpurgo's narrative goes forward, it increases in realism. When Tommo is hit, for instance, he reports that "I find myself suddenly on my knees, and I don't know why. There is blood pouring down my face, and my head is wracked with a sudden burning pain so terrible that I feel it must burst" (175). Before the blast, he was already exhibiting a psychological removal from the scene, feeling as if he was "in a trance, as if outside myself altogether," a common response to traumatic situations, but the blast itself knocks him back to reality, then thrusts him into another realm altogether, where, he says, "I find myself falling out of my dream down into a world of swirling darkness," which he takes to be his own death (175). But there is no agony, no fear, and he shortly awakens to the "muffled sound of machine-gun fire" (177). The "dreadful," to return to that word, is always at a safe remove.

Hartnett's soldier, when he sees something truly terrible, a soldier named Ernie who is hit, looks away, watching as a man distant on the battlefield is wounded, his arms windmilling (149). His distancing of himself also, naturally, protects the reader from gruesome detail. The effect is to impart the knowledge that war is awful without the specific

---

23 Ironically enough, the same theme appears in Iain Lawrence's *Lord of the Nutcracker Men*, which has a soldier shoot himself in the leg, come home, hide in and around town until the boy-hero of the story rescues him, and then live with an altered identity, though known to everyone in town as a deserter, once the war concludes. "Murdoch took a new name, and all of [the village of] Cliffe kept his secret," we learn (205).

detail as to why that might be said to be so. This one properly realized battle scene is the only one offered to the reader, and this is portrayed as exerting enough psychological pressure on the young man that he must flee. The text subtly suggests that he has switched identities with Ernie: "Nor did anyone notice Ernest Whittaker had gone" (158). If this offers the plot enough deniability to sustain its realism, then it does so by the thinnest of threads.

Bringing *Private Peaceful* and *The Silver Donkey* together, then, suggests that the approach of those who write Great War novels intended for a younger audience is to offer moral claims without necessarily taking into account their contradictions. This happens in narratives that, further, appear to presume that a youthful reader needs reminding of the outline details of the war in order to have a context in which to consider moral dilemmas without being exposed to explicit details about the conflict itself.

However, as texts with the social function of imparting "truth" about the war to a new generation, novels such as these do have possibilities. A close look at *The Silver Donkey* reveals that the novel overcomes what appears to be a hackneyed theme (and one unrelated to the war) by using a sophisticated structure that sets inside a general story of cowardice a story of courage that counterbalances the message of the book as a whole: running from the Front will turn out alright in the end.

Structurally, *The Silver Donkey* consists of four retellings of older tales intercut with the (as was said) narration of two girls, and later their brother, who find a Great War soldier who has fled the war, becoming blind by, the clues suggest, a sort of delayed onset of shell shock. The key to validating the text is to observe the relationships of the four retellings one to the other that allows all but one to cancel out, leaving meaning to emerge from the double-coded structure of the text.

Roslin War Memorial, Scotland

One inserted narrative is the story of the birth of Jesus and his "rescue" by the agency of a donkey called Hazel who takes the pregnant Mary and young Joseph to Bethlehem and then agitates to leave because she senses the danger the baby is in when Herod starts killing young males. Hazel dies after the arduous journey of escape, but her sacrifice is explained in the inserted story by her owner, who says, "Nothing lives forever, Joseph.... The lucky ones are those who are remembered after they're gone," after which she encourages Joseph to "[t]each your boy to love animals, to always be kind to them. Hazel would like that, I think" (71).

A second story intercut into Hartnett's text allegorizes a drought in which humans and various animals from an elephant to a tiger to a snake climb a hill and appeal to the sky for rain. Each takes a threatening approach, and each fails. Then without anyone knowing it, a donkey climbs the hill to the highest point and makes an appeal that gains the needed rain. The values of the donkey and its relative "social" position are again what makes the animal effective. A voice in a gathered crowd of people and animals says, "We may be hungry and thirsty, but we haven't lost so much dignity that a moth-eaten donkey must plead on our behalf!" (116–17).

The donkey sidles up to the anthropomorphized sky and is asked why it is there. The narration indicates that, "The sky knew that the people and other animals scorned donkeys" and that due to the species' reputation as "stubborn and thick-headed brutes," they would not let a donkey speak for them (118–19). The sky challenges the animal with the fact that giving rain will only perpetuate the existence of a world in which the donkey is scorned, mistreated, and despised. The donkey's response moves the sky to action, because it says that it will not take pleasure in the suffering of others. The sky relents, speechifying the moral lesson: "You endure much that is unforgivable, yet you forgive. And if you, a simple donkey, can have mercy, then surely I, the boundless sky, can be merciful also" (121).

If at this point the reader is wondering what this has to do with either the war or the soldier-escapee, then such wondering might be forgiven. Story three connects the lines a little more closely, as it tells the tale of a boy who loved donkeys, found himself in the army as a stretcher bearer, and at that point realizes that using a donkey to climb the cliffs where soldiers are fighting allows him to "rescue many more men than he was rescuing on his own" (187). This in turn gives the soldier, Jack, a feeling of home and childhood.

But tragedy intervenes when Jack exposes himself to a sniper position as he tries to rescue a man. He knows in advance the danger of being there, and even pushes the donkey out of the line of fire before going himself. He gets hit, and as he dies, the donkey comes to him, brushing his face with its muzzle to offer comfort (196).

The final story is of the brother of the shell-shocked soldier found by the three children, a boy named John who is everyone's delight but set to die young due to a heart condition. One day, trying to find a remedy for his ailment, he begins to dig. He quickly realizes the futility of the quest: "He had not succeeded—he would never succeed—in escaping destiny. John knew that even if he dug to China, he couldn't make his heart well" (222). Yet as he weeps, and the tears form a puddle in the hole, he spies something—a silver donkey small enough to fit in the hand.

This talisman becomes what helps him accept his destiny, so that he can be like the animals, taking each day as it comes and living each one the best way he can (225), and it is this donkey that the soldier, his brother, has and allows the earlier-mentioned children, particularly Coco, to hold as well.

Her hopes, in fact, run to possessing the donkey herself, and after they have helped the soldier escape on a small boat piloted by fellow villager Fabrice, she returns to the place where the soldier had been hiding. She can't find the silver donkey, until she thinks through the moral lessons the soldier had taught her: to be brave, which she had been, and to try her best, which she had done. She realizes that he has buried the donkey, and she digs it up, kisses it, and the narrative shortly ends (265–66).

All of this makes the point, if not in an entirely complex way, that donkeys, while lowly, sometimes despised, and often abused, have heroic qualities. What does this have to do with the war? Other than the incidental fact that the story is set around the escape of the soldier from his front-line duties, not much. Only one of the animal stories cited, the third, has any reference to the war. Thus we might might move towards a useful interpretation of this novel by drawing a line tracing the trajectory of stories one, two, and four and then setting them aside. This would leave story three as the misfit, but notable because its tale of heroism provides contrast to that of the soldier who is the main character of *The Silver Donkey*. This, then, provides an interesting counterpoint to the ending of the novel, which seems patently unbelievable for any reader (adult or child) aware of the results of desertion from the Front.

As the novel ends, Coco grips her little silver donkey, staring "joyfully into its eyes," and those eyes shine back at her (266). There is but one paragraph left: "And somewhere on a beach far away, footprints crossed and were stamped from the sand as children ran about collecting seashells, laughing and playing in the sun" (266). And so the reader is supposed to believe that the soldier vanishes without a trace, not having thus to face the consequences of leaving the Front, which even he has acknowledged will lead to trouble. Perhaps his hope is a defense of shell shock, though rendering this less possible is that his symptoms, a temporary blindness, gradually recede as the narrative goes on, leaving him vulnerable to a charge of desertion and the concomitant penalty, which could range to execution.

Thus for the knowing reader, *The Silver Donkey* can't logically end as it does, with the footprints of the soldier magically wiped away. And if the novel models the values of the donkey, which apparently allow it to choose right even when the world doesn't see that initially, a critical point of view might suggest that the inheritor of both the little silver donkey and those values, the child character Coco, is not a model of strength so much as of naiveté. However, one might make the argument that Hartnett's point is to show that children may take stances that form moral correctives to the adult mode of thinking that starts wars in the first place, the same thinking that gets the soldier in embedded narrative number three killed and that is thus revealed as inferior to childlike trust in a greater good. In that case, the value of the lowly beast who always manages to find the right in wrong wins out. But it takes childlike faith in not testing the narrative too much against fact to make that seem believable.

Morpurgo also makes the presentation of values key to his text, *Private Peaceful,* and he too uses the wisdom of a young man to upend traditional moral codes, but his novel has an added complication. Its text runs along at two levels. The narrative we follow, the story of Tommo, tests the traditional values of service, sacrifice, and courage, but this story is surrounded by a larger frame narrative in which Tommo's brother, Charlie Peaceful, awaits his execution for desertion. At the end of the novel, he is executed, and this event, combined with the interplay of Charlie's and Tommo's stories, undermines what might have been the simple moral message of *Private Peaceful*, showing instead the complicated and highly contextualized ways in which values work in wartime.

Tommo is just 16 when he joins the British army to fight in the Great War. His twin motivations are to escape his home, heartbroken because his brother has married the girl he has always been in love with (an impossible love—she is the brother's age, older, and she and the brother get together when Tommo is a youth), and to respond to the taunts of an elderly woman who needled him in a market town when a group of soldiers showed up on a recruitment drive. As he describes it, "I came face to face with the war for the first time, a war that until now had seemed unreal and distant to all of us, a war only in newspapers and on posters" (94).

Of course, if he was trusting what he read in the British dailies, he would have had no real knowledge of the events at the Front, as is noted by Randall Stevenson: "The press's expanding powers had been immediately recognized and carefully controlled from the very first days of the war" (23). Reports were based upon an agreement that only certain things would be included, and the language adopted was sunny, even in the worst of times. The reporting on the opening of the Battle of Somme, for instance, indicated that the attack began well: "[W]e got our first thrust well home, and there is every reason to be most sanguine as to the result" was how one newspaper reported it, when in fact, "[a]nyone near the Somme…could not fail to be appalled by these reports and others like them" (25). But Tommo knows none of that, and hears only the speech made to the effect that the Hun will soon be running through the streets of the market village near his home unless he joins up. The man speaking looks him right in the eye, and Tommo undergoes a realization: "Until that moment it had honestly never occurred to me that what he was saying had anything to do with me. I had been an onlooker. No longer" (96). But when the aforementioned elderly woman asks him, "Y'ain't a coward, are you?" he slides away from her and then runs, though by the time he is back at the farm where he works, he has decided to enlist (97–98).

He goes on to detail that this is in part so that he can be with Charlie, with whom he has lived his whole life, but we also learn that he has bought the propaganda line about the Germans invading English soil and that the taunts of the toothless old woman continue to resound in his thoughts (104). Much later, her question recurs in his mind, by which point he can answer, having been "out there," that he is not a coward, in fact (146).

But if this is the story of moral strength, it is set against the fact that Tommo is too young to enlist and only gets in when he and his older brother lie, claiming to be twins (108). Further, there is the complication of his brother's pending execution for desertion, which is presented not as theme, but in the structural construction of the text, in which the hours that pace the chapters represent the last night of Charlie Peaceful's life. That point surfaces as the narrative reports, "I [Charlie] even sent the padre away" as the hours tick through the night (141). The clue is subtle enough that readers, especially youngsters, might lack enough external knowledge for it to be obvious to them that the night is counting down towards the work of a firing squad. It is not until the narrative is near its end that the point is made explicit (176).

So if Tommo joins the war to exhibit the values of courage—or to show himself the antithesis of the coward—there are moral complications that overshadow his actions and stretch outside the text. Morpurgo reinforces the point with an "Author's Note" after the narrative in which he states,

"That a shameful injustice had been done to these unfortu-
nate men [historical persons] seemed to me beyond doubt"
(201). He makes it clear that he is referring to the "over 300"
British soldiers who had been executed during the war (200).
He tells the story, he says, to feel close to them, to understand
"courage and cowardice, [as] a way of understanding more
about ourselves" (202). This attempt to make a moral point is
compromised, according to one critic, by the novel's reliance
on unambiguous moral absolutes, such as Charlie being the
perfect soldier and military commander Sergeant Hanley
being represented as "devious, vindictive, and uncaring"
(MacCallum-Stewart 181). But how is that different from
what Hartnett does? In fact, the two novels proceed similarly,
with any naiveté in moral matters not a flaw but a corrective
to the "wisdom" that created the war.

Another approach to mediating the war to a young audience comes in the most aesthetically pleasing work under
present consideration, Lawrence's *Lord of the Nutcracker Men*.
Categorized by the publisher as part of a list intended for the
teen reader, the novel's (probably unintended) irony is that its
engagement with toy soldiers come to life places it squarely in
a tradition of literature often pitched at children, not teens,
because, as one scholar points out, toys and representations of
them as live characters in fiction serve to help children "project their hopes and fears" and thus have the concept of war
mediated to them (Higgonet 118). Yet the cleverness of the
novel resides in its ability to draw the adult reader into
the observation of play, because scenes of toy soldier battles
staged in the protagonist's auntie's garden predominate. The
toy soldiers themselves, carved individually by the protagonist's father and sent back to him from the Western Front,
form a source of happiness as the reader observes their
description in Lawrence's text.

But the novel does its most clever work as it doubles the events of the games that Johnny Briggs plays into the real history of the war his father is fighting in the trenches in France, details of which are offered to Johnny in a series of letters which begin most chapters. (A few chapters start off with one of his mother's letters. She works in a munitions factory.)

In fact, here is a point of departure for any adult reader who knows anything about the letters soldiers sent home from France, as Mr. Briggs' letters are far, far more explicit in their detail than real-life ones would have been. Consider that he is talking to a ten year-old when he describes being caught out in No Man's Land and fired upon during a trench raid. He uses a dead German body for his cover (67). Another letter offers the realistic detail of how a comrade got hit in the throat by a sniper (85). Nothing so explicit would have made it past the censors, even if a man had decided to tell of such things, which is unlikely.

The novel explores the limit between fantasy and reality as it becomes clear that his father's letters describe the backyard battles the boy has staged. Johnny comes to think that his play trench fighting might have a predictive function, and indeed, he seems to be correct. The toy soldier version of his father, for instance, begins to fade and develop a crack. Johnny panics: "He looked old and pale, not right at all. I lifted him up from the battlefield, a thousand feet up in his scale of little men. I cradled him in my hands" worried that "[h]e's sort of broken" (82). Shortly later, Johnny is playing again, happy to notice that "his paint hadn't faded any more, that the crack in his body wasn't getting any bigger" (88).

Johnny's friend Sarah herself sees the connection between their play in the garden and what's happened to her father, a decorated leader who had been killed. "It was that game…. That stupid game" she accuses Johnny (111). He goes home and tells his aunt that he believes that to be so, asking her opinion. She of course tells him that the idea is ridiculous, but as he surveys his play trenches and thinks about recent events, he realizes that he had put his father-soldier figure in a place where he seemed uncomfortable, and that out in France, as a letter revealed, a "terrible shelter that my real dad had found" made him uncomfortable for a night (115). In the next letter he gets, his father tells Johnny that he had had a dream of being asleep and having the grown-up Johnny standing over him and seeing how he was doing, which is exactly what the boy Johnny had done to the toy soldier (115).

When the town is suddenly alight with the good news that their army has made a major pushback of the Germans, Johnny is not surprised. He tells his aunt, "I had a battle with my soldiers. I pushed the Germans back, and now it's really happened," a point which his aunt naturally dismisses (119). To him, "It seemed that whatever I did with my nutcracker men would happen soon after in France" (122). Yet his teacher-friend, Mr. Tuttle, doesn't take his claims seriously any more than his auntie does. Johnny's conclusion: "It was the sort of thing that adults wouldn't believe" (124). What's worth considering is whether that statement can be applied to Lawrence's novel as a whole if the presumed reader is not a child or teen, but an adult, or whether, in fact, somehow, the story resonates with truth, which it seems to do.

War toys, according to Roland Barthes, "domesticate war," as Higonnet points out (119), though the intention of Johnny's father, a toy maker, gradually shifts from domestica-tion to its opposite. A year prior to shutting his shop to go to war, he had given his boy a set of German toy soldiers. As the war begins, Johnny asks for French and British soldiers to combat them, and his father slowly creates a set, a few before he leaves to fight and more as time goes on and he whiles away his days at the Front. They gradually become more grotesque, the set coming to include one soldier with a dog's face and one so horrible that the aunt immediately burns it: "[H]orrible and twisted, a tortured little man.... It seemed to twitch on the table, its arms groping out, its legs all disarrayed. It looked awful, barely human, like something from a nightmare" (Lawrence 130).

Higonnet claims, "War toys remind us that war is not something that happens on a neatly contained 'battlefront' but [is] part of the everyday" (119). But this toy serves to horrify to the point where her further statement cannot be true in the context: "The toy in the war story as well as in life grants distance and permits us to claim mastery" (119–20). The only mastery offered here is in the toy's destruction, to which Johnny, always careful and loving of his toys—albeit he plays with them and leaves them outside in all weather—reacts: "The thing was more horrid than maggots, more horrid than leeches or great, hairy spiders. I felt a huge relief when Auntie Ivy flung it in among the coals" (130).

For the aunt, the adult in the scene, the burning of the figure serves to bring to the forefront the horror of the war, and she begins to weep, something the boy has never seen before. She covers her face and shrieks; she expresses her fear of the war, saying, "It's such a terrible war. Men dying in ditches; men falling in rows to machine guns"; and she says that if it goes on much longer, she will go mad (131). Johnny embraces her, more out of his desire to get her to stop than to comfort her, and then he goes outside. Surveying the kingdom of his backyard battlefield, he realizes that he is "lord of the nutcracker men" and concludes that "Maybe it *was* true that whatever happened in the garden happened in faraway France" (133, emphasis original). He initiates an enormous attack against the German side. As such, he is fulfilling the dictates of the genre, which demand that "[d]isproportionate size grants the edge of superiority that permits the boy to become the commander of a collection of toy soldiers" (Higonnet 124). But the fact is, his toys seem, to the end of the narrative, not to be diminished in scale, but to have connections to real-life events—to be life-sized, in a sense.

Lord of the Nutcracker Men deploys "the stock narrative trajectory of children's stories…: home-away-home" (Higonnet 122) to govern its plot structure. The father comes home from France. The mother comes back from her work in munitions to make the family intact once more. And Auntie Ivy marries widower Tuttle, the schoolteacher, which allows them to form a home together. And yet in the time to come, the toys are not relegated to a past or lost childhood as Johnny matures. Johnny gives them to Murdoch, a soldier-deserter who is in hiding in the village, and they are put on a bookshelf, from which, as the years go by, they slowly topple, as if they represent the deaths of real-life men who have come back and grown old and are now starting to die off (205). Thus the reader is able maintain the suspension of disbelief that allowed her or him to observe the parallel events in a British garden and the battlefields of France as in fact having an impact on one another.

One might ask why children ought to be burdened with a memory that might otherwise pass them by, even in a story with a compelling narrative hook. Higonnet points out that "[i]n the reflections between toy and human, child and adult, light and shadow intermingle, so that the reader can reconstruct what it is to be human. The toy as simulacrum serves as an imaginative mediator that enables psychic investment and displacements" (130). I might argue that in the case of a text as engaging as Lawrence's, this would work for adults and children alike.

Children's fiction of the Great War either allows or compels the child to understand the world he or she will inherit one day, even while offering to those with complex reading strategies at their disposal potentially more nuanced meanings. The claim these texts seem to offer is that adults can forgive themselves for exposing children to this cultural legacy if the texts themselves are sufficiently stripped of realistic detail. Readers will know the war existed, but they won't carry the weight of it with them. That's something that can, and for many who continue to be readers of this strain of English fiction, will, come later, because at some point, they will come into the cultural inheritance of the war with a more full understanding, one which will be developed by more complex, and at times gruesome and morally compelling, texts.

SECTION 2

FINDING MEMORY IN THE GAPS

CHAPTER 3

Sharing the Burden:
The women's war

As topics more familiar have been written about nearly to the point of exhaustion, fiction writers have turned their attention to areas not as widely treated, giving voice to a range of experience previously unacknowledged. One of these is the women's war or the war at home. Novels on this topic move past tales of lonely lovers waiting for the departed hero and portray women with a clear (contemporary) sense of themselves as complex individuals. As such, they indicate an expression of the desire to see the war as a shared cultural heritage rather than limit it to the province of men. This sharing of the burden of war is dramatized in Frances Itani's *Deafening*, Jacqueline Winspear's *Birds of a Feather*, and Jane Urquhart's *The Stone Carvers*. Each codes the war as a remembered act that must be processed and put into the past in order to move on to life after, a fact particularly true for the women characters.

In widening the field of fiction to include the experience of women and other noncombatants, contemporary writers demonstrate an understanding that the war was fought not by the soldiers alone. George L. Mosse describes the days in the run-up to the war in August 1914 by saying "the nation seemed to act with one voice, heart, and soul—a fragmented people had become a true national community" (64). His further description, "The loneliness of the individual in the modern world was past as he became one with his people," could do with gender-neutral pronouns, but what he suggests further rings true: "A new feeling of national unity…[became] a powerful force" (64).

However, shared participation had a barrier: women, many thought, were to be shielded from the truths of the Front. There were multiple strategies deployed to make this the case. The news stories and images sent home were sanitized. Neil Hanson documents the situation in both the British and German press in *The Unknown Soldier*, explaining that, for example, "censorship ensured that civilians at home remained ignorant of the full horrors of Passchendaele" (230). This happened because "'embedded' war correspondents ensured that only reports of 'great victories' appeared in the British newspapers" (227). Philip Gibbs, the correspondent for *The Times*, also created a "fantastic version of events" that distorted the "story of High Wood to glorify the role of the tanks" (Hanson 194). Juliet Nicolson echoes these ideas in *The Great Silence*: "The soldier's way of life in war remained unrecognizable to anyone who had not experienced it" (25). Letters, as is well known, were heavily censored. Men who came home on leave were often either unable to talk about what they had seen or unwilling to do so, since they were upholding a chivalric code that said the female constitution was incapable of dealing with the kinds of horrors men at the Front would commonly see.

But that assumption was false from the first, as Vera Brittain proved, along with thousands of other women who served in military hospitals as part of Voluntary Aid Detachments (VADs).[24] Brittain indicates that women even

---

24 This is a move that DeGroot describes by saying it "salved their frustration" at the restrictive roles otherwise offered to them (69).

lost their lives in combat, as was the case for several killed in the air raid on her hospital near Boulogne on May 19, 1918. One woman "was evidently slain by a bomb while actually on duty," resulting in her tombstone being marked with "killed in action" (170).

Brittain details the place of women in the war from first-hand experience even as she highlights the tendency to downplay their experience. She first says, "They worked, but they also went on living and suffering and remembering; and immortality—as so many of the disabled and the unemployed have since had reason to realize—is the reward only of a life laid down" (122). She further explains that most of the literature written in the aftermath of the war, as well as other visual-artistic representations of the war, has "ignored the active war-work done by women" (122). "[F]or the most part war memorials, war paintings and war literature reveal to a later generation only the work and agony of the men, because this was crowned and immortalized by death" (122).

Brittain's question was virulent at the time, and it is poignant still: "Why should these young men have the war to themselves?" she queried after seeing *Journey's End* and reading a couple of the early memoirs (193). "Didn't women have their war as well? They weren't all, as these men make them out to be, only suffering wives and mothers..." (193). She then asks, "Does no one remember the women who began their war service with such high ideals or how grimly they carried on when that flaming faith had crumbled into the grey ashes of disillusion?" (193). Think, for instance, of women working in munitions factories, who became casualties of war due to both poisoning and accidents. As one historian says, "Given the volatile nature of the work death was never far away" (Royle 213).[25] Brittain comments, "[T]he two wars made the

---

25 The accident in the factory in Silverton, East London, in 1917 was more destructive than all enemy air raids combined, says Royle (213).

Monument to the soldiers who died in World War I, Coimbra, Portugal

sexes equal, not merely because women proved that they could do the work of men (as they did), but because they could, and did, die the deaths of men. Thus, they shared the 'supreme sacrifice', which made them equals in death as in life" (208-09).

In some circumstances, of course, women could do little more than wait for news, but even that had its horrors. During the time when one expected news, "ordinary household sounds became a torment. The striking of a clock, marking off each hour of dread, broke into the immobility of tension with the shattering effect of a thunderclap" (Brittain 205).[26] "It is not surprising that many women developed an anxiety neurosis which lasted until the end of their lives," Brittain elucidates (206). Perhaps her best synopsis comes in this line: "War was a human event, not a happening which affected one age or sex rather than another" (204).

Itani's *Deafening* cuts two ways: as a novel about the experience of those left at home, particularly women, and as a text which tackles the subject labeled by Donna M. McDonald "the elusive deaf identity" (464). "The rarity of the fully realized deaf person in memoir and fiction shapes the way readers regard deaf people," she claims, but presents the challenge to the writer not to portray the deaf via "the taint of triumphalism or complaint" (McDonald 463). The goal should never be to show the deaf experience as universal, she concludes (463). Itani's novel manages to avoid that potential pitfall via its particularity, focusing on the experience of one young woman from the age of about five through her early twenties, as the war concludes. Much of the beauty and complexity of the text is in the private moments of this main character, Grania, first as she grows up and later as she watches her husband, Jim, go to war from the tiny Ontario town where they live. Itani herself described her thematic goals as being to portray a series of

26 Brittain describes one such ordinary day in *Because You Died*. See 205ff.

oppositions: "sound and silence, love and loss, hope and despair" (Fisher 50). She develops these themes through the characters' involvement with the war.

Though McDonald indicates that many of the portrayals of deaf people (often by the hearing) involve stereotype or focus on the theme of loss, Itani's emphasis is elsewhere (465). Speaking of this novel as well as Vikram Seth's *An Equal Music* and TC Boyle's *Talk Talk*, McDonald says that they "position their reader to…witness, be immersed in, and navigate experiences of deafness" (465). Itani in particular "draws the reader into the deaf experience through the narrative device of the interior monologue of the deaf heroine, Grania, which is supported by an omnipotent narrator's observations of other people's responses to her deafness," which allows the reader to be "immersed in Grania's preoccupation with her deaf self and social isolation" (McDonald 466). The critic also notes that the love story of Jim and Grania is set during the Great War, "against the imaginative soundtracks of the gunfire of the war in Europe and the quiet of small-town life in Canada" (466).[27] In fact, it is not the sonic difference between the two geoscapes which signifies so much as the physical and emotional distance that separates actors on each stage, and Itani's text, to the degree that it is a narrative of those (mostly women) who have been left at home, dramatizes and finds meaning in the unbridgeable gaps in space, time, and knowledge which exist between the soldier and those he leaves behind.

The couple has been married for just weeks when Jim leaves for training and service. He survives four years of the war before he returns. Much of the narrative of *Deafening*

---

27 Note, however, that McDonald adds to her discussion that she is disappointed with the way that this novel portrays deafness for a contemporary audience. "I feel resentful, angry, embarrassed, and sullen because I do not want *this* to be the story of deafness that is told today," though she admits that the historical point of view it offers is important to understand and preserve (467).

occurs in this four-year gap. Itani's challenge is to fill this space meaningfully. She does it by her portrayal of Grania's life as a deaf person, but also by showing just how hard the waiting is, by using a series of indications to show that the war is far away, largely unfigurable to those who are not participants. The point is summarized in the last scene, which has Jim coming off a train to greet Grania, whose narrative informs us, "She would never know where he had been. Nor would he know where she had been" (Itani 377). The first half of the proclamation is cliché; the second half raises the sentiment to art because it suggests complexities in the everyday, present, (woman's) world that he will never understand but that mirror those in his (wartime) world. As critic Neta Gordon says, details of combat activity are "an interlude within a narrative chiefly concerned with the home front and an expanded examination of particular Canadian communities in the early twentieth century" (79).

Earlier on, when Grania is visiting her sister Tress, herself dealing with a husband who has returned from the war physically wounded and emotionally unstable, unable to leave his home, Grania thinks, "[W]e seldom have a chance to laugh or have fun. All we do is wait out the war" (314). Nothing happens while one waits, except waiting itself, which becomes the focus of the narrative. So, for instance, the narrator reports that "[Grania] had no idea when that [Jim's return] might be or where they might go. Some future time connected to events unseen and far away. Others were in charge of determining outcomes that affected her life and Jim's" (Itani 282). She concludes, "Thinking his name made her feel alone and unconnected. Everyone has lost something in this war.... We have waited so long, and we have all lost something" (282). The narrator later adds, "War was a nightmare they were trapped inside," but if the details offered are not themselves nightmarish—and indeed, in this text, very little of the war itself is seen—then what constitutes a meaningful narrative in this four-year time of conflict (284)?[28] Itani answers the question with her claim, stated in an interview: "I was trying to show…that the war affected everyone—most certainly the women and men left at home and those who had to deal with the young men returning" (Fisher 53).[29]

Waiting is dramatized by figuring the war, for those at home, as distant and unreal and presented to them only in documentary form. This is mostly text-based: letters, (dreaded) telegrams, and newspapers. But it is also, in this "new" era, filmic, as when Grania and Tress attend the cinema in Toronto (312–13). This experience disorients both women.[30] Grania is put off by the rapid cuts, which make it impossible for her to follow the action. Tress, who is a hearing person, meanwhile, grasps and releases her sister's hand, often recoiling at what is happening. When Grania later asks her why, she is told that the music was "so intense, so rapid, my heart started to pound" (313). The narrator informs, "[T]hey both look as if they have come through the war themselves" (313). This gives a nod to what David Williams points out to be the disorienting aspect of cinematic experience for this new generation of media consumers.[31]

---

28 This is not to ignore Gordon's argument that trench life, when it is depicted, is portrayed "with gruesome, terrifying, and heart-rending detail" (79).

29 Itani explains in an interview that it was reading the school newspaper for the actual institution where her grandmother was a student, called the Ontario School for the Deaf at that time, that inspired the novel. She read editions dated from 1900-15, which interested her in setting the novel when she did. "All of the news from the next five years [following 1914] dealt directly or indirectly with war" (Fisher 50).

30 Hochschild describes what they might have seen: "[J]erky, flickering, sometimes blurred footage interspersed with the printed titles of the silent-film era," suggesting that the medium had the ability to "electrify" audiences (227).

31 See, for instance, Chapter 2 of *Media, Memory, and the First World War*, "Mediated Memory."

Text in the form of newspapers is prevalent, both in the narrative of the novel and at the meta-textual level, with many chapter headings comprised of clippings about the war. From the first, with news reports flooding the papers, people are inundated with the war, to the point that one comment from Grania's school newspaper poignantly says, "*I am tired of hearing about this war*," the subtle irony being that the newspaper is produced for those concerned with the deaf school that Grania had spent her youth attending (121). While we learn at one point that the printer of the paper is a hearing man, many of those who read it are not, and thus to "hear" about the war bears double meaning. Even not hearing, they are surrounded by it.

Grania has great hopes for letters from the outset. With their marriage coming just two weeks before Jim's departure, she is sure that Jim "would not withhold information. Withholding meant keeping her out and that would be worse than everything else put together.... If he wrote enough to enable her to create a picture of him there, she would be able to keep him close" (135). In fact, he does, and as the years go by, she creates bundles of letters, one for each year, but as she adds to the one for the third year of his absence, she feels distant from them, despite having the contents memorized, their language having become so familiar as to almost, it seems, have lost its meaning (269–71). This conviction hits her full-force in 1918: "[A]fter each letter had been read and added to its bundle—a fourth bundle now, for 1918—she had to fight the fading of that belief" that her life and Jim's would be merged (323). Contrast this with the early days of Jim's absence, when she feels so close to him that his absence affects her bodily: "She felt as if she would be forced to take shallow breaths for days and weeks and months, until Jim would come home" (194).

Jim also quickly realizes that hoping in letters is false, and so he composes what he calls letters in his head, which will not be sent—the reason being that the details are too graphic and that much of what he would like to say would not escape the censor. "Every time I sit before a piece of paper, four eyes instead of two stare at the blank sheet. I will store what I can in memory," he explains (169). But he also knows, having seen a man's brains blown out, that "the knowledge would be kept inside the matter of his own brain—forever" (205). The distance to the Front means that "no one at home could have any idea of what this stretch of earth in the Salient now contained" (205). This includes "death, and the memory of impossible acts. The terrible thing was that no one at home would ever know. Because what was happening was impossible to be told" (206). His statements are closely echoed in Tom Sherbourne's statement to his wife in Stedman's *The Light Between Oceans*: "You *don't* understand, Isabel. No civilized person should ever *have* to understand. And trying to describe it would be like passing on a disease…. I did what I did so that people like you and Lucy could forget it ever happened" (116, emphases original).

The strategy of relying on text doubles back and leads not to clarity, but to confusion. Here is the start of one of Jim's (imaginary) letters: "Sometimes I can't remember what I have actually written and what I have told you from the mind's eye" (165). Add to that the difficulty with time lags in delivery, which Grania quickly realizes makes conversing via letter impossible (even trying to correlate a parcel sent to the much-later acknowledgement of the kindness proves a headache, cf. 248), and it is obvious that text is not enough to keep memory alive. Grania describes one letter she got from Jim as "like a document of dark history that had no connection with her at all; reading it made her realize more than ever how her own life was suspended" (285). Jim keeps writing, but he more or less gives up trying to communicate. "[H]ow could he write to [Grania] of love from a place where body parts worked their way through mud?" he wonders (239). After he is hurt and sent to England to recover, he thinks, "I see now that no civilized person would understand how we live. It would be pointless to try to explain….*Over there* is a life invented by and known only to ourselves" (261, emphasis original). This, perhaps, is as much commentary on what the people at home, particularly the women, were allowed to know, or not know, as it is a gloss on his frustration at the inability to put the nightmare world into words. The result, of course, is that the images in Jim's head, like the ones in Tress' husband Kenan's (home now and shell shocked), linger, torture, and paralyze. What do the people at home know to do? To wait. "They were all waiting," the narrator tells the reader. "It was difficult to think of the war in any other way except loss" (265). But think of that ("loss") not as death so much as "gap"—the war, because it happens somewhere else, is *time between* for those waiting at home. It is an experience of non-experience.

Jim, for his part, thinks while at the Front, "War ground on like the headless, thoughtless monster that could not be stopped. The bad fairy tale that refused to end" (237). A fairy tale is also a text, one must note, and a bad fairy tale in this context would be one that enacted horrible scenes rather than magical ones. Yet because the point of view from which *Deafening* is told is largely Grania's, war scenes are few in this text; in fact, when a late portrait of battle comes in to explain how Jim lost Irish, his best mate and fellow stretcher-bearer at the Front (Itani 330), the reader is somewhat surprised, because so much narrative space and time have passed since the prior scene from France (the last being c. 239). The death-of-Irish scene seems most important as a bookend to earlier graphic displays of Jim at war, the point being that all of this waiting that Grania, her family, the town, and everyone else has done is *for* something. However, I would argue that it is not coincident *with* that something itself. Rather, waiting exists as an entity of its own, albeit one which is composed of nothing, as a reality that opens endlessly from the present to the future. While it is there, memory is not possible, because the past is not significant. Only after the war is over can it be quantified, measured, examined. And that is what Grania and others feel, and show the reader, as the narrative progresses— the frustrating emptiness of the wait, for which there is no solution.

Grania's answer to the distance between her world and Jim's once she sees him again with the war over is to decide that they will live devoid of memory: "For now, we will live in the present. That will have to be enough. Until we are better" (378). The implication is that the unseen war, and the absent four years, have not been harmful to the soldier alone, but that neither does he have a way of understanding it now that it is over, because his memories of wartime do not coincide with those of the civilian. Itani presents much of what happens at home as life going on, but the shadow of the war, the threat of a death telegram, and the emptiness of a community missing its young men linger, a point made clear by the novel's foregrounding of the lost possibilities of text as carrier of meaning. Once the soldier is home, the need for the letter is absent, but like Kenan, Jim is probably not going to be able to bring his experience into words anyway. The gap that existed between home and away will continue to exist, making memory something which divides rather than unites. One might imagine that between Jim and Grania, even recognizing that there is a gap in experience would be a way of getting past living in an eternal present tense, but events in *Deafening* end before this longer aftermath of the war can be coded. In any event, such a dramatization is not the point; the subtleties of Itani's text are precisely in its portrayal of the inability of those (women) at home and those who went to war to share discourse concerning the events they experienced, a fact which renders their experience equally significant.

Maisie Dobbs, the heroine of Jacqueline Winspear's popular *Birds of a Feather*,[32] acts as another example of a woman sharing the burden of the war, a fact very much central to her character. Having suffered a shrapnel injury while on nursing duty, Maisie is representative of the small number of women with specific memory of the physical horrors of war, as only a very few who served ever incurred such wounds.[33] Now ten years have passed, and the novel dramatizes her transformation over the course of the several weeks of the plot from a woman stuck in the past of the war to a woman looking forward to a new future, albeit one with overhanging shadows of economic turmoil and the possibility of another war. This feature allows a text otherwise focused on plot—*Birds of a Feather* is, after all, a whodunit—to be contextualized into the contemporary canon of World War I fiction as highlighting important social questions of the post-war period. The motif turns, as I will indicate, on a crucial formulation of the function of memory that highlights the distinction between *remembering* something (inevitable given the experience of the war) and *being reminded* of it (being forced to encounter memory against one's will). Growth comes—for Maisie, as a woman finding a modern sense of herself—only with the ability to resist the latter demand.

---

32 Part of a series that began with the novel entitled *Maisie Dobbs: A Novel*.

33 Among others, nurses who served in Boulogne with the Third General Hospital (McGill), which was my grandfather's regiment (see this book's dedication), were subject to shelling in the summer of 1918. See *The War Diary of Clare Gass 1915-18* (Mann xxxvii).

The central plot begins as a mystery for investigator Maisie Dobbs to solve: to where has heiress Charlotte Waite disappeared? It gradually becomes a murder mystery—who killed Philippa Sedgewick, Rosamund Thorpe, and Lydia Fisher, and will that person make an attempt on Charlotte's life next? And this in turn is overlaid with a more important question: what are the lingering effects of the war, especially for women, and can they be overcome in the attempt to forge a modern consciousness?[34]

Memories of the war, now more than a decade in the past, hang over Maisie and most of the others who populate *Birds of a Feather*. When Maisie walks into the grocery/department store of Joseph Waite, she observes post-war capitalism at work under the banner, literally, of war. That is, "her eyes [are] drawn to the wall above the doorway" to a "mosaic crafted at great expense....Upon each tile was the name of an employee of Waite's International Stores lost in the Great War," and over all, "IN LOVING REMEMBRACE—LEST WE FORGET" (40, font original). As she feels tears coming, we learn that such grief has a way of taking her "when she least expected it, when the sharp and dreadful memories came to her unbidden," but she knows she is not alone: "A shared grief often seemed to linger in the air" (40). This was a "fear or reality...[that had] to be negotiated anew every day" (40).

The timeframe is Spring 1930, and the war has, in one respect, frozen Maisie in the past, because she remains wedded, though not literally, to her still living but lost love, Dr. Simon Lynch, wounded along with Maisie by artillery fire while working at a casualty clearing station. He is in convalescence at the same hospital that holds the son of a Mrs. Willis

---

34 Note, however, that this question arises only in the lives of the two more privileged young women in the novel, Maisie and Charlotte. While women at other social stations are pictured and even realized as characters, they do not develop a consciousness of themselves as choice-making beings.

(who will eventually be revealed as the murderer Maisie seeks), but as Maisie has told us early on, Simon has not recovered (28). Thus, though Maisie is intent on becoming a "modern" woman, a move she appears to have made by the end of the story, while signaled by economic independence, choice-making regarding her appearance, and a sense of a modern (Freudian) definition of personhood, this shift is also hindered by the plot device of her needing to find love. Her ability to move on from the war, in other words, must be accompanied by her continuing, at least in one aspect of her life, to be a nineteenth-century heroine.

As the mystery plot is untangled and the crime solved, it becomes apparent that three healings must take place. One is in the mind of Mrs. Willis. The second is in the body and mind of Maisie's assistant, Billy. The third is in the life of Maisie herself, and in affecting that change, the narrative leaves room for a new, modern Maisie to emerge.

Winspear shows early on how, despite Maisie Dobbs' success in running her own investigations firm, she is lost. She can't leave her wartime love in the past. And she does not know quite how to grasp her social position, having raised herself from servant class to the class of women whom the servants address when upstairs as "Miss" rather than by name. In a conversation with one of the servants in Belgravia, where Maisie lives, they mutually contemplate the changing nature of the British working class. "Not as many staff as there used to be, are there?" Sandra asks, to which Maisie replies, "Certainly not as many as before the war, Sandra" (161).[35] This is repeated almost verbatim in the chat to follow, and then Sandra says, "I think people are trying to forget the war,

---

35 Nicolson discusses the matter of the shift in domestic help after the war, claiming that "[t]here was…a strong reluctance to accept live-in jobs" after the conflict, a "growing antipathy to a lifelong career in service," a trend she indicates Virginia Woolf said began "well before the war" (237).

don't you, Miss?" (161). And then she drops a key formulation about memory into their conversation: "I mean, who wants to be reminded? My cousin...he said that it was one thing to be remembered, and quite another to be reminded every day" (161). For this soldier, the fact was, "He didn't mind people remembering what he'd done, you know, over there. But he didn't want to be *reminded* of it. He said that it was hard, because something happened to remind him every day" (161, emphasis original).[36] "Remember" versus "remind" in fact becomes the crux on which all of the transformations and plot events turn in *Birds of a Feather*.

The point is taken up later by the doctor at the war hospital that continues to house Great War vets. He indicates, "[W]e all know a veteran of the war when we see one in the street... but when we are close to that person, in a setting like this...it's a reminder, a terrible reminder" that "can make people recall events and feelings that they would rather forget" (211). For some, the pain is so intense that they cannot deal with it, and this prompts the murder spree that turns out to be the central plot mystery in *Birds of a Feather*. It is in solving the case of who committed these crimes that Maisie Dobbs comes into her own as a modern (woman) by figuring a middle way between remembering and being reminded.

Part of Maisie's shift to the modern is being willing to let go of the past represented by her lost lover Simon, whom she comes to accept as irretrievably damaged by the war. The narration had revealed him as "the former love who had sustained such serious injuries during the Great War that he was now in a convalescent hospital" for care (134). The narrator had reported that Maisie visited once a month, but even at

---

36 Note here that the person speaking these words is a below-stairs servant, but the crucial declaration comes not in her voice, but that of her *reportage* of the voice of her (male, soldier) cousin. Thus Winspear is able to make the claim, let it be voiced by a woman, but shield it behind the persona of a man, in a sense.

this point, she does not see Simon as "real" and, in fact, feels guilty that she uses the unseeing, unhearing Simon as a sounding board for her current case. We are told that "[i]n speaking aloud to one who could not comprehend, Maisie was aware that she was using this time to reexamine the details of the Waite case" (135). She is not, in other words, living a contemporary relationship with Simon, and indeed, that is impossible.

The culminating moment comes in an act of self-performed psychoanalysis that is supposed to grow out of Maisie's character as an astute reader of clues and knower of the human mind and people's motivations. This is her realization: "Had it been her rupture in her relationship with Frankie [her father] that had prevented her from making other associations...[?] Never able to open her heart to another?" (227). And at this point, she remembers, not coincidentally, Andrew Dene, the handsome and eligible doctor who shortly will make his interest in her clear. Reading this, one might say that if she is to become a modern, then perhaps she ought to start by coming to a sense of her own desires, but even though she makes moves in this direction, Maisie is still caught up in old-think when it comes to women's (sexual) liberation. However, in the manner of this text's narration, when she does find closure to this problem, her transformation is immediate, and it is signaled by the outward symbol of her getting her long hair cut into a style which prompts Billy to respond: "I mean, Miss, well, it's a bit of a shock, innit? But it suits you, really it does" (308). He follows up with, "It suits you, makes you seem more...sort of modern" (308, ellipsis original). The outward symbol of the hair complements her inward decision regarding Simon, articulated later as, "Yes, though she would continue to visit, probably forever, it was time to move on, to set her cap for...whatever fate might bring her way" (308, ellipsis original).

Having resolved her attachment to the past, Maisie is able to spread her new, proto-feminist consciousness to at least one other woman as she works at the end of the novel to heal the relationship between her client, rich merchant Joseph Waite, and his daughter, Charlotte, essentially by challenging Waite to see the woman as the more-capable balance to the son he lost in the war. Shortly thereafter, Maisie uses Charlotte as a decoy to catch the killer of Charlotte's three white-feather comrades, and as Mrs. Willis stabs what she thinks is the drugged, unconscious body of Charlotte (but is in reality a stuffed dummy created by Maisie), the past is perhaps symbolically killed and the new Charlotte born. Maisie acts as midwife to this birth by prompting a conversation between Joseph Waite and his daughter: "Talk *with* Charlotte, not *at* her. Ask her how *she* sees the past, how she feels about losing Joe [her brother]," Maisie suggests (299, emphases original). She further urges, "And give her a job…. She needs a purpose, Mr. Waite. She needs to stand tall, to do something, to gain some self-respect" (299).

Maisie has thus started the fashioning of Charlotte as a modern and allowed her to move past the crux of remembering and reminder that bound her to her wartime activities, though what she can do nothing about is Charlotte's need to confront her grief every time she enters the main London Waite store, which has the memorial plaque on it bearing the name, among many others, of her brother, Joe. It will only be in getting past this reminder of the war that she will be able to remember her brother in a constructive way.

Jane Urquhart's *The Stone Carvers* is concerned similarly with a protagonist, Klara Becker, who takes a circuitous path towards awareness of herself as a woman in the post-war milieu. Becker disguises herself as a man to go to and work on the Canadian memorial there. Perhaps a good place to start in discussing her in the present context is to cite Urquhart's statement from a 2004 interview with Herb Wyile: "Women have always had a history, of course, but I believe that they should be put into the official history. But I don't think that I'm the person to do it. I think that I am as intent as I am upon giving the female point of view because I am a woman; it's that simple" (83). Yet Urquhart's focus in this novel does not reside in creating Klara as a symbol of the new woman. Rather, the novelist portrays her protagonist as a person, like many others, whose grief at losing someone in the war drove her to seek purgation. Klara does this by surreptitiously carving the lover's face into one of the male figures represented on the Vimy Memorial. As Urquhart portrays the aftermath of the war through this character, she makes an argument (not rooted in the protagonist's gender) that reveals the complex dynamic which holds personal grief in tension with the monuments themselves intended as symbols of collective mourning.

Klara is literally mid-stroke with her hammer and chisel when the memorial's designer, Allward, a character fashioned after the historical person in charge of the Vimy Memorial, finds her working. Observing what she has done, he accuses her of taking the universality out of the figure, instilling it instead with particularity. As the narrative indicates, "He had wanted the stone figure to be the 66,000 dead young men who had marched through his dreams when he had conceived the memorial. Even in its unfinished state this face had developed a personal expression, a point of view" (337). Yet his anger quickly (too quickly to be realistic) turns to sympathy: "He had to admit the work that had been done here in the early hours of the morning was careful, skilled" (337). In portraying the abandon with which Klara pursues purgation of her grief, Urquhart dramatizes the urgency to memorialize and points to the power of Vimy itself as a site of mourning. Klara is able to let go only through carving his name into the memorial, a task given her as a gift by her new lover and future husband, Giorgio (375). The resolution of Klara's grieving comes about as she completes the inscription: "Klara knew this would be the last time she touched Eamon, that when they had finished carving his name all the confusion and regret of his absence would unravel, just as surely as if she had embraced him with forgiving arms" (376).

Klara's purgation of her grief through this highly symbolized, if somewhat rhetorically exaggerated, scene, however, points to the power of the monument itself, and it is working out the question of what the monument means that preoccupies Urquhart at least as much as the concern with Klara as post-war woman. A clue to this theme exists when Herb Wyile suggests to Urquhart in an interview that she is very much concerned with remembrance and asks whether "Lest we forget" is not a sort of unofficial motto of her fiction. She replies, "The word forget is important to me, but I'm more interested in how people forget or why people forget, or, for that matter, why they remember or how they remember, than whether or not we should or shouldn't" (76–77).

In the Wyile interview, Urquhart describes the Vimy Memorial by saying, "[I]t really is quite a staggering work of art and the best war memorial in Europe; there's no question in my mind about that. It's a very powerful, powerful work of art. And then there is the size!" (78).

Everything about Vimy in *The Stone Carvers'* fictionalized version of events, as in the real efforts at building the Vimy Memorial, is out-of-scale. The stone it would be made of had to be sourced in Yugoslavia (now Croatia). Roads had to be built simply to get the raw material to the site. The monument itself has a scale almost unimaginable. The first time Klara and her brother, Tilman, approach, the enormity awes them:

"Above all this [ground-level war graves amongst other scenes], on the horizon, rose the twin white towers of the monument, their shape distorted by five-storey-high [sic] scaffolding and canvas bunting" (300). We are told that "[a]lthough Tilman and Klara were viewing the monument from almost a mile away, the structure had begun to dominate the entire landscape" (300–01). In fact, it is so large that it blends with the skyscape itself. "Distant grey woodlots, this miraculous road, the ridge itself, even the stratified clouds in the sky leaned toward it as if a construction of this magnitude could not be ignored, even by the surrounding disarray, and even by nature" (301).

It is as if the designer had Kant's notion of the sublime in *Critique of Judgment* in mind. Compare, for instance, Kant's discussion of a view of a similar structure, but note that he makes the point that appreciating magnitude is partly a matter of maintaining perspective through carefully controlling one's proximity to what is being observed:

> [W]e *must keep from going very near the Pyramids just as much as we keep from going too far from them, in order to get the full emotional effect from their size. For if we are too far away, the parts to be apprehended (the stones lying one over the other) are only obscurely represented, and the representation of them produces no effect upon the aesthetical judgement of the subject. But if we are very near, the eye requires some time to complete the apprehension of the tiers from the bottom up to the apex; and then the first tiers are always partly forgotten before the Imagination has taken in the last, and so the comprehension of them is never complete.* (112)

Kant also explains what to consider in judging such a structure: "We call that *sublime* which is *absolutely great*. But to be great and to be a great something are quite different concepts," by which he means to distinguish magnitude (in the first instance) from quantity (in the second) (A25/p. 106, emphases original). He elaborates to say, "That anything is a magnitude…may be cognized from the thing itself, without any comparison of it with other things…. But to cognize *how great* it is always requires some other magnitude as a measure" (107, emphasis original). He later adds, "[I]f we call anything, not only great, but absolutely great in any point of view (great beyond all comparison) i.e. sublime, we soon see that it…is a magnitude which is like itself alone" (107).

Kant's depiction of the size or magnitude point might fit as an inversion-corrective to the enormity of Allward's (and hence Urquhart's) Vimy: "*The sublime is that in comparison with which everything else is small*" (109, italics original). That he is not talking about physical size is obvious when he adds this proviso: "*The sublime is that, the mere ability to think which shows a faculty of the mind surpassing every standard of Sense*" (110, italics original). He further says, "The feeling of the sublime is therefore a feeling of pain arising from the want of accordance between the aesthetical estimation of magnitude formed by the imagination and the estimation of the same formed by reason" (A27/p. 119).

As a gloss on Klara and Tilman's perception of Vimy, this points out what they do not see as they focus on the monument's enormity, which is the power of vision and the feeling of grief that reaches the viewer emotionally when confronted with the memorial—in Kantian terms, the sublime itself, which cannot be measured. The fictional Allward's vision came in part due to his inability to encompass the grief which tormented his soul during the war years, a process not unlike the one Kant describes when he talks, as cited above, about trying to grasp the sublime. Witness the narrator's explanation of Allward's feelings: "[T]he last years of the war came to him as a great awakening that let all the horror in, and he dreamed the Great Memorial well before the government competition [to commission it] was announced" (Urquhart 266). The scope of Vimy is intensified by the narrator: "Nothing about the memorial was probable, even possible. Allward wanted white, wanted to recall the snow that fell each year on coast and plains and mountains, the disappeared boys' names preserved forever, unmelting on a vast territory of stone that was as white as the frozen winter lakes of the country they had left behind" (267). He wants, in other words, something that gleans its power from being impossible to understand, and if he conflates complexity and magnitude, that is perhaps a reflection of his historical counterpart's obsessions.

The historical Allward fascinates Urquhart in his singularity.[37] She says of him, "He was a greatly obsessed man, and the memorial stands there as a kind of tribute to his obsession, because it worked. I think in order to accomplish something like that you almost have to be obsessed" (Wyile 78). In order to get his great vision built, as Urquhart tells it in the novel, Allward nearly gave his life. As the government of Canada prods him regarding the long delays in construction that come about as a result of his perfectionism, it is revealed, "I will be emptied, he thought, when this is over. I will have put every drop of my life's blood into this already blood-soaked place" (272). As he observes Klara and Giorgio carving Eamon's name, he comes to believe that he has accomplished his task: "The weight of the sorrow he had carried for fifteen years was leaving him. The emotion was working through the

---

37 Urquhart never meant to be purely historical. "Facts are points of embarkation for me rather than a final destination," is how she explains the research process that led her to write *The Stone Carvers* as she did (Wyile 62).

arms of these people…and he knew that passion was entering the monument itself, the huge urn he had designed to hold grief" (377).

And yet collapsing grief onto the personal doesn't account for the true power of the memorial any more with Allward than it did earlier with Klara. The next chapter after the above description starts by tearing Allward's hopes apart, pointing to what we might now code as a failure of reading from a Kantian point of view: "The larger, the more impressive the monument, the more miraculous its construction, the more it seems to predict its own fall from grace. Exposed and shining on elevated ground, insisting on prodigious feats of memory from all who come to gaze at it, it appears to be as vulnerable as a flower, and its season seems to be brief" (378). But this is so only if one forgets Kant's claims about sublimity being recognized as a magnitude which refers to itself alone. With that in mind, the text does leave room for the monument to have meaning: "Whole oceans of grief were revisited, especially by women. Stories concerning the brief lives of young soldiers were told" despite the fact that those who hear have now largely forgotten those commemorated (379). This is the monument at work as sublime creation, able to inspire a sense of its own incomprehensibility.

Having done this work, devoting fifteen years of his life to the memorial, Urquhart's Allward returned home not quite broken, but finished. His friendships had disappeared. "Few people wanted to discuss the monument," and yet "like a long love affair that had ended in sorrow, the Vimy Memorial would not relinquish the large space it had occupied in his heart" (379).

Sadly, for everyone else, this was no longer true, for, "the world beyond Allward's walls was beginning to forget about the tragedy of a distant slaughter. The grief was losing its sharpness, could perhaps bruise, but could no longer really cut most hearts" (351). Funny what Kant says: "[A] long peace generally brings about a predominant commercial spirit and, along with it, low selfishness, cowardice, and effeminacy, and debases the disposition of the people" (B28/128). Perhaps these words would comfort Allward in his lost quest to believe in the transcendence of his masterpiece, which itself has lost nothing. At the very least, he might have taken solace in the fact of Klara's healing, facilitated by his creation, if at the price of a tiny piece of its magnitude.

Taken together, the works of Itani, Winspear, and Urquhart indicate that for women and those removed from the physical action of the war through distance or time, loss and separation must be dealt with somehow. That it takes time, as portrayed by the delayed grief in the latter two novelists' works, and that it is in all cases an uncertain process, is simply the nature of dealing with such a cataclysmic set of events.

CHAPTER 4

The Empire Against Itself: Facing the Irish question

Egyptologist and theorist of cultural memory Jan Assmann points out that at the turn of the prior (i.e. 20th) century, collective or social memory was generally understood as a biological function, even in Jung's theory of archetypes. The notion that a people-group's identity was "inheritable," that "'racial memory'" existed, held until challenged by sociologist Maurice Halbwachs and art historian Aby Warburg, each working independently of the other (Assmann 125). After their rethinking, "The specific character that a person derives from belonging to a distinct society and culture is not seen to maintain itself for generations as a result of phylogenetic evolution, but rather as a result of socialization and customs" (125). Being part of a group, in other words, came to be seen as a function of memory passed down, a point Assmann makes as he plays off of Darwinian language: "The 'survival of a type' in the sense of a cultural pseudo-species is a function of the cultural memory" (125-26).

Assmann cites Nietzsche's point that genetics determines survival amongst animal species while human culture survives because of strategies undertaken to ensure continuity from generation to generation. The overriding strategy, and the one that offers an explanation of how cultural identity persists over time, is "cultural memory," which is "a collective concept for all knowledge that directs behavior and experience in the interactive framework of a society and one that obtains through generations in repeated societal practice and initiation" (126). Assmann's concern is to figure out the delimitation between what he calls "communicative memory" (that which is based in everyday shared experience) and cultural memory. John Kirk offers another vocabulary for an essentially similar phenomenon when he cites Fentress and Wickham, who edited *Social Memory*. That term may be defined as "a 'collective experience…identify[ing] a group, giving it a sense of its past and defining its aspirations for the future'" (qtd. in Kirk 607). Kirk goes on to point out that the definition as Fentress and Wickham offer it is not a "'passive' phenomenon but rather…a 'performative' act" (607).[38]

Those who live in social groups participate in the creation and sharing of communicative memory. This could take place in a myriad of ways including telling jokes, gossiping, sharing memories—any context in which two people can interchange roles and listen, speak, and listen again (126–27). Bakhtin talks about a similar idea in "Discourse in the Novel," where his particular concern is to show how the dialogic process governs what is said and how worldview is formed. He claims that "in the everyday speech of any person living in society, no less than half (on the average) of all words uttered by him will be someone else's words (consciously someone else's) trans-mitted with varying degrees of precision and impartiality (or more precisely, partiality)" (339). He is speaking specifically about the voices that appear in the construction of a literary

---

38 Note too that these scholars suggest that such memory exists first to "define a national community, enabling the bourgeoisie to legitimize its 'structures of political and economic dominance'" and also as a tool used by the elite to maintain their dominant position (Kirk 607). Class memory is thus incredibly important, "particularly in times of rapid change" (Kirk 608).

text in much of what he says, but he also makes the claim for worldview: "Within the arena of almost every utterance an intense interaction and struggle between one's own and another's word is being waged, a process in which they oppose or dialogically interanimate each other" (354). That is, as a person goes about being in the world, she plays with, chooses between, and re-presents the voices that she has heard, albeit in a "dialogized" way, or as a product of the negotiation that takes place between the various voices constructing the utterance.

Assmann would appear to pick up the point when he suggests that "[e]very individual memory constitutes itself in communication with others," a point he qualifies by saying that these "others" are not just anyone, but "groups who conceive their unity and peculiarity through a common image of their past" (127). Each person belongs to many of these units, from the smallest one like a family to the larger unit of a nation, he adds. However, if this form of memory is useful for creating identity, its limitations are its "temporal horizon"—the length of time that its cultural formations hold, and this is at the outside a period of 100 years (Assmann 127). Halbwachs thought that "once living communication cristallized [sic] in the forms of objectivized culture" a change would occur because "the group relationship and the contemporary reference are lost" and thus you end up not with memory ("mémoire") but history ("histoire"), but Assmann disagrees, seeing instead the similarity in the way that groups use objectivized culture to form identity and the way that everyday memory works to do the same (128). In either case, "a group bases its consciousness of unity and specificity upon this knowledge and derives formative and normative impulses from it, which allows the group to reproduce its identity" (128).

Communicative memory has a limited time horizon, as noted, where cultural memory does not. It does, however, have fixed points that allow identity to be constructed against it. These can include "fateful events of the past, whose memory is maintained through cultural formation…and institutional communication" (Assmann 129). The former might be exemplified in things like texts, whereas the latter might be seen in something like recitation, and the idea, following from Warburg, is that objects (and the examples Assmann names include high art but also pop cultural artifacts like postage stamps and costumes) have the ability to retain their power to communicate cultural meaning even across a distance of millennia (129). Taken together, "The concept of cultural memory comprises that body of reusable texts, images, and rituals specific to each society in each epoch, whose 'cultivation' serves to stabilize and convey that society's self-image" (132). Members (or potential members) of a group become familiar with this body of knowledge, and on this the group "bases its awareness of unity and particularity" (132).

This idea is complicated, however, where the dominant narrative exists in tension with that of a sub-group, which is then represented as an alien "Other." As postcolonial scholar David Lloyd says, such a group may code itself (or find it impossible to do so) as the product of what can be neither forgotten nor spoken. With respect to the literature of World War I, this might be seen in the case of the Irish, and Lloyd says that the Irish worldview even up to the present is informed by the singular tragedy of the Famine of the 19th century, even if this is not spoken of. As he expresses it, "[T]he trace of unredeemed and unredeemable loss continues to glimmer cryptically in post-Famine Irish culture…. The afterlife of silenced or diverted grief appears everywhere" (175). Following this claim, he gives examples of "the silencing of

Mud Corner Cemetery, Belgium

grief, the afterlife of loss, and the encryption of survival" in Irish literature from Joyce to Beckett (175). "The destruction of the Famine and the silencing of mourning that followed in its wake are the very conditions of a nationalist subjectivity that is melancholic in not even being able to name the loss that it mourns," Lloyd explains (175). Into that vacuum pour the words of the colonizer, in the case of the Irish, this being, obviously, the British.

To go back to Assmann one more time, cultural memory has what he calls a "binding character of [its]…knowledge," and this is "*formative*" and "*normative*," as was mentioned earlier (132, emphases original). The first has "educative, civilizing, and humanizing functions" and the second the "function of providing rules of conduct" (132). This would be as true for the Irish subject as for anyone else, of course, but observing several examples of Irish Great War literature will indicate that while Assmann's ideas may serve as a guide to identity formation, cultural memory may become fragmented and complicated to deploy when it exists either as a dominant (in the sense of dominating) narrative or as a site of resistance to one.

Lloyd perhaps provides a gloss on how this works in the case of Ireland when he says, earlier in his article than what was just cited, "[T]here is no shortage of images, and especially of misery, especially of hunger, especially of humanity on the verge of animality" available in the "visual representation of Ireland in the nineteenth century" (161). He adds, "The iconography of Irish poverty, if intensified by the globally registered horror of the Famine, has an enduring and more ingrained history than the handful of images drawn from those years could suggest" (161). Put in the terms that I am using here, any attempt to code Irish cultural memory will have those images of the subjugated, starving Irish superimposed over it, and will thus beg the reader to ponder the relative position and motivation of the person drawing the portrait (or narrating the story).[39] Frank McGuinness in *Observe the Sons of Ulster Marching towards the Somme*, Tom Phelan in *The Canal Bridge*, JG Farrell in *Troubles*, and Sebastian Barry in *A Long Long Way* offer varying versions of this postcolonial tension which pits what can be remembered and by whom against what cannot be remembered but which nonetheless constitutes an identity—one born from struggle and tragedy.[40]

The characters in Frank McGuinness' play *Observe the Sons of Ulster Marching towards the Somme* have two touchstones by which they form identity: one is communicative memory based in their own declarations about their role in the Great War, and the other is cultural memory in the form

---

39 There is a quite particular type of Irish postcoloniality, as Lloyd and many other recent scholars have pointed out. See also Eoin Flannery, who provides a useful short overview of the field.

40 Farrell was born in Liverpool of Irish descent. He died prematurely of drowning and is buried in Ireland.

of myth that they draw on based in their knowledge of the past. This they articulate without questioning its normative function. However, the play itself, and its insertion into a particular reception context (Dublin in 1985) when first performed, leaves the question open as to whether this identity construct can maintain its formative/normative function over time. This is in part signaled, as will be discussed presently, by the title of the play, which presumes future action as it demands something of the audience ("observe"), a command that is belied from the play's first lines, which show that the Sons of Ulster *have already* marched.

Jacqueline Hill points out that "[t]he twentieth century, with its questioning of the integrity of the self, of authorship, and the reliability of human memory, prompted skepticism in some quarters about the extent to which the past is knowable at all," adding that these "issues lie at the very heart of *OSU* [*Observe the Sons of Ulster*], since so much of what happens on stage is a function of the memory of the elder Pyper" (EP7). As the play opens, the war-and-identity theme is immediately complicated by the fact that all of the characters, except for Pyper, have died at the Battle of the Somme. They are ghosts, and Pyper is an old man, the only one to have survived the war. Yet as the chronology of the drama goes back in time to boot camp and then forward to the Battle of the Somme—which is not depicted except in its anticipation and its aftermath—the Irish soldiers' brotherhood is established. This happens first (in time) because they overcome their class and culture differences in boot camp, but primarily (in motive) because they unite under the notion that they are Sons of Ulster, connected in meaningful ways to a past narrative. And yet if they know what that means and why it motivates them, with even the outsider[41] Pyper buying in (it is he

---

41 He is different in many ways. Socially, he stands apart from the rest, having come from a family of some means. In terms of his personality, he seizes upon the misfit role. And, of course, he is the only one to have survived the war.

who yells, "Observe the sons of Ulster marching towards the Somme" as the play ends and the soldiers are about to make the charge which kills all but him), the play itself is problematic as an act of remembrance or commemoration (80).

Assmann's "fateful events of the past" for the Sons of Ulster is in the form of the long-distant Battle of the Boyne, which gave King William III victory and ensured Britain's continued Protestant dominance in Ireland. This is added to by the more proximate events of the Somme. Pyper invokes this history unselfconsciously. He declares in his opening soliloquy, "The sons of Ulster will rise and lay their enemy low, as they did at the Boyne, as they did at the Somme, against any invader who will trespass on to their homeland" (McGuinness 10). As he does so, it becomes clear that he does not address just the audience, but the ghostly Sons who were his army mates. He invokes their shared history when he calls out, "The last battle. I died that day with them" and later addresses the boys particularly when he adds, "[Y]ou will always guard me. You will always defend Ulster" (11).

The men share an identity in which their memories allow them to form a bond. As young Pyper says early in Part 2 ("Initiation"), "You are here as a volunteer in the army of your king and empire. You are here to train to meet that empire's foe. You are here as a loyal son of Ulster, for the empire's foe is Ulster's foe" (16). The logic he uses allows him to slide from one communal memory (being a Son of Ulster) to another, larger one (being a subject of the King) to yet a third, albeit one that is in the future rather than in the past (defender of the Empire). To put it another way, here Pyper deploys cultural memory rooted in the past (which it is by definition) to predict a future in which these men will act. And yet in the early going, he is not part of them, and both he and they know it.

Pyper is of a social class that the (other) Sons are not. He has had an odd range of past experience, including having married a French prostitute who may have been suffering gender confusion.[42] And he simply acts in a way that is aloof and separate from the group. Moore asks him in their barracks, "What's a rare boyo like you doing in an army?" (19). Pyper does little to dispel their notions of his difference, including his reasons for being there in the first place. Whereas the others share an identity construct rooted in the past and their wish to defend their homeland, Pyper says, "I enlisted, before I was conscripted, because I'd nothing better to do…. I'm dying anyway. I want it over quickly" (19). But though he says it, of course, he is not dying; he outlives them all, surviving to share in their story and later to share it.

When the boys start to talk about why they are in the King's army, it takes little time for Craig to name the truth: "I'm in this for Ulster" (22). He and the others, save Pyper, share past participation in various branches of the citizens' army that was meant to keep Ulster free of "Fenian rats," as Craig says (26). As the "Initiation" section ends, Millen challenges Pyper about his difference, asking him, "Is that what you want, Pyper? Death?" and in response, Pyper positions himself with them for the first time: "I might survive from what I learn here. Right? And who'll teach me? Other sons of Ulster, marching off to war. A good war. A just war. Our war. The war of the elect upon the damned" (36). They are not yet ready to accept him, but shortly after, as the scene closes, Craig says, "Ulster," to which Pyper responds, "Ulster" (37). It seems that they have folded together into this identity as Sons. It is a scene that will be echoed at the end of the play, where the word "Ulster" is repeated as a mantra in the dying moments of the action (81).

---

42 See Kiberd 286 on this.

The Ulster Tower, Thiepval, France

Pyper, as the one who stands out as different from the group for many reasons, claims in the "Pairing" section (Part 3), which portrays the men in a dream-like state on Boa Island, that he tried to escape to Paris, he tried to escape Carson's dance (participation in the Unionist cause, of which Sir Edward Carson was a leader), but that he couldn't do what he wanted to do in France. He had to continue doing what his ancestors demanded of him: "I could not create. I could only preserve. Preserve my flesh and blood, what I'd seen, what I'd learned" (56).

By this point, however, the other Sons of Ulster are starting to see their cause in marching towards the Somme as problematic. Roulston confesses that he joined the army because he could not be a preacher like his father (47). Crawford says, "I am a soldier who risks his neck for no cause other than the men he's fighting with. I've seen enough to see through empires and kings and countries" (48). McIlwaine says, "We are the sacrifice. What's keeping us over there? We're all going mad" (51). Anderson tries to keep them all on track with his declaration to McIlwaine, "You'll go back to the front, if I've to carry you. You won't disgrace yourself or your breed or where you work," and Millen declares, "I do as I'm told…. If they order me to put my hand in the fire, for the sake of what I believe in, what they believe in, I'd do it willingly," and he urges Moore, "You have to do that as well, Moore. That's the only way" (52, 53). In the end, they do go on to fulfill their mission (and to die), but it is Pyper who has been transformed by his recognition of communal memory, as signaled by his declaration, "I would take up arms at the call of my Protestant fathers. I would kill in their name and I would die in their name" (57).

However, they are not where they are, on the Western Front, to defend their homeland. They are there to propagate war on the Germans. And history shows that the actual Sons of Ulster, who made up the 36th Division, were successful. Jacqueline Hill points out that "on 1–2 July 1916 its members had succeeded in penetrating further into German lines than any other unit: four VCs were subsequently awarded to individual members for heroism" (EP3). However, this was somewhat for naught, as "their success had been negated by poor support and the rigidity of the British battle plans" (3). The men/ghosts in this play, because of the fractured chronology of the events presented, are facing a battle that they already know the outcome of, since, as has been indicated, the play begins long after their end has come.

Yet in Part 4 of the play, perhaps because they need to reinforce their sense of communal identity to bolster their courage for the battle upcoming, the men reach back into the deepest recesses of their Unionist history, pairing up to reenact the Battle of Scarva in the section called "Bonding," which happens just before they are to march towards the Somme.

The irony is twofold: they don't explain why they're reenacting the battle, and the reenactment goes awry and has their side losing.

Before the mock battle starts, Anderson cautions the group: "And remember, King James [played by Anderson], we know the result. Keep to the result" (70). As they play fight, Anderson narrates the action like play-by-play at a modern football match. The problem is, Pyper, the horse for King William (the character Moore), trips and falls, thus losing the battle. Millen pronounces the feeling of all of them as they circle the fallen Pyper and urge him to get up: "Not the best of signs" (71).

They are all stunned—this is not how the narrative typically ends, or, to put it in the terms I am using (and interrogating) here, cultural memory has taken a hit, because the outcome of their mock battle runs opposite to what they all know the outcome always has been, and what they think it always will/must be. They immediately deploy strategies of collective memory to make things right. McIlwaine says, "It was only a game," and Moore adds, "Prepare us for the real thing" (71). But the mood is ominous. Their cultural memory has not prepared them for this alternate outcome to the battle, but its occurrence suggests that it function as predictive, so that the outcome of the Battle of the Somme, their next engagement, will be different than what they would have wanted. And that is indeed the case.

What's coming is the battle that will kill them all, save Pyper, and Craig tells him so: "This is the last battle. We're going out to die" (74). Pyper offers a final prayer for the men, invoking as he does all of the collective memory in their shared history while also inserting the Somme battle into that set of images: "Let this day at the Somme be as glorious in the memory of Ulster as that day at the Boyne, when you scattered our enemies" (80).

History shows that the Somme did add to the store of memory that identifies this group. As Kiberd says, the Battle of the Somme, until now, is "a milestone in the history of Ulster loyalism" (279). But that heroic narrative does not stand as significant for itself alone. Kiberd claims of the trench experience in general, "New and unprecedented ideas of Irishness emerged, as so often in the past, as a consequence of an intense experience overseas. In the muddy fields of the Somme, a generation achieved a form of self-definition" (280).

As the Sons turn toward the Battle of the Somme, they make Pyper one of them, giving him an orange sash like the ones they wear, and when he asks why they are doing so, Anderson tells him it is a gift, and asks him whether he will wear it like the rest of the men. Pyper asks why, and the answer is, "So we'll recognize you as one of our own. Your own" (77). This identity, one might say, is forged through a melding of an immediate history, early 20th-century Unionism, embedded in a longer one, identity as a Son of Ulster going back to the Boyne in 1690, but with the accretion of a contemporary event, 1916's Battle of the Somme, which functions to unite and extend the early communal memory by forming a prism through which the notion of "Sonship of Ulster" might be viewed. They are now all Sons with no qualifications, no differences of class, past, or goals.

Yet Pyper, even while envisioning himself a part of them, separates himself from them, marking out his difference, which leads critics to suggest that his strategy (or McGuinness' through him) is to invoke the contemporary 1980s play-going audience, challenging their ideas as to what the significance and shifting definitions of membership in the Sons of Ulster might mean. Hill points out that "the elder Pyper recalls the events of the Great War through the prism of 'the Troubles'" (of the 1980s) and elaborates to say that in the reception context, Dublin in 1985, the production of the play "generated considerable controversy" (EP8).[43] This because "[McGuinness'] interpretation of his group's wartime experience...almost certainly is influenced...by later events, and specifically, it appears, by 'the Troubles,' to which he alludes" (EP8). Declan Kiberd reiterates the point, saying that the play "seemed to capture that new mood" that saw "[c]alls for the abandonment of the constitutional claim on the six counties of Northern Ireland...[coming] thick and fast" as well as the rise of "attempts to come to a deeper understanding of the unionist tradition" (279).

To go back to Assmann, the formative aspects of memory might function in a familiar way, but the normative aspects will be observed to have shifted in the period between the events described in the play and the production of the play itself. Declan Kiberd may help here. He says that the "ultimate nightmare of World War I [was] [i]ts destruction of a developmental notion of history" (291)—the war, in short, destroyed the idea that a narrative could have that normative function, because in the face of the Somme, as is said, nothing could make sense any more.

The definition of Ulster Protestant Unionism, which Pyper and his wartime comrades take to exist in reference to historical events such as the Battle of the Boyne and in contemporary commemorations of those events, had undergone change in the period between the Somme and the time the play was first performed. Hill explains this by saying, "What has been called their 'multi-layered' sense of identity, comprising

---

43 See also Tom Herron, who talks about the state of Northern Ireland at the time the play was written and performed: "It is tempting to read [the play] as a parable of the betrayal felt by many unionists and loyalists at the signing of the Hillsborough Agreement (15 Nov. 1985) behind their backs" (139).

Ulster, Irish and British Imperial elements, was becoming more problematic" (EP8). Hence audience reactions to what Hill codes as "an indictment of the traditional values of loyalty to king, creed, and empire that rendered men willing to sacrifice their lives at the behest of a faceless and incompetent 'top brass'" (EP8). "That such values are presented in the play as having enduring power, reaching into the late twentieth century, can be seen as rendering them all the more malign and destructive," Hill notes (EP9).

Thirty years on, in our time, or in another place, the sting might not be so great, however, and so to the degree that the play lives into the present, it might be worth noting Hill's point about the rejection of *Observe the Sons* by its reception audience: "such a verdict is not sufficient" (EP9). If nothing else, the play offers another way to look at the mechanisms by which memory functions in part because it conflates history and memory, allowing one to stand in for the other without the demand of an objective truth test. This is particularly true with reference to the orange sashes the men don as they head out to battle, a historical artifact, if not a fact, as Hill points out (EP7).

Speaking of a history of the war written in its immediate aftermath, Hill says, "[T]here was a sense among Ulster Unionists that a record of the Division's achievements would not alone memorialise the dead and comfort the bereaved but also reinforce and justify their own claim to special treatment in the settlement of the Home Rule issue" (EP3). What they did always already referred outside itself to the politics of Ireland. That, however, makes it ironic that the play, unlike the fiction to be discussed below, makes little reference to the contemporary issues in Ireland. The Easter Rising is discussed just once, as aftermath, in jest, with McIlwaine telling the story as a tale of incompetence and cowardice and concluding,

Stone of Remembrance, Irish National War Memorial Gardens, Dublin

"So you see, Fenians can't fight. Not unless they're in a post office or a bakery or a woman's clothes shop. Disgrace to their sex, the whole bastarding lot of them, I say" (65). It is barely noted that Pyper, recognizing the nonsense offered in this version of "history," asks, "Who gave you this version of events?" to which he finally gets the answer, from McIlwaine: "I'm very imaginative.... To hell with the truth as long as it rhymes" (65). In part, this is because McGuinness was filling in a gap in the record, which had stressed understanding Northern Ireland in relationship to "the Troubles" rather than to the Great War or the Somme in particular (Hill EP5). Declan Kiberd puts it cryptically: "McGuinness's play was as much a product of the 1980s as it was a story of an Ulster mind-set which achieved definition all of seven decades earlier" (280).

By the time the play was first performed, says Kiberd, the role of those who had joined up to (they thought) preserve Ulster and their ideal of Home Rule "had been all but forgotten: and even the rebels of 1916 were no longer commemorated with the fervor which once they had aroused. There was a real danger all the dead would be forgotten" (280). Pyper, fortunately for their sakes, becomes the unlikely vehicle through which this gap in memory would find a remedy.

In fact, the significance of the play is as much in how it complicates memory by employing a shifting chronology as in how it portrays what is remembered. From the opening, we know that the men we will yet meet—those we expect to see marching towards the Somme—have acted, because they have died at the Somme. The future (predicted) identity formed by the communicative memory of being a Son of Ulster who so marched has already happened, though the play exists to show us how it did happen. Of course, this makes the command of the title, which demands that the viewer observe the Sons of Ulster on this *marche funèbre*, impossible to achieve, because we shortly realize that they have already so marched. 44

In offering up the theme of "Remembrance," the title of Part I of the play, *Observe the Sons* demands that its audience, both when the play was first performed and now, think though the matter of what is remembered. That this is contradicted in Pyper's opening words "I remember nothing today. Absolutely nothing" is only a foil (9). He pauses, and then, addressing both the audience and the gathered ghosts of his dead comrades in arms, says, "I do not understand your insistence on my remembrance" (9). They may not, but the audience does, because "the elder Pyper represents not just one Ulster Protestant but millions of survivors, who were faced, like him, with the task of finding meaning in such appalling losses" as had happened at the Somme (Hill EP9). Note, though, that the act of finding meaning may be read as distinct from that of remembering, rendering McGuinness' section title ironic.

---

44 The article by Herron takes up at length the matter of the dance of death and these characters as ghosts.

Tom Phelan's novel *The Canal Bridge*, while taking place mostly in Ireland, all but guts the notion that Irish unity surrounding 1916 had heroic qualities tied to cultural memory. In fact, representatives of Irish nationalism are portrayed as laughingstocks, as stupid, illiterate, blind followers of a set of ideas that they don't have any full grasp on. This perhaps happens because the novel mostly takes place in a tiny village whose relationship to Dublin is distant. Irish politics in Ballyrannel are like a game of telephone in grade school—the message may have started out pure, but by the time it has reached this village, its tone is decidedly local.

For the two main male characters, Con Hatchel and Matthias Wrenn, going off to join the British army has nothing to do with rejecting their Irish roots, as those who mock them would have it.[45] In fact, their reasons have nothing to do with fighting at all, as they leave in 1913 to see the world on the British army's shilling. Even would-be Irish revolutionary Ralphie Blake understands as much (21). The townspeople don't necessarily understand, however, and the gossip cited in Blake's narration goes like this: "They're traitors to their own country, them lads. The English army is the army of our enemy," this from an unnamed speaker (21).

The novel does cite the "problem" of an Irish man joining the British army in a number of places, including bringing it up at the end, in the form of a set of tragic actions, but the novel occurs in layers, where the Irish theme is embedded inside revelations about memory and how it functions, which is in turn embedded inside the local Canal itself functioning as both a thematic and symbolic element.

This text occurs in chapters each featuring the voice of a narrator different from the last (with a few exceptions where a character has two consecutive chapters), so readers

45 Though like anyone who answered Kitchener's call, they would have had to learn the lesson that "once a man enlisted, his body—whether alive or dead—belonged to the King" (Stamp 87).

hear the story from a number of points of view. In an early chapter told by Father Kinsella, the local priest, we get a glimpse into the Irish question as seen from someone distant from the center of the action, Dublin: "[T]hat cross-eyed Pearse and his crowd; so badly he wanted to be a mythical or mystical hero he just couldn't wait to get himself killed…. Him and his crowd just couldn't wait for the War to be over. There was no need for anyone to be a martyr for Ireland…. Home Rule was on the books in London" (85). His interest is only in getting permission to have a festival (Feis), and he wants that to restore Irish culture and language when Home Rule comes to be (86).

Meanwhile, would-be local rebel Johnjoe Lacy continues to try to convert people to the cause, most notably simple fellow Ralphie Blake, who is unable to resist his demands despite his fears, but who also shares the priest's and Matthias' skepticism about the cause (105–06). "If the English had only given them [the martyrs] all a good kick in the arse and sent them home to their mothers the whole thing would have been over and done with in a matter of days," he informs us (107). The English firing squad turned them into heroes, he says.

In a chapter narrated from Matthias Wrenn's perspective, he speaks about July 1, 1916, telling the reader that "[t]he lads from Ulster got farther than anyone else. They all did it because it was expected of them, climbed out of holes and faced into a slanting storm of terrible bullets," and 27,000 were lost (92). The point is not what ethnicity they were, though, but the scale of loss: "[A] mother and a father to cry for each one of them. Twenty-seven thousand young lads! If you squeezed all that sadness into a bomb you could destroy half the world with one explosion" (92). But then he turns the screw. "Twenty-seven thousand down in four hours, and we saying that the people in Dublin thought they had something to cry about with the twelve lads shot in Kilmainham that same Easter" (92). He says it once more: "Twenty-seven thousand lying in the muck in front of us, many of them from Ireland, but all that Ireland could think of was twelve bastards who stabbed in the back every Irishman fighting against the Germans. Couldn't they have waited? Did they need to be heroes so badly?" (92–93). He might well have added, "Which memory will mean more in 100 years?" though he might not have gotten the answer right.

Irish independence as a motif returns at the end of *The Canal Bridge*, albeit once again as a figure of parody. The war has ended, Matthias is home, Con is dead, and self-fashioned local rebels turn up at Enderly, the estate where Matthias farms and lives, and threaten to burn it down. Their plan is not at all well coordinated, taking no account, for instance, of Matthias' potential to defend against invaders because he is trained as a soldier. When he kills one of the group and threatens the rest, this too is the legacy of the war, as Ralphie realizes: "It must have been the War that did this to Matthias, taught him to size up a situation while his eyes were still taking it in, and then to act without thinking about acting. Maybe this was what had brought him safe home from France and Belgium" (267). The events seem to be about to conclude, but Johnjoe Lacy, unwilling to let his failed plan fade into the night, demands that his men attack once more. Both he and Matthias end up dead, and with that, the narrative of Ballyrannel concludes with a brief coda in the form of Kitty recounting events from the distant perspective of 1970.

Kitty's words indicate that cultural memory, in a town like Ballyrannel, exists in concretions like the Canal rather than in abstractions like what Johnjoe Lacy would spout to encourage his "rebels." Kitty nostalgically says, "The Canal was ours.... The Canal was everything we did with each other until the

Island of Ireland Peace Park, Messines, Belgium

two lads went away; it was us knowing everything about each other" (278). Then she brings us up to date, saying that while they believed that "it would always be there.... now [50 years on], the Canal is fading out of the fields and out of memory" (278).

We learn in the last scene, which takes place in 1970, that the Canal has dried up. Its disappearance prefigures what Kitty fears regarding the gravestones marking her friends' and husband's place of burial—that it, and they, now exist only as sites of knowledge about the past, a sign that points towards something having happened, rather than a place that can hold living significance in itself.[46]

The Canal, too, is slowly being erased both physically and from memory—farmers have dug into the beds and put roads across, and in places, the bank is leveled for miles, according to Kitty, which means that "all traces of the Canal are gone, as if it never was" (277). The very way of life that saw the Canal

---

46 This could be Pyper talking about the memory of the other Sons, if he were to be honest about their erasure.

as a passageway of both goods and information is lost on the present generation. But in becoming desiccated, the Canal ironically becomes something else—a trench. The irony of this, of course, is that for those who have this recognition, this physical space marks England's war having come home, despite Irish resistance and even the belief of those who fought for England that, after 1918, they had left the war behind.

As is well known, the Irish question in the aftermath of the wartime Troubles was very much on people's minds in the 1920s, with Sinn Fein hearkening back to 1916 as they pressed their demands for the British to vacate. Decades later, we see this conflicted time demonstrated in two novels, JG Farrell's *Troubles*, which details the events of 1919–21, and Sebastian Barry's *A Long Long Way*, which takes wartime itself as its setting.[47] Together, these novels reveal the repressed psychological trauma of British colonialism in the Irish cultural imagination, but only if we read one in context with the other to reveal that the background to *Troubles* (1970) may be asynchronically found in *A Long Long Way* (2005).

In *Troubles*, the war is over, but it still filters into the language of the people who populate the grand but dilapidated Majestic hotel in Ireland where much of the action is set. To them, British subjects, World War I forms a familiar point of reference, directing attention away from the immediate reality that the Sinn Feiners are wreaking havoc in the countryside surrounding the hotel. It is, in the way that the term is commonly understood, a Freudian repression of traumatic experience, odd in that it chooses one trauma as a replacement for another, as I will unpack in what follows.

The Troubles, in this way of thinking, are rendered a post-war problem that may be "solved" (really covered over or

---

47 Farrell's novel falls outside the timeframe I work with in *Mixing Memory and Desire*, but its receiving of the Lost Man Booker prize in 2010 warrants its inclusion.

ignored) by pulling the contexts of 1914–18 forward into 1919–21, a period in which, according to cultural historian Geoff Dyer, "everything about the war—except the scale of loss—was suspended in a vacuum" (35). *A Long Long Way*, however, demonstrates that it is not possible to elide the Troubles by referencing the war as a tool to repress the trauma of their presence, because in invoking the war, the British must inevitably invoke 1916, when Irish conscripts in the uniform of the Empire were forced to fire on Irish protesters. Hence any reference to the war, properly read in the context of 1916, does not represent successful psychological repression, but in fact an intensification of trauma.

Siegfried Sassoon, the war poet who famously underwent psychoanalysis at Craiglockhart War Hospital, wrote the following in "Repression of War Experience":

> …[I]*t's bad to think of war,*
> *When thoughts you've gagged all day come back to scare you;*
> *And it's been proved that soldiers don't go mad*
> *Unless they lose control of ugly thoughts*
> *That drive them out to jabber among the trees.* (4-8)[48]

Here he puts his finger on the triggers of repression: guilt ("bad"), fear ("scare"), and aversion ("ugly"). Sassoon's goal, as expressed in his diary entries, was "a ferocious and defiant resolve to tell the truth about the war in every possible way" (qtd. in Murray 107).

In 1915, Freud said the following, which sounds very much like it could have been a source for Sassoon: "the essence of repression lies simply in turning something away, and keeping

---

48 The poem first appears in Sassoon's 1918 volume *Counter-Attack and Other Poems*. For further discussion on Sassoon's time at Craiglockhart, see Murray 116–27. Oliver says that Sassoon's doctor did not see him as mentally ill, but merely war-weary (254–55). Williams discusses the poetry in his sixth chapter, "'Spectral Images': The Double Vision of Siegfried Sassoon" (*Media, Memory* 138–57).

it at a distance, from the conscious" (qtd. in Boag 74).[49] The idea came to Freud as early as the 1890s, when he described the loss of traumatic memories as a process of "*motivated forgetting*: '…it was a question of things which the patient wished to forget, and therefore intentionally repressed from his conscious thought and inhibited and suppressed'" (Breuer and Freud, qtd. in Boag 75, italics original). The types of memories which might be repressed include those creating "shame, self-reproach or psychical pain" (Boag 75). Repression was named by Freud as the central tenet of his theory of psychoanalysis in 1914 (Boag 74). He claimed in the middle-1920s that "it is possible to take repression as a center and bring all the elements of psycho-analytic [sic] theory into relation with it" (qtd. in Boag 74).[50]

Freud's theory, in fact, divides repression into two types: psychoneuroses and traumatic neuroses. The latter will be of service here, dealing as it does with the process whereby "traumatic memories are forgotten, arising from 'shocking' experiences such as war" (Boag 77). Freud himself said in 1919, "[T]he war neuroses are only traumatic neuroses, which, as we know, occur in peacetime too after frightening experiences or severe accidents, without any reference to a conflict in the ego," hence detaching the theory of traumatic neurosis from the psycho-sexual (qtd. in Boag 77).[51] His words reflect the mechanism of displacement that the characters in *Troubles*

---

49 This characterization is taken from Simon Boag's recent article tracing the history of the theory and arguing for a renewed understanding of the concept.

50 Boag details how repression relates to the sexual impulses, which he says are inaccurately translated as "instincts," when "drive" is a better rendering of the German, though still only an approximation (75).

51 Boag goes on to detail how the primary definition of repression Freud offered beginning in the 1920s was the psycho-sexual one, with the repression of the instinctual drives, which begins in childhood, the foundation for psychological repression. He critiques the common view of repression for ignoring the instinctual element of Freud's later emphasis (78–79). However, the volume of citations he offers indicates that most researchers do use "repression" in the sense of repression of traumatic experiences.

enact when dealing with the problems literally outside their front door.

In *Troubles*, there is a constant undertone of reference to the war. The trenches, particularly, figure into the thoughts and speech of many characters. Is it, perhaps, that the lingo of the time was simply rich with allusion to the events that had dominated people's thinking for five years? On the surface, it makes no sense that one would invoke a traumatic event in order to forget it, so this almost-constant act of remembering must have another cause. In fact, recalling the trauma of the past allows the characters to forget the trauma and guilt of the present. In Farrell's novel the (British) characters, when faced with a choice of remembering what was horrible in the past or dealing with what is horrible in the now, choose to use memory of the past as a way to deflect their guilt in the present. In choosing war memory over the presentness of the Troubles, the characters can maintain the fiction that England will survive. The now-past war is thus both symbol of and simulacrum for the attempt of England to stave off decline.

Troubles features almost as many references to the Great War as to the Troubles (both those that happened in 1916 and their aftermath going on in the present of the novel) happening in and around the Irish manor house/hotel (the Majestic) that forms the physical setting. The fact that the nation, and by extension the Empire, was at war allowed the English to shield themselves from the reality of the ruin all around them by telling themselves that all under the British flag sought a common purpose. Carrying the discourse of the Great War into the period after 1918 allows Farrell's characters to continue in this state of ignorance. Thus when one figure in the novel says to another, "[G]ive the bloody war a rest, will you?" he points out the ubiquity, rather than the scarcity, of such references (Barry 413).[52]

Easy references to the war include characters or the narrator tossing off military terms. "[S]he had been 'confined to barracks' by her military-minded father," the narrator says when talking about a woman who had been prevented from leaving home with her fiancé (Farrell 128). The Troubles themselves are coded as "a war without battles or trenches" (167). The trenches come up frequently, with characters referencing their time there, as the Major does when answering Edward, who wants him to pass judgment on whether Sarah, the woman he loves, should play cards with him over Edward's objections. "I think it's better than being in the trenches. Does that answer your question?" he says (265).

Thinking about the way that memory functions helps explain this preoccupation. "In neural terms, the past is only ever a construct of the ever-changing present," Williams says, referencing the fact that "personal memories are bound to change in the light of new experience" (*Media, Memory* 38). In *Troubles*, war references exist from past to present. However, they do not form a continuum, nor are they unrelated to what is going on in the immediate context, in this case, the acts of rebellion of Sinn Fein. Hence the habit of measuring present experience against the experience of the war is seen in the way various characters reference the war in *Troubles*. The Majestic hotel has a number of young men staying at one point, and they are described by Edward, the owner of the place, as "just schoolboys, really (though they've done their bit, mind you, they've been in the trenches)" (161).

---

52 The plot is relatively simple, though the narration of the novel is intricate (on which see Moseley 492). A Major from England comes to stay at the Majestic and marry his fiancé. She dies, and he then falls in love with a local woman, and stays over the course of a couple of years, during which time the twin trajectories of the hotel's final physical decline and the rise of "Troubles" related to Irish independence intersect.

The Major, late in the going, awakens from a dream and walks into a darkened hallway. Hearing a voice, "an image flashed into the Major's mind—of a man he had seen mortally wounded sitting hunched in a shell-hole with his intestines in his lap like a mess of snakes" (348). In defining themselves, additionally, the British characters often revert to the war. The Major's personality is entirely collapsed onto it. "[S]he wanted the Major to tell her about himself. And so the Major, feeling strangely at peace, found himself talking about the war," when speaking with Sarah, a woman he falls in love with (134). All of this is quite natural, given the background experiences of these people, although unusual in one sense— veterans were famous for not talking about the trenches (Parker 74, 232).

However, the war is coded quite differently, that is to say, strategically, when deployed in the Irish setting, which is imbricated into the war as the wartime experience is laid over it via the characters' strategy of repression indicated earlier. In fact, the template is given in narration early in the text, when the narrator is recounting the Major's memories of Peace Day (July 19th, 1919). He recalls that the pubs were full, the song "Tipperary" and others being sung lustily. The trouble was, from his point of view, those songs were "from the first year of the war" and for that reason, "[t]o the Major they sounded incongruous and pathetic. Dublin was still living in the heroic past. But how many of these revelers had voted for Sinn Fein in the elections?" (95). His memory, of course, might be selective. Perhaps other songs were being sung, and it is thus not Dublin that, in 1919, lives in a "heroic" past, but he who does. Yet in recalling just those songs that represent 1914–15, he signals his repression of the events of 1916 and his projection of that repression onto the Irish. The Major is hearing with British ears, which select the moments of the war, a traumatic experience, rather than those which might induce guilt, such as those connected with 1916.

In understanding Sinn Fein post-war, the war experience is a template. The Major thinks to himself as he is walking on a city street, "[H]ow does one recognize them? They wear no uniform. They're like spies" (97). And when looking at the Irish out one day en masse walking the country roads while he rides with Edward in a Daimler, he sees them as "refugees… moving back from the Front" (267). The narrator reports his interior monologue: " 'What a rabble,' he thought unsympathetically. He hated the Irish" (267). By this point in the text, the rebellion has reached the gates of the Majestic, with events such as the killing of Edward's prized piglets just around the corner (397).

Indeed, the Irish are moving back from a front, but not from "the Front," the war being over for them in one sense, though very much alive in another. Thus as the novel enters its denouement, Anglo-Irish strategies of repression (and hence suppression of Sinn Fein in the novel's present) begin to fail, and the events of 1916 start to push to the forefront of character consciousness. "[H]ad there been one, even one, honest-to-God battle during the whole course of the rebellion?" the narrator reports Edward thinking. "Not a single trench [the measure of warfare in this context] had been dug, except perhaps for seed potatoes, in the whole of Ireland! Did the Sinn Feiners deserve the name of men?" (390). The response to this is telling, as the Major invokes the key event of the Rebellion. "Of course, there *was* Easter 1916" he says (391, emphasis original). Here he suggests the repressed background to all the war references made by all the English characters who populate the novel. But Edward does not take the reference up, and indeed, it is essentially singular in *Troubles*.

The book ends with two significant events: first, the Major is buried alive on the seashore by Sinn Fein, to be drowned by the incoming tide. The experience becomes a wartime one for him: "[H]is mind wandered away, buoyant and aimless as a drifting balloon, to the trenches—to some 'show' or other in some godforsaken wood without a name" (443). In a portrayal of the decline of English influence, which will be more fully realized in the next scene, he is rescued not by the men he has stood with in opposition to Sinn Fein, but by the elderly women left to fend for themselves as the last guests at the Majestic.

In the second notable moment that closes the novel, the Majestic, crumbling ruin that it is, is set ablaze and burns to the ground. This is the same place that its master, Edward, planned to defend as if in a World War I battle. "Edward was making plans for the defense of his estate," we are told, because "fields of fire, enfilading machine-guns, flanking attacks and suchlike" were the strategies he believed his enemy Sinn Fein would use (429).[53] The hotel, the symbol of British excess and repression, is reduced to rubble, and the narrator tells us, "Now that these rooms were open to the mild Irish sky they all seemed much smaller—in fact, quite insignificant" (453). Like the Empire they represent, they have been humbled, and not even by the act of a gang of rebels with no proper technique nor training. A single, elderly, angry Irish servant sets the place ablaze. The words of Harry Patch, the last surviving veteran of the trenches, are apt: "The war might have been over, but its effects were never far away," he said later on in life (qtd. in Parker 261).

The British in Farrell's novel never come to grips with the claims of the Irish, and they never face their own guilt for

---

53 He means this figuratively, of course, since, as he knows, Sinn Fein does not have military equipment that would make such a coordinated strike possible.

the British suppression of the Rebellion of 1916. If the Majestic can be taken for the symbol of their repression of the Irish in the interests of maintaining their own over-reaching lifestyle as center of the Empire, then Edward's comment on the condition of the house, made to the Major, is delightfully ironic in its understatement. Pointing to a pile of plaster rubble that has come down in a heap large enough to look in the semi-darkness like a snowdrift, Edward says, "The place needs doing up a bit" (313). The fact that it is never "done up," but rather, in the end, undone, suggests that the attempt to repress the moment of 1916 and the current claims of Sinn Fein and the Irish on their land by focusing on the war has failed. But Farrell never says that, and his text presents little of the Irish point of view, except as seen by the English. For that, we must turn to Barry, who points readers towards an explanation of why the war matters when it comes to understanding Sinn Fein's actions after the war.

The nearly invisible underside in *Troubles* is the unvoiced dissent that lives in the shadowy Sinn Fein figures seen as little more than peasant rabble by the Anglo-Irish at the Majestic. Barry allows us to hear those voices by focusing attention on the background to the post-war Troubles and demonstrating their rootedness in the events of the war itself. Used as a gloss on this, *A Long Long Way* dramatizes that World War I is paramount in the worldview of the Irish for the exact opposite reason Farrell's novel seems to suggest through its focus on the English. Rather than being a tool by which more painful realities (the Troubles) may be ignored, it becomes a symbol of exactly what the British are repressing: the events of 1916. By showing that the Irish trauma after 1916 was not simply traceable to their need for independence, but a direct result of the suppression of their rebellion as an act related to British militarism during World War I, Barry uncovers the reasons for the final denouncement of England via the actions of Sinn Fein in Farrell's novel.

The experiences of Barry's main character, 19-plus year-old Dubliner Willie Dunne, are typical of what happened to enlisted men during the war. Throughout the novel, Willie searches for the truth amongst the competing and fragmentary views he gets of the Rebels as his experience goes from confusion to repression of traumatic detail about the 1916 Rebellion, a process that might be taken as more than just his own, but rather to symbolize the struggles of the Irish as a whole in the wake of both the Great War and the Easter Rising (not to mention, in the longer context identified by Lloyd, of the great Famine).

He joined the war effort for two reasons: to defend women from the Germans (52)[54]; he did it also because the British had promised Home Rule (14).[55] He is a naïve young man, but a convinced patriot at the events' outset. The narrator reports early in the going that he feels that he has enlisted to heal Ireland. "[H]e was sure that all Ireland was, and all that she had, should be brought to bear against this entirely foul and disgusting enemy [Germany]" (23). His sympathies are confused, however, when he is home on leave during the Easter Rising. He is on board his troop ship ready to leave when everyone is ordered off. Standing on the dock, he is about to take a flier from a man when a captain tells him not to talk to the enemy. "What enemy, sir?" he asks, incapable of conceiving of a man in street clothes in Willie's hometown

---

54 The Allied side claimed German atrocities in Belgium from the outbreak of the war. Most commentators believe these stories apocryphal. For a discussion of some of what was believed, see Vance 22–26, 35.

55 This was such a sensitive issue that, as historian Hew Strachan says, "the commitment of the Liberal government to home rule [sic] for Ireland promised to drive Ulster loyalists into rebellion" in the early days of the war (16). O'Malley says that "a wide range of social groups were able to read their own aspirations into the war" (116).

that way (88). The captain takes out his pistol and holds it to the man's temple until Willie steps back into line.

Shots are fired, and his column is ordered into action to suppress the Rebels, an enemy that Willie, at least, does not know exists. A fellow soldier exclaims, "Is it us against us? What in the name of Jaysus is going on?" (90). They are ordered to charge at a building that has Rebels firing from it, and in the din, a young man with an ancient pistol comes up behind Willie and tells him that he is his prisoner. Willie asks, "Are you a German?" to which the young man says, "German? What are you talking about. I'm an Irishman. We're all Irishmen in here, fighting for Ireland" (92).[56] A fellow soldier shoots the boy, and Willie hears his act of contrition, then holds him while he dies.

Willie still has no idea what has gone on. His friend, Jesse Kirwan, who will later be executed for refusing to continue carrying out his military duties, tries to explain. He says that the Irish Volunteers went to war for England "because Home Rule was as good as got. But a few broke away and that's who you just saw on the lovely streets of Dublin" (95).

Willie returns to the Front questioning which side to sympathize with. The narrator reports that "[a]lthough Willie might be hard put to describe…what happened in Dublin, it was harder nonetheless to get it out of his head" (102).[57] To put this into similar terms to those I used to describe Farrell's novel, one might say that Willie's process of repression of the details in his memory is complicated by the fact that he doesn't understand them. Repression, in this equation, takes two steps: recognizing the horror and then burying it.

---

56 In fact the Rebels' headquarters featured a sign that said, "WE SERVE NEITHER KING NOR KAISER, BUT IRELAND" (van Emden 184).

57 Neil Oliver takes the positive side of this, exclaiming that "[t]he men of the South joined the 10th (Irish) and the 16th (Irish) Divisions; the men of the North joined the 36th (Ulster).… In the Great War they fought not as rivals but as Irishmen, and honoured one another as they did so" (229).

When the men he fights with are behind the lines resting and catching up on old newspapers, he can't talk about what he saw in Dublin. "Willie didn't want to say anything, to describe what he had seen and done at that very Mount Street. He didn't know why exactly. It was as if he wished he had never been through there, seen those things. It was foul enough where he was betimes without having to think back to other foul things—confusing, awful things" (137). This may signal the start of repression. As Richard van Emden comments when talking about men who went over the top and experienced the mind detaching itself from the experience and instead offering the soldier "uncontrolled thought," this appears "to imply that the mind was protecting itself from the prevailing horrors" (53).

As the novel progresses, it winds through the familiar World War I tropes of gas, machine guns, field punishments, and trench warfare, but underneath these is Willie's questioning of the events of Easter 1916. As in Farrell, the war and the Rebellion end up becoming entangled with one another, with the men's reaction to those executed in Dublin to "curse," "praise," "doubt," and "despise," but "all in a confusion complicated infinitely by the site of war" (144).

The regiment Willie is a part of, the Royal Dublin Fusiliers, loses strength after the Somme, and they are replenished by Englishmen. Some, including their priest, hold to the idea that "you are fighting at the end of the day for Ireland, to bring Home Rule and all the rest, to gather the raveled ends of Ireland together" (214). Meanwhile, Willie has written a letter to his staunchly Loyalist father suggesting his sympathy with the Rebels, because of his feelings for the young man he saw killed. His father reacts violently to this because he is sympathetic to the English, being a policeman who has risked his life and lost his men in the effort to suppress the Rebellion. Willie, in discussing this with him while yet again on leave, says, "It's a funny, dark world out at the war, Papa…. It brings your mind to think a thousand thoughts, a thousand new thoughts," thereby indicating that the process of repression engenders a mix of old memories with new, and the attempt to recapture traumatic moments leads only to confusion (247).

Shortly after, as the events of the novel begin to point toward the end, he mulls over the Home Rule question once more: "Something had come to an end before even the war was over…. The aspirations of poor men were annulled for ever [sic]. Any fella that had come out in the expectation of Home Rule could rest assured his efforts and his sacrifice were useless" (275). But this is not accepted simply by Willie. Rather, the narrator goes on to report, "Willie thought that was very sad. Very fucking sad. And very mysterious" (275). When he makes up his mind that he has been duped, the narrator reports Willie's interior monologue as asking, "How could a fella love his uniform when that same uniform killed the new heroes…? How could a fellow like Willie hold England and Ireland equally in his heart, like his father before him, like his father's father…?" (287). He says it with "his heart clean and pure, as pure as a heart can be after three years of slaughter" (287). For Willie, the war has become a conflation of what happened in Flanders with what happened in Dublin.

As such, the war proves to be beyond Willie's ability to code. He feels like he might dig in with his mates and be at the Front for another thousand years (288).[58] As for Ireland, or any country with a defined identity, it is left behind: "[S]o far they had come that they had walked right out to the edge of the known world and had fallen off into other realms

---

58 van Emden similarly cites a soldier who says, "[W]e had abandoned all hope of peace and hardly ever thought about it" (65).

entirely.... There was no road back along the way they had taken. He had no country, he was an orphan, he was alone" (289). Having become detached from Ireland, having demonstrated that beyond memory and repression lies a shadowland where neither time nor place exist concretely, having outlived his usefulness in asking this question of what can survive of memory or place, he is killed off, a sniper's bullet quieting him as if he were a "busy owl" (289).

Foregrounding Willie's confusion over the Troubles provides an answer to the question posed by Farrell's *Troubles*: why the focus on a past war when the very present Troubles should be demanding the characters' attention? Willie, in this reading, is Ireland in microcosm, his struggles the psychological profile of the "rabble," to invoke again the British characterization, who were Sinn Fein (Farrell 267). Reading the post-war moment depicted by Farrell while taking Willie Dunne into account demands that one recognize that any attempt (by the British) to use the war as a distraction from the present Troubles in fact does the opposite, because it surfaces the repressed trauma of the Easter Rebellion.

Willie Dunne's fellow soldier makes an ironic comment after a visit to the Front by King George: "It kind of suits an Irishman to curse the King of England, all things considered. But he spoke to us, man to man.... Like he was one of us" (226). It suited the British to be seen this way because it served their political ends, though neither they nor the Irish, if the postcolonial theorists are correct, could be fooled into accepting this conflation of their identities, because after the war as before it, the Irish had a deep store of repressed memory which separated them from the British. Sadly, long practice made it possible to repress yet more—the memories of what the British did during the Great War and after, even using Irish troops in suppressing the Easter Rebellion.

CHAPTER 5

Aftermath and Other Scenes: Times and places beyond the war

Returning home from trench life was, in mid-1919 when most survivors were released from service, a joyful event. But most combatants, and their loved ones, did not realize what they would have to live with in the time to come, because the war was taken back home after the peace. If the war created heroic characters of ordinary men, most didn't carry that quality back to "normal" life. In fact, the aftermath of the war was for many a chaotic and difficult period filled with longing for the grand ideals they had lived by in the trenches mixed with the desire to forget their horrors.

For most former combatants, the aftermath of war was lived far from the scenes where they had experienced 1914–18—at home in Canada, Australia, India, or somewhere else. And for all of them, time had passed, but the surface appearance of the places of their return remained largely the same. Much of the time, these places bear no resemblance to the geography—physical or psychological—of their wartime experience. They would more likely resemble portions of the former battlefield area as described by Vera Brittain:

"Aveluy is now rebuilt—new red-brick houses, white mortar, bright blue painted railings" (158). Observing such a scene, it seems on the surface as if nothing has happened. The same is true for the faces the former soldiers put forth to the post-war world. But inside their minds, they experienced a constant tension between the past and the present or, more poignantly, they lived with an entwined struggle to remember and to forget.

Few were close enough to the former battlegrounds to use them as reminders of what had been, and even those who might have been would have seen memory gradually erased. Brittain, taking a tour in the 1930s, makes this cryptic statement: "Impossible for anyone living in [the] Somme area to forget the War" (151). This for reasons both horrible and (dare one say) beautiful: the land was still scarred, the danger of unexploded ordinance still lurked (and does until today—at mid-day, shells found in plowing are detonated), but most significantly, because the whole place struck her as "[o]ne vast open-air museum filled with memorials," as indeed it will until now for anyone with a car to drive around (151). Every country lane seems to have a sign that points to another beautifully tended graveyard.

The Thiepval Memorial was a late addition to the rostrum of spectacular monuments dotting the former Western Front. And it appears today much like it did when Brittain described it (albeit with much effort at preservation having been expended over the years). It sits on the top of a rise, looking over scenic countryside, immense and silently powerful. But as Brittain says, it is a "cheating and a camouflage" that helps "create the illusion that war is a glorious thing, because so much of its aftermath can be rendered lovely and dignified" (176). It is a representation in brick and mortar of the need to simultaneously remember and forget.

Johannes Fabian provides a gloss on the process of forgetting while remembering when he talks about what anthropological subjects do when they relay their memories as stories.
Often, they leave gaps "that reveal the interplay of remembering and forgetting" signaled by moves like skipping ahead in
time, concentrating long periods of memory into stories surrounding a few objects, or eliding large amounts of time by
remembering just the beginning and ending of events but
pointing to what is left out using speech fillers (85, 85–87).[59]
Fabian labels the process by which large swaths of a life are
explained using relatively few concrete details to stand in for
elaborate detail "typification," and he says that this kind of
narrative adds up to "a remarkably thin story," one in which
the person turns into a reported biographical version of himself; in the case of the African man he is using as an example:
"a strangely absent colonial subject" (87).

One possible meaning of this willingness to let summary
stand in for detail on vast eras of one's prior experience is
"a narrative stance equidistant from remembering and forgetting" (89). This allows the person to stick to the grand detail
but still be vulnerable to recall of specific detail if prodded.
Thus when Fabian's subject claims not to remember the popular cultural craze for ballroom dancing that stretched through
the Depression, the researcher redirects the question to the
personal level: "Did *he* ever dance the *malinga*?" and gets an
affirmative response (89, italics original). He summarizes the
point by saying that "[t]ypification causes Baba Ngoie [the
interview subject] to sacrifice—to forget—detail and
concreteness in his life history" (89). This process quite ably
describes the manner in which aftermath is presented in
several novels about the period following the Great War
including Jack Hodgins' *Broken Ground*, Allan Donaldson's

---

59 He relates the example of a man who was interviewed in French, with "alors"
(so, well) and "donc" (so, therefore) as the fillers. See 86+.

Maclean, John Boyne's *The Absolutist*, and Pat Barker's *Toby's Room*. Each dramatizes a world in which the war is present yet absent, close yet not quite tangible, often elided yet still understood to have constructed the world of the (fictional) present.

In a review essay on several pieces of Canadian fiction, WH New describes Hodgins' *Broken Ground* along with several other novels: "All four novels look back to an event or person in the past, revisiting the geographical space in which events happened in order to understand the mental space in which the persons lived—and asking for that mental space to be re-imagined" (567). The reason this must happen is that the present lives of the people, at least those in the Hodgins novel, are fragmented—broken—with two sets of memories determining who they are. One is that of a forest fire that devastated their rural BC community. The other is memory of the Great War. As they focus, or attempt to focus, on the former memory, they find that no one person can hold it whole. Each has just a piece.

> [And the] *problem is that the stories of the fire (true up to a point, within the borders of bias and faulty memory) are the townspeople's way of avoiding the memory of the real critical moment in their past, the years of the First World War, when the men returned from France maimed and determined to forget.* (568)

This is not without effect on their material existence, because "[t]heir repressed memories—of loss, guilt, fear, self-justification, responsibility—fragment their presumably normal lives just as the War fragmented the entire century's belief in a stable community of values, a uniform 'point-of-view" (568).

As New explains, *Broken Ground* "tells a gripping tale of the fact that an entire community must come to terms with its attempt to live outside its own history," which is, they find, impossible (568). This is dramatized most poignantly by Charlie, the narrator of the novel's final section, who must deal with the aftermath of the war, despite not fighting in it. His struggle, and that of his generation, is to cope with the problems of his parents' generation, "loss, guilt, fear, and self-justification," the irony being that he "finds them to be just as dislocating, just as much the consequence of 'broken ground,' as those of the European battlefields" that his father and the men of the town had gone to fight in (569). They did it because they felt called to. He and his generation feel no such calling, because there is no cause to support—only the broken ground of the farms granted to their fathers as "reward" for their service but which are as defeating as any Western Front trench. The younger generation, in a manner of speaking, is as much shell shocked into numbness as their fathers had been, despite not having experienced the war.

From the start of *Broken Ground*, the veterans' alienation is clear. "This was the sort of reward they gave you for spending three or four years of your life being shot at for the King," Matthew Pearson thinks (18). The land these former Great War soldiers have been granted is such wooded and rocky ground that it's next to impossible to clear, and the novel opens with Charlie's father blowing himself up attempting to remove a stubborn stump. As Pearson says, "We were farmers who had never farmed land like this before, or cleared land like this before, or for that matter ever *seen* land like this before the War" (18, emphasis original). They live there not just to farm, but to forget. One of the female narrators in what is constructed by Hodgins as a set of alternating narrative viewpoints is Christina Ahlberg, whose take is that "[o]ne of the better things about living here was that the War did not get mentioned often" (29). Deconstruct that and it means, of course, that in its silence, the war lurks and lingers over everything which *is* said.

There was once a timber mill nearby, but even that wasn't put there to fulfill its obvious function, but to qualify the

14th Light Division Memorial, Zillebeke, Belgium

logging company for a timber license. "It was a ruin without ever having been anything else, a thing of the past in a place that had no past," which in one sense would seem like a good place to forget (103). But the war doesn't simply go away, even with the preoccupation of trying to make a living out of this impossible ground.

Like other communities, this one agrees to erect a memorial, but not by raising money. Instead, the farmers "came together on a certain day with their wagons and stoneboats and trucks, to drop off their contribution for a memorial to the men killed or lost in the War" (88). "[T]hey only wanted hand-picked stones, one or two from each family, so the memorial would represent the entire valley" (88). In a situation where every possibility seems to suggest its exact opposite, this memorial would force the focus back onto something, but not the now-receding war years. Rather, it would remind each of the men/families who used it to commemorate how bad their present material conditions were, though these were a "reward" for their wartime service.

This is perhaps why Matthew Pearson, in response to a visitor's question about whether they talk about the war, asks, "Do they talk about it anywhere? Most of us are trying to forget" (91). His disaffection is palpable: "When you suspect you've been taken for a fool you don't talk about it much.... We're still trying to figure out what we're supposed to have accomplished" (91). When Pearson tries to relate a story from the war to the visitor, Wyatt Taylor, he himself finds it fragmented ("typified," to return to Fabian), ending his tale with, "I haven't been able to tell you even this one small episode without leaning on the passive voice and that faceless 'they' for support. And you wonder why you don't hear me telling tales of my 'war experiences'? I am ashamed of the words I would have to use" (101).

Broken Ground exists in three sections. The first takes place in 1922; the second, which is quite brief, covers 1918–19; the final one moves ahead to 1996, when a film that documents the wartime and aftermath has been shot. The most striking depictions in the 1996 section are of Matthew Pearson's visit back to the battlefields of France soon after the war had ended. He was stricken, we learn, by the silence: "[T]here was not a single echo here of the uproar that had sometimes filled his head at home" (264). Yet the war does linger, in the form of a farmer who tells Pearson that he continues to plow up ordinance, body parts, and other remnants. In fact, he was himself a casualty, losing a leg herding his cows. "I suppose I will be plowing up bayonets and shells and human limbs every year for the rest of my life," he comments, and the narrator (an elderly Charlie, whom we met as a boy at the start of the novel) says, "He seemed to find this amusing" (265). It is, at the least, a great contrast to the harvest of stone and stump which the men from BC dealt with for the balance of their working lives. Pearson's quest, Charlie informs us, was "[l]ooking for fragments of himself that he may have left behind" (271). He recorded what he found in notebooks, which were eventually passed down to Charlie.

These depict a post-war France in the years when battle-field tourism was popular, and in them, everything ends up appearing absurd. Matthew Pearson encounters a farmhand who was a colonial soldier—either New Zealander or Aussie, he's not sure which—and that man, now working for a French farmer, had simply not gotten back on the boat to go home. He disappeared, exclaiming to Matthew, "Makes you wonder if it ever happened" (303). Swimming in a pond, a former shell crater, Pearson concludes, "War forced you into middle age when you had hardly lived out your boyhood," and he thinks to himself that "[a]ll around them this regenerated flowering landscape was green from the fertilizer of men" (304, 305). Time, the landscape, and memory—all three are altered by the war.

Charlie concludes while he watches the documentary film that these effects extend well past the wartime generation: "I began to suspect that I had already lost something impor-tant that I didn't even know about, before I was born or soon afterwards. We all had. All had gone on losing even more of it ever since, whatever it was" (325). This is perhaps why even until now writers have the impulse to scribe this war into fic-tion: "Behind the colorful parade of this century's gains and losses was a huge absence of something that was neither iden-tified nor regained nor replaced" (325).

Matthew Pearson, a teacher after the war, slowly changes his approach to it. At first, he avoids mentioning it. When he must because his history class demands it, he uses only "facts and figures" so that it becomes dull, dead. Later, Matthew "would sometimes offer opinions, but only those that had become commonplace by then" (329). Though "[e]ventually,

he would use the War to issue warnings to younger generations," even these don't move past vague claims that perhaps
the world that those (Germans) who rejected Victorian cer-
tainties and the Empire had fought for in a losing cause was
being created in any case (329). Pearson would end his lessons
by focusing on the futility of the 20th century's focus on the
individual and its rejection of morals. It became his mission
to confront students with their own responsibilities in the face
of this alienation (329).

But when he is gone, and what remains tangible of the past
is the movie, Charlie is left to sort out where truth comes
from. He asks, "Would it *become* the true story, erasing from
our memories the versions we'd heard a thousand times
from those who'd been there and from those whose parents
had been there? Had we been honoured and immortalized
by celluloid, or had something been stolen from us that we
would never get back?" (330, emphasis original). He decides
that "[f]or some the movie would provoke a whole new round
of remembering, and remembering of earlier remember-
ings—new tellings of old versions, as well as variations that
had not been represented on the screen," but for those youngsters who had no tangible link to the war, the movie would be
adopted "as though it were gospel, forgetting the facts" (330).
Like the town's war memorial, the film would point to something, but rather than the event it sought to commemorate, it
would, inevitably, at least for the self-conscious viewer, point
more to itself and the problematic matter of its own construction than beyond itself to any sort of authentic past. But then
again, perhaps that's all that a memorial, or a documentary
film—or a novel—could ever do.

Donaldson's *Maclean*, also set in Canada, begins with
a vivid scene of battle, though it's been decades since the war
concluded, and the scene is only a dream. Between that time

and the 1943 World War II moment the novel portrays has come the Great Depression that has cost John Maclean his livelihood as the bookkeeper at a furniture factory. This loss has left him an underweight 50-something semi-vagrant with just his army pension to live on. Gas got him in the trenches, and his penchant for alcohol, perhaps used as a salve to deal with the cruelties of his childhood, consumes his thoughts and his budget as the novel spans the course of a Saturday and into early Sunday morning.

The novel concludes with him sitting, alone, at night, on the German field gun resting next to the town's Cenotaph, thinking about all the fellows he knew who had been lost. Their names come to life again as he reads them. "He knew where every name was of the boys who had been his pals" (160–61) we learn, and he puts his remembrance into larger contexts: "They shall not grow old, the dignitaries at Remembrance Day were fond of intoning, as we that are left grow old. Age shall not weary them nor the years condemn. And so forth" (161). But he has already provided the gloss for these thoughts when thinking of the loss of the McIntyre boy, whose death in World War II has just been announced.

> [M]*aybe none of them had ever come home. Maybe only their ghosts had come home, as some poet had said. Maybe one way or the other, quick or slow, they had all died of their wounds. And maybe that wasn't so different, after all, from the way life happened for everybody. Maybe the whole thing was a war, leaving behind its trail of dead and wounded.* (159)

Maybe the only difference is that "[i]n his kind of war, it had happened a lot quicker than in what they call peace, condensing into a few months what otherwise took decades" (159).

This is the surprising coda to a story that features a character consumed by present-day problems, including dodging the local riff-raff with whom he both hangs out and has running feuds. His wartime experience, further, is so far in his past as to seem irrelevant to the present. Add that to the fact that his major problem in life is cruel treatment by his father during childhood and the fact that the man forced Maclean to quit school, for no good reason other than because he didn't want his kids to be better than he was, and you have a person with a set of traumas much more front-of-mind than the war (96). And yet the war is still there, dancing in and out of Maclean's mind and life as the narrative progresses.

In fact, in the early part of the text, which is to say earlier on this same day, Maclean had wandered past the Cenotaph, noticing the gun, "the only German gun he had ever seen," and the names, which "leapt out at him" as he passed. "Robert Cronk. Charles Simpson. Frank Gallagher. Old pals whose faces he sometimes had a hard time remembering now" unless he was drinking, in which case "one or the other of them would suddenly without warning take shape so clear he could imagine him speaking" (24).

The significance of the war thus toggles between two things in Donaldson's narrative, at times being simply a time marker for something other than itself and at times being the locus of memories that have constructed Maclean's life down to the present. To take one example, Maclean goes into town in the morning and sees some friends sitting on a wall. One is Leveret Hershey, who was with Maclean at Ypres and elsewhere, where they mutually suffered gas and machine gunning (37). But another is Ginger Coile, who is described as being "young enough to have missed the Great War and just old enough not to have been called up for this one" (38).

Maclean's deepest thoughts are about the quality and meaning of memory, and the Great War is, of course, high in his mind at these times. Often, these moments of recollection come suddenly, with no transition as the narrative breaks into

a distant third-person point of view. Such is the case when he
and Leveret are talking and drinking with other men, and
"[a]ll of a sudden, the glass of memory wiped clean by alcohol," Maclean has a visual recollection of a trench scene (47).
The narrative proceeds with him and Leveret trading memories, and then a section break shifts to the following voice:
"You men, you men there, what are you doing here? Get out
where you belong. Lieutenant! Lieutenant whatever your
name is!…You Canadians are a disgrace to His Majesty's uniform" (50). But then right after this, the voice is once again the
more familiar narration of Maclean, albeit still in third person, and the trench scene is summarized by, "That day is one
of the worst he could remember" (51).

Once again, we recall Fabian's notion of "a narrative stance
equidistant from remembering and forgetting" (89). Yet
unlike Fabian's interview subject, Maclean is fully aware of the
meta-discursive question of how one person's life relates to
history/History. That he has considered the meaning of the
events he witnessed on the day in question, and thought about
how history has coded them, becomes clear when the narrator
says, "He's never had the faintest idea what that battle was
about, and neither had anybody else he had ever talked
to" (56). He had looked through a history book in the Legion
when one became available, but found nothing but
"a reference to some 'brisk' skirmishes," which leads him to
conclude, "Whatever all the killing had been about that day, it
evidently hadn't qualified as history" (56). This is exactly the
point that *Maclean* the novel emphasizes most keenly. The war
exists in the past; it exists as memory; but there exists
a disconnect between what had been done in the years of
1914–18 and how official history recorded these events. "All
that stuff was a long time ago," it is true, and thus hard to
decode in the now (56).

Tyne Cot Cemetery, Belgium

The things that have happened since—Maclean's having lost his job around the time he turned 30 and his subsequent submission to alcoholism—while perhaps traceable to the war, exist beyond it also as factors that determine the later course of his life. The war, in short, is both there for him at all times and yet distant enough to be out of his reach as a cause of his current condition.

Still, Maclean's memories, which are very much like those of many ex-soldiers one encounters in the contemporary canon of World War I fiction, affect how he relates to others. He has flashbacks at the most odd times, sometimes with no context. Anyone nearby would have a hard time knowing what was going on in his head. Consider the scene where Maclean is telling of his good days, walking to the furniture factory. Suddenly, someone he sees coming along the road appears to be the man they called "Sergeant Death" (86). He quickly realizes that it is just a harmless man who works in a local clothier's shop.

In any case, he has no time to get lost in reflection on the past, what with dealing with his rivals in the town of Wakefield, trying to scrape together money for drink, and, at least on this day, working hard to find the money he needs to buy his mother a birthday present, since her birthday is the day after the story takes place. One prevailing irony of Maclean's life related to this quest for resources is that without the war, he wouldn't have any livelihood at all, since he is on a small military pension for having been gassed (107). Even at that, he worries that one of his yearly medical reviews will determine that he no longer qualifies (111).

The aftermath of the war is just one thing that has been carried into the present for Maclean, with his painful childhood being the other. It prevents him from having a relationship with his sister, and when he does stop by Alice's house, they end up arguing, because she sees no point in bringing up the past. Significant is that Maclean doesn't even know why he is compelled to recite his memories. "What had he come here for?" he asks himself (99). He attempts to explain: "Someone, something, sneaking past the sentries he had posted, had thrown wide the gates of memory" (99). Memory thus becomes a graveyard of ghosts who slip past the guards to haunt the present. And while the war is always there and often in benign details—the watch he borrows money on for his mother's present, for instance, was one he brought back from the war (120)—it also reduced Maclean to a being devoid of spirituality. He says through the narrator, "God is dead. A shell full of mustard gas got him while he was having a glass of wine and a loaf of bread beside the Menin Road" (111). However, this shell also left Maclean with a body which is itself the repository of recollection. When he hears a train thundering towards him while he crosses a rail bridge, we learn that "[h]is body had memories, and he was shivering like an animal under the battering weight of the noise" (110).

It was the war that taught him, above all, how random death is. His current-day enemy, Willie Campbell, is hit by a truck and killed. "Bad luck or no luck, [Maclean] still couldn't feel sorry," the narrative indicates (152). It's like when Sergeant Death had been killed. The company all thought that it was good luck, that now they would be saved. "But, of course, Death hadn't died, and their next turn in, they lost ten men killed without any real fighting at all, just to snipers and random shrapnel," no doubt deaths which would not be worthy of the history books, either (153).

Maclean ends with John Maclean, having delivered his present to his mother for her birthday the next day, making the aforementioned visit to the Cenotaph. Then, as he walks away, he steps off the curb and into the street: "[H]e began to march, first close to the sidewalk, then out and straight down the middle, his arms swinging wider and wider arcs as he passed the store windows and the darkened displays" (161). As he proceeds, "out of the great gulf of the past, the boys took shape around him. Bob, Frank, and Harry. Dan. Bill. Charlie. All just the way they had been before the bad things started to happen, swinging along in the close-packed, khaki lines of the old battalion, marching at ease" (162).

John Maclean thus marches into tomorrow as if the distant yesterday of the Great War determines his steps, and to a degree, perhaps it does. But what we know, and he ought to realize, is that tomorrow will be no better than today, because tomorrow, like today, he will still be broke, living where there is little opportunity but where he is haunted by his past, and with the desperate need for alcohol still driving his choices. None of this is entirely the fault of the Great War, but the one thing the war has done for him is teach him that memory resists even the best efforts to contain it.

By contrast, Tristan Sadler, the main character in John Boyne's *The Absolutist*, discovers a means of articulating what living in the shadow of war is like quite readily, if by accident.

Menin Gate Memorial to the Missing, Ypres

He is in Norwich on an errand with grave and far-reaching consequences, but that's a day away, and so he happens into a pub for an afternoon pint. A man takes him up as a friend, asking him whether he'd been at the Front until the end, to which Sadler says he had been. The man then tells the story of his two boys: "[O]ur Billy would have been twenty-three now and our Sam would have been about to turn twenty-two" (21). And Sadler as first-person narrator reports, "He smiled when he said their names, then swallowed and looked away. The use of the conditional tense had become a widespread disease when discussing the ages of children and little more needed to be said on the matter" (21). The grammar of memory, its entanglement between present and past and the complicated possibilities presented by its modality, comes to the forefront as Boyne's narrative proceeds, forming the means, however fragmented and ineffective, by which aftermath is experienced and dealt with.

The novel's structure itself demonstrates the tangled nature of time when it comes to war and remembrance. The first section, from which the above is drawn, takes place in

September 1919. The second is back in wartime, 1916, and the time frames alternate through the book until the last section, which flashes ahead to 1979. The narration throughout is first person, but Boyne pulls a switch in that the more distant times, 1916, are told in present tense while the more recent time (indeed, the "now" of the novel until one encounters the 1979 section) is in past tense.

One reason for the present-past conundrum posed in this narration is symbolic: because the main character, Sadler, lost his great love in the war, he thinks of his life as having ended at that time. He thus speaks of the time leading up to the death as present, as if to signal vitality, while the aftermath, be that 1919 or later, is dead time, indicated by the use of the past tense.

Physically too, Sadler, though just twenty-one in 1919, is a past-tense version of his own bodily self: "My chest...had lost much of its definition in recent times; it was pale now. Scars stood out, red and livid across my legs; there was a dark bruise that refused to disappear stretched across my abdomen. I felt desperately unattractive" (29). He goes on into even more lurid and repulsive detail: "my body...[was] beaten and bruised from more than two years of fighting...my left hand veined and discoloured in places, my right prone to the most inexcusable shakes and shudders...my sex mortified into muteness," and he concludes simply, "I was hideous, a spent thing" (31). For this reason, he imagines that were he to take a lover, that person would see him and get "spasms of revulsion" and thus that he himself "couldn't abide any touch that might suggest intimacy. I was twenty-one years old and had already decided that that part of my life was over" (31). The aftermath, for him, obviously is as visible and real as the reflection in the mirror in his room every morning.

He lives to be an elderly man, yet he is never able to live again in the form of being close to someone. There has been,

Sadler confesses, "Not a single person. Not once. No liaisons of any description" (306). Based on just this knowledge, it might be said that Boyne's point is complete—aftermath puts the person experiencing it into a permanent conditional tense, rendering him (in this case) unable to act, unable to feel, and unable to live in the present (tense). And the fault would be charged to the war. This might have been true in the case of the father in the pub who lost his sons, but in Tristan's case, his inability to act wasn't to the war's charge at all. It was Sadler himself who ruined his life, physical scars from battle notwithstanding. The clue comes in part in the physical symptom of shell shock that he described, the trembling index finger, which points to his true psychological condition and its causes.

As the plot events unfold (in the chronology of the novel, as we move forward, we move back in time, as indicated, to 1916), we learn that Sadler has fallen in love with another soldier, Marian's brother Will Bancroft, who appears incapable of recognizing another male, Tristan, as more than a physical lover. They are sent to the Front and see combat action, and then, in the book's apparent climax, Will is executed for refusing to go on fighting in the war effort. Worse than that, Sadler participates as one of the six men firing into Will's chest, with his last recollection of Will being his surprise declaration at seeing the lover he denies standing with gun raised. "'Tristan,' he says, his last word" (292). It is this, of course, which precipitates what would turn out to be a lifelong internal conflict which leaves Sadler, by his own admission, unable really to live. At the point of Will's execution, not coincidentally, the novel is finished with its telling of the past. The only section that remains is set in 1979.

Boyne's alternating uses of the present and past tenses as the novel has progressed offers a level of complexity to what is a somewhat melodramatic plot. The 1916 sections, told in present tense, seem most alive, as in this description of Tristan and Will's first physical encounter: "He reaches over, takes my face in his hands and pulls me to him…. [I do not feel] any of the great urgency that I thought I would, should this moment ever come to pass. Instead, it feels perfectly natural, everything he does to me" (100).

Over against this, the 1919 sections, occurring in past tense, suggest aftermath in the sense that no more action can be taken. By Tristan's declaration, as has been indicated, his life and his hopes remain in suspension from the moment of Will's execution. Everything that happens to him, and by implication to other survivors of the war, both soldier and civilian, happens in a kind of conditional tense—never quite being what it might have been.

There are hints of this through various characters—the boy David Cantwell, just too young to fight and still unhappy about it in 1919 (9); Marian's parents, who have to deal with the shame of their son's seeming cowardice when their village decides to erect a war monument but leave Will's name off (235); Marian herself, who expresses the point so well when she says, "[Y]ou men all feel things so deeply now…. Friends of mine, boys who fought over there. You have an intensity now, a potent sadness, even a sense of fear. It's not at all like before" (136). The implication is that action is some- how infinitely suspended, or deferred. If the conditional is what might have been, Marian here describes what must be an incredibly frustrating feeling—the need to act but the over- whelming anxiety of not being able to because of sadness and fear. For Tristan Sadler, this comes in the form of regret at what he has done, which can now never be undone.

Talking with Tristan, Marian's father echoes these ideas. "Sometimes I think that many of them [soldiers] half believe they died over there and that this is all some kind of strange dream. Or purgatory. Or even hell" he says, and then adds, "You've become a generation of response" rather than action (234). This only adds to what Sadler had earlier said to Marian: "I don't think I did survive it. I may not be buried in a French field but I linger there…. I think I'm just breathing, that's all. And there's a difference between breathing and being alive" (137).

As they sit in the aforementioned café having met for the first time, Marian and Tristan discuss aftermath. "Do you think things will ever get back to normal?" Marian asks, to which Sadler replies, "Some days, yes" but when pressed as to when, he says, "Not this century, anyway…. Perhaps the next" (107). Posed another way, he might have said something like, "In a hundred years from now, the war will be seen to be over," or "One day, we will have been able to recall the war," pulling that notion of grammatical tense into the dialogue to suggest distance not only of time but also of memory. At some point later, in other words, it will be possible to remember in a way that is too immediate to enact now, in time so close to the events.

But even when sixty years pass, not enough time has gone by for Sadler *to have acted*, although he is by this point past eighty. He meets Marian again, and while he has by now become a successful novelist, he has not dealt with his lover's death and his own responsibility in it. She confronts him and asks about his life. The claim the elderly Tristan makes in 1979 is that he has lived a life less fulfilling than what he might have had the war not unfolded for him as it did. Marian presses him as to why. He mentions, "What I did to him in the end," but can summon no more specific language, prompting Marian to respond, "Murdering him, you mean?" (307). All Sadler can do is look down and murmur an assent. At this point, it looks like he will live to the end in a conditional way—suspended between the known past of the war and an unknown and never-arriving future. Perhaps as an explanation of his ability to act at some level, he tells Marian that he has written about these events, but when she asks why he hasn't published this work, he says that he wouldn't be able to live with the way people would look at him (308). They part, Marian vowing that they won't meet again.

Inaction, living in the aftermath, dealing with a grammatical use of the conditional tense—all of these have characterized Tristan Sadler's life since 1916. Yet now, in 1979, having been confronted by Marian Bancroft, he decides to change things. "[W]aiting for the story to find a conclusion of sorts, sure that it would come sooner or later," he decides after seeing Marian that "it has finally come tonight," and so he goes to his room and shoots himself (308).

Before he does the final act, however, he contemplates his obituary, concluding that it will say "that I was the last of that generation to go and what a shame, another link with the past gone" and yet that his writing was left behind as a "legacy to honour his memory" (309). This might be true, except that before killing himself, he places in plain sight in the room the manuscript he has just described to Marian, the one which tells the whole story of his life in the war, and with Will, and the firing squad. He knows, then, that people will know who he was, and that his legacy will be entirely tarnished as soon as this final book appears: "There will be outrage and disgust and people will turn on me at the last, they will hate me, my reputation will forever be destroyed, my punishment earned, self-inflicted like this gunshot wound" (309). He has finally *done* something. And yet has he? His final words are, "[T]he world will finally know that I was the greatest feather man [coward] of them all" (309). In so stating, he perfectly suspends himself in aftermath. His death will now be forever looked at as owing itself to the war.

Tristan Sadler recognizes his cowardice by his final words. But he also makes the point that the war, no matter how much time goes by, leaves its participants in a forever version of the conditional tense, where what might have been will never be and the speculation as to what that is will never cease. Marian's mother says to Tristan in 1919, "The war is over now at last," to which he replies, "There'll be another one along in a moment, I expect" (232). For him, that other one was the one that had already happened and would keep happening all his life, its grammatical tense past, present, and future collapsed in one, like the narration of Boyne's novel.

Pat Barker's 2012 novel *Toby's Room* simultaneously demands that we reckon with the aftermath of violence and visualizes the effects of that aftermath, a point best understood by thinking about wartime violence as an extension/correction of the concept of medieval carnival described by Mikhail Bakhtin. Carnival is not innocent of violence, though Bakhtin describes carnival violence as if there is no aftermath, no consequence. This is possible because death is always connected to rebirth, carnival violence to regeneration. Bakhtin, talking about Rabelais' fourth chapter, where Pantagruel visits the Island of the Catchpoles, whose job it is to be thrashed, says: "Abuse is death, it is former youth transformed into old age, the living body turned into a corpse…. But in this system death is followed by regeneration, by the new year, new youth, and a new spring" (197–98).

In order to elide the effects of carnival on the individual body, Bakhtin makes a subtle shift from singular to plural, from the *person* receiving the blows to *the people* as a collective. "The individual feels that he is an indissoluble part of the collectivity, a member of the people's mass body" (255). If death or mutilation of the carnival participant occurs, that is rendered irrelevant by the fact that the whole body of the people is the beneficiary: "[T]here is no room for fear. For fear

Cloth Hall, Ypres

can only enter a part that has been separated from the whole, the dying link torn from the link that is born. The whole of the people and of the world is triumphantly gay and fearless" (256).

One particular scene of Catchpoles' beating sounds very much like it could be describing, at least metaphorically, the results of battlefield conflict: "Beside the direct injuries inflicted...there is a long list of indirectly hurt organs and members: sprained shoulders, black eyes, crippled legs and arms, injured genital parts" (207). He even says, "There is a combination of the battlefield with the kitchen or butcher shop" (207). The logical question about carnival violence, then, concerns the effects of physical injuries. Bakhtin makes the individual disappear by shifting his point of view from "them " (the Catchpoles) to "it" as he describes the aftermath of the above-referenced beating. He repeats this formulation in his chapter on the grotesque body: "The death of the individual is only one moment in the triumphant life of the people and of mankind, a moment indispensable for their renewal and improvement" (341).

British propagandists used precisely this kind of language during the war of 1914–18 to keep the people believing in the righteousness of the cause while ensuring their blindness to the consequences of trench warfare. But as I read Bakhtin, and as the English read their newspapers and began to realize that the troop trains leaving Victoria Station were increasingly mirrored in hospital trains returning to it, we both might have ringing in our heads the question, What happens when Mr. Catchpole survives, though wounded? In historical terms: what are the aftereffects of the war on the physical body of the British soldier, and is it possible to claim that the good of the group supersedes individual suffering, or, in other words, that aftermath shouldn't be thought about?

Bakhtin does not ignore the matter of time altogether: "Carnival celebrated temporary liberation from the prevailing truth and from the established order," he says (10). The offer of a time marker—"temporary"—suggests both the before and the after of carnival. By marking out time, Bakhtin might equally have been talking about a prevailing condition of the physical body—that it too is temporal, and that put under carnival-induced stress, it would break down, with consequences apparent in the time after carnival. Further, he develops an opposition of terms in describing the grotesque body—closedness versus openness—that suggests the margin between health and injury that would characterize the body after carnival: "[T]he grotesque body is not separated from the rest of the world. It is not a closed, completed unit; it is unfinished, outgrows itself, transgresses its own limits" (26).[60]

In fact, though he likely didn't mean to, Bakhtin nearly perfectly describes the type of injury that soldiers received in a conflict like the Great War, the first fully mechanized war

---

60 Immediately prior to this, Bakhtin does discuss the matter of time and the grotesque body (24-25), but he resolves what he initially says is development in time into the more cyclical notion of the grotesque, saying that even in Rabelais, the grotesque images are incomplete and ambivalent (25).

in human history: "The stress is laid on those parts of the body that are open to the outside world, that is, the parts through which the world enters the body or emerges from it…. This means that the emphasis is on the apertures or the convexities…the open mouth…the nose" (26). Shellfire in particular created a category of injury not seen before, with facial disfigurement a particular feature. However, *contra* Bakhtin's Catchpoles, the wounded soldier did not embrace the newfound openness of his body, but rather sought surgical repair—and other means—to close himself off once more from the outside world.

Toby's Room is populated with the disfigured soldiers who survived the war but cannot "face," literally, its aftermath because their visages are all but obliterated by their wartime injuries, which have left them missing jaws, noses, or entire portions of the skull. The chief of these is Kit Neville, a painter, who now lives in a convalescent hospital dedicated to repairing facial trauma. Walking down a hallway of this institution, Kit's friend Elinor Brooke becomes our eyes: "Men with no eyes were being led along by men with no mouths; there was even one man with no jaw, his whole face shelving steeply away into his neck. Men, like Kit, with no noses and horrible twisted faces" (156). When Neville's friend Paul Tarrant describes Kit's face after surgery, he quickly treads into Bakhtinian territory: "He looked like a man with a penis where his nose should be: obscene, grotesque, ridiculous" (Barker 262). Kit demonstrates the opposition Bakhtin develops between the "open" and "closed" body, a concept which offers a way to understand the grotesque injury that comes as the aftermath of battlefield carnival and foregrounds memory as a product of the differentiation of carnival time from not-carnival-time.

Katherine Feo describes the surgical technique developed in 1917 to deal with, for example, the loss of a nose: "[T]he tubed pedicle graft...allowed the successful grafting of skin from one part of the body to another by maintaining a continuous circulation to the reattached area" (19). A tube of skin would be detached from the forehead above the hairline or from elsewhere on the body and grafted onto the face.[61] The end of the "pedicle" would grow into the place where the original tissue was lost. Neville explains his own surgery: "They cut a strip of skin off the chest, here, and then they roll the edges over so it's a tube—that's to stop it getting infected—and then they stick the other end...Well, wherever it has to go. Nose, in my case" (Barker 262). Ironically, this suggests that the body can only be closed by opening it yet more.

After the graft took, the pedicle, which provided bloodflow, was removed. The face was "closed" again. Unless the procedure failed. Kit Neville's experience indicates the continued openness of the area. He gets a pedicle, but it fails because he gets a cold. Much later, he has a second surgery, and a second pedicle is attached. As he comes out of the operation, he feels that "it was like returning from the dead," and he experiences "fierce joy" (Barker 244, 245). This, too, sounds almost Bakhtinian.

Sometimes, surgery was not an option to return the body to the closed state. In those cases, when the injured man expressed a desire to close his body off (in the language I am using) from outside scrutiny anyway, this was done through the production of a tin mask which replicated the (prewar) face. In an ironic inverse of carnival, this closing, because illusory, has a generative function. Feo explains that facial injuries were "especially deleterious forms of disfigurement

---

61 Nicolson describes the invention of the technique by surgeon Harold Delf Gillies, picking up the metaphor of openness and closedness: "This procedure...ensured that the underside of the healthy tissue was no longer open and exposed to possible infection" (74).

for men…understood to be worse than other injuries for their social and psychic ramifications" (20). The language of the day equated "the loss of productivity and a decrease in social identity/self-esteem from disfigurement as one and the same" (Feo 20). The assumption was that facial disfigurement, even more than the loss of a limb, made it extremely difficult for a man to make a living. Feo explains further: "Whenever discourses of masculinity were directly engaged regarding facial disfigurement, economic independence…was cited as the main motivation for restoration" (20). The connection of being economically independent with the hope of having a family—literally merging one's body with another's—is taken as a given in this formulation.

Derwent Wood, who opened the tin noses shop at Third London General Hospital, describes his work in language that resonates with Bakhtin's notion of the open versus closed body: "My work begins where that of the surgeon is completed. When the surgeon has done all he can to…heal wounds…to cover areas by skin grafting, I endeavor by means of the skill I happen to possess as a sculptor to make a man's face as near as possible to what it looked like before he was wounded" (qtd. in Feo 22). In fact, the masks so closely approximate the look of the man before the war that they can be read as reversing the injuries that the war's violence inflicted.

Yet these masks are sterile, with even the appearance of the open mouth or the nose an illusion. Thus we might say that the grotesque body is doubly closed because it is both shielded and lacks ability to move.[62] But if the masks close the case as they close the body off from the outside, that does not imply that a person must be happy with that closure. Neville

---

62 This is a point remarked upon by Kit Neville more than once in the novel, for instance when he discusses with his surgeon what a woman would think of the mask (226).

comments on that, explaining, "[I]f you had to wear it all the time it would be absolutely bloody intolerable" (Barker 213). It's not just the physical aspect that bothers the wearer, though, but the inability to engage in human interaction. "[O]bviously behind the mask there are all kinds of expressions going on, and you forget nobody can see them. As far as other people are concerned, it's like talking to a brick wall," he says (Barker 226). Nicolson uses similar language when she talks about the products of the "Tin Noses Shop," a term she capitalizes: "[F]acial masks made of galvanized copper... would hide the effects of damage. Concealment, it seemed, rather than repair was the only option for those who no longer had noses, eyes, jawbones, cheekbones, chins, ears or much of a face at all" (65). This impulse to close off is rooted in the modern sense of subjectivity, which Bakhtin describes by saying, "The new bodily canon...presents an entirely finished, completed, strictly limited body, which is shown from the outside as something *individual*. That which protrudes, bulges, sprouts, or branches off...is eliminated..." (320, emphasis added).

Earlier in his Rabelais text, he claimed that "the theme of the mask, [is] the most complex theme of folk culture. The mask is connected with the joy of change and reincarnation, with gay relativity and with the merry negation of uniformity and similarity; it rejects conformity to oneself" (39–40). When he mentions "reincarnation" and "negation of uniformity," Bakhtin could, one supposes, be talking about the masks used to recreate the faces of the disfigured of the war. But when he uses language like "joy" and rejecting "conformity to oneself," he is thinking obviously of a mask that is not a replication of the face of the individual, but a representation of a type. He adds, "The mask is related to transition, metamorphoses, the violation of natural boundaries" (40).

War Memorial, Woodstock, England

The mask of folk culture in the Middle Ages carries forward his notion of carnival play as regenerating.

But when he shifts his discussion to how the mask appears in its Romantic iteration, Bakhtin loses his hopeful tone: "[T]he mask is torn away from the oneness of the folk carnival concept.... Now the mask hides something, keeps a secret, deceives. Such a meaning would not be possible as long as the mask functioned within folk culture's organic whole" (40). And when he moves on to the following statement, it as if he is thinking directly of the alive-but-dead looks of the faces replaced by the post-war tin noses: "The Romantic mask loses almost entirely its regenerating and renewing element and acquires a somber hue. A terrible vacuum, a nothingness lurks behind it" (40).

The soldiers themselves, particularly Kit Neville, dance between these two ways of looking at the mask, though their reactions are the inverse of what Bakhtin describes. On the one hand, Neville's mask hides his disfigurement, which is actually a source of joy for him. On the other, it tells a lie by making him other than who he is/was. Yet that denies him the possibility to live as he would without it. Kit rhetorically asks, "[W]hat would be the point of kissing *this*?" and answers his own question, "No bloody point at all. Better the gargoyle underneath" (213, emphasis original).

This conflict informs the key scene in *Toby's Room*: Kit Neville's voluntary unmasking, which in turn foregrounds the tension between remembering and forgetting at the center of this text. It happens when he and Paul are out for an evening of drinking. Neville has borrowed a mask from a fellow patient, but even then, not one that resembles the man's lost face. It is the likeness of Rupert Brooke, renowned for his attractive visage and known as a public figure and poet.[63] The two men get into a cab in London, and the driver

---

63 If the novel took place today, the face would be Brad Pitt's, or Hugh Grant's.

immediately recognizes the face, and Neville jokes about it (Barker 216).

But when he and Paul go to the Café Royal, their drinking place from pre-wartime, it seems people recognize him as Neville, despite the face. Nobody blanches at the mask, though neither are they sure what to do. Unlike carnival participants, they do not view the mask as a sign of "joy of change and reincarnation, with gay relativity," nor do they see that "it rejects conformity to oneself" as the folk mask does (Bakhtin 39–40).

Perhaps disappointed by the failure of the mask to inaugurate merry time, Kit becomes enraged.[64] He stands up, bellows, and rips the mask off, confronting the room with the grotesque face that has been given to him by the war (218). The reaction is much like what one might expect after carnival, were Bakhtin not so careful to seal carnival time off from its aftermath. "One or two people cried out. Others were blank with shock" (218). Being confronted with a face like Neville's forces the audience to come to grips with the moral consequences of war. Paul Tarrant says as much, his interior monologue upon seeing Kit's pedicle post-surgery being, "What must it be like, having that thing on your face? To know you looked grotesque? To know that people would find the sight of you repulsive or ridiculous, despite continually reminding themselves it was tragic?" (Barker 269).

In fact, every character in *Toby's Room*, whether physically scarred or not, is deeply mired in the question of the aftermath of war, though the plot events take place while hostilities with the Germans are ongoing. A doctor speaking to Paul encapsulates this idea after telling Tarrant about his lost son: "'Nothing,' he said, as they parted at the door, 'would ever be the same again'" (Barker 273).

Elinor, for her part, lives in denial of the events taking place, spending much of the time the novel encompasses being purposely uninvolved. "Yes, for a long time...I was

---

64 Another term Bakhtin uses for carnival.

French National War Cemetery at La Targette, Neuville-Saint-Vaast

determined I was going to ignore the whole thing," she says, but she admits that, "It gets you in the end" (Barker 160). In fact, her strategy was more purposeful than that. Her brother Toby had told her on his last leave before dying at the Front that he wished that she would involve herself in the war effort. They argued about it, and she makes the point that the war "leached time and energy away from all the things that really mattered" (Barker 175). Even near the end of the narrative, she retains the following naïve idea: "[W]hat I really think, deep down, is that the dead are only dead for the duration. When it's over they'll all come back and it'll be just the same as it was before" (297).

She is caught between remembering and forgetting. Toby haunts her thoughts, not least because they had earlier had an incestuous affair, which she has tried to forget. Memory, for her, sounds very much like carnival aftermath, as she records in her diary: *"I'm aware of something happening to me that I can't explain. It's almost as if I'm turning into Toby. It's not just me thinking it either, other people have commented. As if you cope with loss by ingesting the dead person*" (Barker 236, italics original).

Elinor is tortured by the need to know how Toby died and to deal with the loss. The latter she does through painting, but what comes of the work is the ongoing visible reminder of Toby. She shows Paul the art, and he notices that "every painting contained the shadowy figure of a man, always on the edge of the composition, facing away from the center, as if he might be about to step outside the frame" (Barker 108). Paul says to her, "He's in every painting. Toby" and she replies by way of correction, "A male figure," then admits, "Oh, all right, Toby. But I'm not running away from it, you know" (108–09).[65]

Kit Neville is painting as well, his subject "the moment of death," as Paul describes it when looking at Kit's work. "Paul knew he was looking at the moment of Toby Brooke's death," and seeing that it is depicted "not exactly as Neville had related it" makes Paul wonder (289). As the closest eyewitness to Toby's demise by suicide on the battlefield, Neville was the only one who really knew what had happened to Brooke. He tells Paul the story, cautioning him against telling Elinor but admitting that Paul can do with the information what he likes, and yet perhaps even that story is not true. Tarrant admits, "Oh, Neville had set out to tell the truth—he didn't doubt that for a moment—but was it possible that, in the end, he'd ducked out of revealing something too dreadful to be told?" (289). His further thinking on the matter reveals the memory question that lingers in this novel: "There came a time when you simply had to let it go and accept an approximation of the truth" (289).

So it is with war/carnival itself. "[T]he masks were invented to cover the shocking reminder of violence apparent in

---

65 Barker discusses war art in her novel *Life Class* as well, but a completely hackneyed first half consumed with a trivial love story makes it less worth extended analysis by far than does *Toby's Room*.

disfigurement, and attempt to recreate a familiar, pre-war face in an unachievable realistic, and so obviously artificial, way" (Feo 18). The need to fashion the tin noses (masks) had "to do with memory, repression and the representational substitute for the loss of humanity that occurs during war" (18). But the strategy did not, indeed could not, work, because "the masks themselves became wearable indicators of tragedy by their suggestion of the gruesome face underneath. The masks took on themselves what they intended to conceal" (18). The grotesque body, even when it was not revealed, was apparent, and the masks "memorialize by inadequately concealing the unsettling, unresolved and horrific consequences of the first modern war" (Feo 25). Paul Tarrant in Barker's narrative echoes this, saying that "though it hid the ruin of the face it also directed the imagination towards it" (213).

Further, because the mask does not age while the man wearing it does, there is a curious dual reference in time, irreconcilable to the present: "[M]asks…were modelled [sic] on photos taken before enlistment" and thus "would already have become outdated, locked into a moment that occurred at least two years in the past…a physical backdating that cruelly juxtaposed the recipient's actual face with the time before the trauma of violence" (Feo 24). Bakhtinian/Rabelaisian carnival, by contrast, is atemporal. Neither faces nor bodies age, because death is always replaced by life.

What memories exist of carnival? None, because the individual is elided into the group and the look is always forward, to the next time. However, the masks might be seen as "deny[ing] the viewer, and indeed, the wearer, the ability either to remember or forget" (Feo 25). Carnival appears to do that as well, because "while carnival lasts, there is no other life outside it" (Bakhtin 7). Yet the difference is that in wartime, violence is not about renewal. Rather, this violence defaces the person, shutting him off from human discourse and making it impossible to really know what happened when events conclude.

The mask-wearer becomes a type of himself, a summary or an indicator pointing past the now—what is seen—to some other, but now unrecoverable, self. The same could be said of all of those who live in the suspension of remembering and forgetting which is the aftermath of the war.

CHAPTER 6

Alt-text Versions of the War: Humor via incongruity, the graphic novel

Mixed in with the familiar form of fiction in the canon of recent literature are two alternate ways of looking at the Great War, humor rooted in incongruity and graphic fictional representations. Each relies on the reader's willingness to suspend the serious tone that accompanies, or seems like it should accompany, literature concerning the Great War as demanded by the deaths of ten million combatants and millions of civilians. Taken together, however, comedy and what might be called "comics" serve as "alt-text" versions of the war, enacting memory in unique ways, as will be indicated via readings of William Boyd's *An Ice-Cream War* and Pat Mills' and Joe Colquhoun's *Charley's War*.

In most war fiction, the loyalty of the soldier is unquestioned and the purpose for which the army fights indisputable. However, at times, the cause is not just and the direction given by those in charge is anything but orderly. Such situations can produce chaos, but they are also given to comedy. Invoking the absurd by portraying unfamiliar settings provides the perfect background for such explorations. Such is the case with William Boyd's *An Ice-Cream War*, which dislocates the war from the familiar Western Front action in order to make its point about how combat is experienced when bureaucracies meet the bumbling British officer class.

As an entry point into how humor can come from tragic events, consider the words of Barnes' narrator Tony Webster in the previously discussed *The Sense of An Ending* when describing his attempt to remember a tragic event from the long past: "Again, I must stress that this is my reading now of what happened then. Or rather, my memory now of my reading then of was happening at the time" (45). Tangled? Yes, and true. He was trying to recall from the point of view of his elderly years what had happened when, in his school days, one of his best friends had written to him to say that he had taken up with Tony's former girlfriend. His point is that there is no way to get to the truth of what his failed relationship with Veronica meant, but as he throws up his hands and declares the conundrum unsolvable, he opens the door to laughter by making a tongue-twister out of what had been a painful moment of his past, and one for which he never did get any proper resolution.

The friend who stole the woman, Adrian, ends up killing himself during that same school-days era, and after that, Tony and three others, inseparable from Adrian as friends, gather to commemorate his life. It's one year since he died. Tony takes up the description: "We tried to invoke and celebrate our friend. We remembered him telling Old Joe Hunt [the history teacher] he was out of a job, and instructing Phil Dixon about Eros and Thanatos. We were already turning our past into anecdote" (58). He ends the recounting of the day by saying that Adrian "retreated from us rather quickly, slotted into time and history" (58).

There are two foci here—the pain of the memories themselves, and the fear that they will become unrecoverable. In that vein, it is significant that Webster uses the word "anecdote" to describe what Adrian has become. Not as trivial as "joke," certainly, the word nonetheless has none of the gravity of "memory" or even "story." Anecdote—something tossed off, a snippet told in the brief space between floors in an elevator, or to a colleague at cocktail hour when there's nothing else to say. Trivia, absorbed into the atmosphere, but retold when the context demands it. It edges right next to comedy in the pecking order of what is recalled.

Offering a standard definition of humor, Jeroen Vandaele explains that "two traditions…have been mainly associated with humorous stimuli: *incongruity* and *superiority*" (222 italics original). Vandaele explains that incongruity may come as six types: linguistic, pragmatic, at the level of narrative, as parody, as satire, and what he calls "unlocated" or "absolute" incongruities. Each one breaks audience expectations or has "transgressive" qualities (238).

Note, however, that prior knowledge must exist—there must be something to measure against to detect superiority or incongruity. Thus when the child, or the person from outside the culture group, asks, "Why is that funny?" he or she is not saying, "Teach me the principles upon which humor rests." She is saying, rather, "What is the norm on which this group measures itself?" A joke about the British Raj in India or the colonial Brit in other parts of the world—indeed, the subject of entire Evelyn Waugh novels—might not be in any way universal, even if the idea of a group thinking itself morally superior but proving itself inferior is. But it is funny when the audience has prior experience to compare it to.

Three incongruities particularly interest me in the context of Boyd. Linguistic incongruity occurs when one's expectations for language are misdirected (as for instance when an expected response is not given or the tone is clearly inappropriate for the situation, [Vandaele 229]). *An Ice-Cream War,* portraying as it does a diverse group of people with a world of languages uniting and dividing them, often plays on this for humor at a micro level. Narrative incongruity occurs when what we have in memory about events already depicted does not help us to sort out future events that occur in the text (232). For Boyd, this provides humor at a macro level in that, in fact, nothing that audiences know about World War I fiction will help them understand the plot twists taken in this novel. Even within the events depicted themselves, in fact, there is constant redirection of expectations, since nothing happens as it seems it might from one day to the next. This, in part, is what gives the novel its parodic quality (the third type of incongruity under consideration here). As the novel proceeds, Boyd moves among and between these three incongruities to create the conditions that make for humor.

Vandaele defines parody as a form of humor by suggesting that it, along with satire, has "a dual structure of following-and-breaking the rules, in which the aspect of 'following' is more explicitly present than in many other forms of incongruity" (234). That is, there is "a necessary cognitive fore-grounding of specific schemes to be transgressed" (234); again, with respect to Boyd and in the present contexts, this becomes the entire logic of expectations brought forward by the canon of contemporary Great War literature.

If it seems like using humor is transgressive, or if the excuse made for it is that the war is long past, that mixes up cause and effect. A novelist can joke about the war not because enough time has passed to take it lightly but because enough time has passed for the humor to be understood because the audience has context for it. In *An Ice-Cream War*, Boyd manages to create humor through establishing the conditions of incongruity/superiority in readers, and he does this through spoofing and pointing up the foibles in how a war is run and in how those involved in it, either as combatants or bystanders, conduct their affairs.

All family life is parodied, but particularly that of the Cobbs as observed through younger son Felix. Looking at his father, the patriarch, in the scene where we first meet the aristocratic family, we learn his thoughts: "A thoroughly unpleasant-looking man, all in all, Felix thought. He prayed earnestly that his own old age wouldn't leave him similarly disadvantaged" (66). As the man barks about Home Rule (this is July 1914), "Felix sat back and rubbed his eyes. Disembodied sentences filled his ears. He felt something like panic course suddenly through his body" (71).

Logistical miscues also form a source of spoof, as for instance in the difficulty with which character Gabriel Cobb moves from England to India. He realizes at one point that "The war had been going on for three months" and that "[f]or two of them...[he] calculated with some sarcasm, he'd been on board ship" (136). The crossing continues, with the entire ship seasick. "The sides of the *Dongola* became streaked and spattered with dried vomit," he observes, hardly the sign of heroism Gabriel might have expected from his time in the army (138). If his experience is not unique, Boyd might be said to suggest, then how could a war be propagated successfully at all? Indeed, Cobb is not sure where he's going or why, and he muses that "it was typical of the army's Byzantine reasoning to send him all the way to India just to send him back to Europe" (139). He is, in fact, rerouted to East Africa, wasting even more time.

British intelligence strategy is also parodied. When he and his shipmates get to talking about the war, Gabriel realizes that the British are going to inform the Germans that there is "an official abrogation of the truce" that prevented fighting in Tanga (151). He realizes that this means that the Germans will know an attack is coming, and yet when he informs his cabin mate of this, that fellow agrees, but immediately refocuses the conversation on the minute: "Remember…whatever happens, don't forget your pillow and basin" (151). This sounds absurd, and is funny therefore, but underneath might be Boyd's point: for most combatants, the war was experienced in the details of ordinary life rather than at the grand levels of history and strategy.

When he finally gets where he is going, Cobb finds that engaging in battle does not work on the simple attack-and-counter equation that he believes it is supposed to. He walks up to the house where command is headquartered, but his impression is that "[i]t certainly didn't look like an invasion force, and there was a complete absence of danger" (156). He feels like he's on a stroll once the actual battle starts, and when they attack, it's with no response. "It made no sense at all" to him, nor do the orders he receives (169). They say, "Your men should bring their left shoulders up and march toward the point" which prompts him to raise his own "left shoulder experimentally," which makes things no clearer (169). That, in fact, is how war goes for everyone in this story.

A couple of years later, in search of both vengeance for now-dead Gabriel and for personal redemption, Felix Cobb makes a similarly tortured journey to Africa. Again, there are misdirections and problems in his getting there. But when he finally does, the absurdity is not over. Felix finds himself in an area cut off from the mainland due to the rains. Rather than combat wounds killing the soldiers there, eating poisonous roots is doing so (315). He realizes that during this three months when he was supposedly at the front lines, "he'd never seen a single enemy soldier;" in fact, his "'quest' had fizzled out in the mud of Kibongo, his high ideals and passionate aspirations replaced by grumbles about the damp" (318).

The irony is clear in his summation: "What kind of war was this? he demanded angrily to himself. No enemy in sight, your men slowly being starved to death, guarding a huddle of grass huts in the middle of a sodden jungle" (318).

The Great War, or any war, Boyd points out, is mostly a collection of inefficiencies masquerading as strategies that, when attempted to be activated, end up curling back on themselves and, mostly, failing. But in the eternal logic of the military mind, things must be seen to be moving, and so even disasters are reported somehow as gains.

Take as a further example the initial engagement of the Germans and British in East Africa as fictionalized in this novel. In June of 1914, Walter Smith, an American, and Erich Von Bishop, a German, get along cordially as neighbors. By August, the latter is at the Smith farm seizing it on orders of the Germans. Smith "tried to summon up a rage or a sense of injustice, but Von Bishop's easy-going manner made it appear somehow inappropriate, an over-reaction, even a discourtesy" (112). Smith's first thought at being put off his property, one he clings to for quite a number of months, is, "I can demand reparations," but in truth, "It didn't feel the least bit like a war" (114).

Where this becomes absurd occurs when, as he tries to get help for his loss of land and livelihood, he realizes that he was "the only person in the whole of British East Africa who had had his land overrun and occupied" (129). When he decides to file an insurance claim for reparations, the inspector comments blithely, "This war; it causes endless inconveniences" (129). That, too, is doubled back ironically as when, shortly thereafter, the inspector and Smith attempt to go to the Smith property to survey what has been lost, and Inspector Essanjee is shot dead (133). Earlier, Smith had asked that the Germans not mess around with his threshing machine, called a "Decorticator" (113). That is promised, though much later it becomes clear that the promise has not been kept. After many different efforts, Smith happens to return to the house and finds that the walls and every other visible surface have been covered in human excrement (267). The machine is gone, and nobody knows what has happened to it (406). Walter Smith and Felix Cobb, having discussed that, part with, "At least it's over, anyway," in the words of Smith (407). Cobb replies, "What?" to which Smith says, "The war" (407). Walter bids him to come back soon, urging him, "Don't wait for another war" (407). Absurd, indirect, and not focused—that's the dialogue of Boyd's novel, where characters as often talk to themselves in the guise of responding to other people as create meaningful discourse.

Boyd's novel does its best work when focusing on the microscopic ridiculousness inherent in human discourse. People don't even recognize themselves in their conversations, as in this exchange between Walter Smith and Liesl Von Bishop: " 'We have nothing like your botanical garden in British East [Africa]. But, I must confess I wanted to see Dar and, um, your splendid new railway.' He wondered why he was talking in this ridiculous manner" (23).

Absolutely hilarious is the Scottish underling of Felix, who uses a hybrid of English and his local dialect language to express himself, though in a way that Felix understands only slightly. His height is reached when, having endured months of rain together, Gilzean says, "This cackit place…. I'm a snool, a glaikit sumph. Nocht but rain, howdumdied all day o'boot. I've lost my noodle. Camstereerie bloody country" (319). He goes on, his words making just enough sense to keep the reader aware of the meaning of his syntax while being unfamiliar enough to prompt a chuckle.

The Pipers Memorial, Longueval, France

The war exists, in the early going of the novel, as something distant from whatever scene is being portrayed. From Stackpole, the Cobb family seat, it is a distant battle in France, then later Africa. From Africa, it is a distant European engagement with some local tendrils, which is why near the start, locals are being drilled for the army, and Smith and Von Bishop discuss matters. Smith says, "I can't see there being any fighting out here, can you?" to which he gets, "I doubt it" from Von Bishop, who adds that the local troop drills are just precaution (32). As the war goes on, troop movements are erratic, if not entirely accidental, and while the Germans are gradually being driven back, the reader is not privy to any successful engagements of the British with them. When Felix's battalion finally does go to war, he and his men are digging latrine trenches (326), which may be why his final thoughts about the conflict are reported to be, "Felix wondered if anyone really knew what was going on in this war" (356). Of course they don't, because if they did, things would make sense at the micro and macro levels, robbing Boyd of the power of incongruity, readers of their sense of superiority, and the novel of its humor.

The collection of combatant deaths and injuries in *An Ice-Cream War* does well to point out Boyd's method. In all, there are at least seven people of those we meet killed or maimed in this war, but two conditions prevail: either they are not injured in combat, or their combat injuries occur offstage. Witness this: Gabriel is hurt by bayonets when he is running away after having landed amongst the enemy accidentally (179). Former family servant Cyril is killed offstage, "in the war. For King and Country, my mam says. In France, like," according to his son (210). A pilot is killed doing a foolish training run (244). Bathe loses his hands in a training accident (249). Walter's fellow combatant Youell is sniped after they are sure there is nobody over on the German side and after Walter has stuck his head up into the line of fire several times (263). Charis, the wife of Gabriel, kills herself over guilt about an affair with Felix, a death described as making her "as much a victim of the war as our young men who have bravely given their lives in France" (291), so said by someone who didn't know about the affair. And Aristedes Pinto is killed by the foolish actions of British soldier Weech-Browning as he pulls a trigger by accident while he and Felix are trying to sight in a mortar gun. His explanation? "The lanyard, Cobb. I sneezed. I was holding it in my hand. It just went off" (383).

Nothing heroic happens in *An Ice-Cream War*. Nothing even particularly gripping happens in this novel. That's not a criticism of the book, but rather a diagnosis of what Boyd is doing, so that when, at the end of the narrative, Felix sums up by thinking, "since July 1916…he had never fired a shot in anger" the reader is able to understand his follow-on question: "What kind of a war was it where this sort of absurdity could occur?" (393). The problem is, as he says, the one that most soldiers eventually realize is the reality behind the sought-for glory: "[H]e was not responsible for the way events had turned out, that it was futile to expect that life could in some way be controlled" (393).

In the end, this novel remembers by forgetting. What it forgets is the Western Front, France, and all that is familiar to readers of the World War I canon. What it also forgets, as alluded to above, is the macro view of strategy and engagement that typically characterizes the big picture of a war but which is most often invisible to the troops on the ground. In that way, *An Ice-Cream War* is no different from a novel like Boyden's *Three Day Road* in its portrayal of what happens to real soldiers on an everyday basis. But while the war on the Western Front, for instance, had little in the way of breakthroughs and only the occasional significant movement of the line, at least there, combatants had a sense that they were engaged in a campaign, however fragmented their perception it might have been.

For Boyd's characters, no sense of plan or purpose exists, and the absurdity continues right to the end of the story. Having "sworn to himself that before he left Africa, before he was done with this mad, absurd war, he was going to…fire at least one shot in anger," Felix Cobb decides to "put a bullet in Von Bishop's brain," because he believes him to be the murderer of his brother (393). He is mistaken, but it doesn't matter anyway. Having found a way into Von Bishop's house, he finds him in his bed, already dead (403). As he says when he sees the man lying there, before he realizes he is dead, "This was absurd" and indeed, that could be stretched to the conclusion that Boyd suggests should blanket the entirety of the events he portrays, and, by extension, World War I as a whole (403).

Another form of alternative fiction is the graphic novel such as Pat Mills' and Joe Colquhoun's *Charley's War*. The genre has been given a number of titles over the years, from adult comic to sequential art, picto-fiction to graphic novel, as Elaine Martin details (170–71). In fact, some dispute the idea that one title—graphic novel or another choice—can subsume such a complex and varied genre (Labio 123).

Scholar Elaine Martin describes the recent (she is writing from the point of view of 2011) flood of such work:

> *The phenomenal growth of graphic novels—a veritable tsunami—in the past decade, but particularly in the past five years, would indicate that the genre is here to stay. It would seem to attest to fundamental changes, at least in western cultures: first, an increasingly visual orientation due to the internet and second, the increasing interpenetration of*

popular culture and high culture. Due to its cooptation and
replacement of traditional purely "textual" literature for
the younger generation and its increasing sophistication
and stylistic innovation, we ignore the graphic novel at
our own peril...and at the risk of our intellectual
impoverishment. (178)

With this in mind, it is imperative to ask, "What is the social function of these novels as it pertains to the war, and how do they accomplish it?" Are they able to supplement in a meaningful way the plain text that we see in the other selections on offer from contemporary fiction writers?[66]

One scholar, James F. Wurtz, speaks to this: "It seems to me that a fundamental requirement for representing the violence of the Great War is that images and words must work in concert, both to maintain...precision...and to deliver the emotional assault the visual art (such as the monuments) can achieve" (205). He continues, "[I]n their narrative complexity, the intrinsic tension between verbal and visual storytelling, and their challenge to the ways one reads, they are particularly well suited to the commemorative and interpretive requirements of representing the Great War" (205).

Of necessity, a graphic novel will have to make sacrifices—there aren't pages and pages of dense narrative text offered to the writer to fill, after all. "Still, trimming the story and cutting down the number of characters does not automatically result in scaled-down sociocognitive complexity" (Zunshine 124). As Jennifer Williams says, to read these texts successfully, one must not concentrate on the words only, but rather observe the special protocols and form that are the graphic novel (194). And at least one other critic sees what he calls

---

66 Certainly the cartoon form itself has a history that crosses through the war's timeframe. Joseph Morewood Staniforth drew approximately 15,000 cartoons during his career, approximately 1,300 during the war alone, according to Chris Williams (43). Many were recently digitized at cartoonww1.org.

"comics" as demanding more from readers than what pop culture (TV or film) does: "[C]omics offer readers the chance to actively construct, critically interpret, and consciously reflect on and relate to specific messages. Unlike popular media such as film and television, comics require more from their readers to establish basic meaning" (Carleton 161).

Carleton talks about the styles of the art used and the need for interpretive savvy in decoding the images offered, concluding, "In short, comics readers must use both textual and visual literacy to be active agents of the storytelling process" (162). He adds, "Moreover, unlike novels, comics are deliberately incomplete and require readers to extract meaning from the implied relationships between partial sequences of words and images" (162). This process is known as "closure," where the reader negotiates the gaps between panels and (though Carleton does not state this in the present context) the implied or inferred relationships between text and image to forge meaning (162–63).

The classic instance of a properly complicated approach to the graphic war novel is *Maus*, which became paradigmatic because it inaugurated a number of elements that would become standards in the genre. Particularly important for the present context are two: "a frame/tale construction which includes a multilayered narrative" and "metatextual representations of the artist in the narrative" as well as graphic innovations like intercut photographs (Martin 172). The work, though it has a Holocaust theme, exhibits "visual wittiness and ludic irreverence" (172). *Charley's War*, by Pat Mills with art by Joe Colquhoun, similarly aspires to extend the possibilities of the genre for complex presentation of its themes, at least according to Mills.

Writing an introduction to a 2004 hardcover edition of one section (the Somme battle) of the comic which originally came out in *Battle Picture Weekly* in 1979, Mills says that he is disappointed that "*Charley*," as he calls his work, "never influenced, in any meaningful way, other writers to produce similar dramas with such subversive subtexts" (Introduction, np).[67] He cites three levels to the work. First is that it is a "humorous, tragic, heavily researched drama with strong characterization, drawn in mesmerising detail" (np). Second, it "does not endorse macho hero values" (np). Finally, the work is "an anti-war story, often with polemical comments and footnotes that I deliberately wrote 'head on' so that they couldn't be ignored" (np).

Mills goes on to name his main message in the work: that World War I was, as other wars since have been, "a class war, a war against the poor": "Charley and his mates were actually fighting to make someone else rich," he says (np). His tone turns acerbic as he comments about the contemporary graphic novel publishing industry, "[W]e're not mature enough in mainstream comics to risk publishing an equivalent of this drama documentary," by which he refers to the critical film *Fahrenheit 9/11* by Michael Moore, with its indictment of U.S. policy that sent poor young men to be "cannon fodder" while no sons of U.S. Congressmen went to the war (np). In fact, he might be happy to know that, according to Carleton, the 2000 decade saw an explosion of comics with politically progressive themes, alternative views of history, and "accounts of resistance…that challenge readers to think and act differently in the world" (158–59).

Neil Emery, writing a further introductory piece in the *Charley's War* volume called "Into *Battle*: A Chronology of *Charley's War*," says that Mills' avowed approach was to turn the tide on pro-war comics, which *Battle Picture Weekly* was. The first skirmish to be fought in this effort was to make

---

67 As Wurtz notes, the original was in comic book form, but the re-issue is in
    what he cites as " 'graphic novel' format" (206).

World War I interesting as a subject of the graphic novel. Up until that point, the war had been a failure in boys' comics, he says, because, "The static nature of the subject made it difficult to hold the interest of readers more familiar with the fast paced adventures of heroes blazing their way across the many theatres of World War Two" (np). With that accomplished, Mills could go on to assert his alternate telling of the war centered on the anti-industrialist theme. As Emery says it, the strip was "[a]n anti-war story in a pro-war comic" (np).

Peter Hughes Jachimiak argues that texts written long after the Great War itself may make a reappraisal that earlier histories could not, claiming that comics in particular should be acknowledged as "justifiably relevant literary versions of history" (164). His emphasis is on the many versions of masculinity portrayed in *Charley's War* as well as the educative function of the strip, which, when it appeared originally in *Battle Picture Weekly*, stood in opposition to what the publication normally featured, which was World War II stories. As do others who argue the merits of the comic form, Hughes Jachimiak claims that narrative intertexts enrich the text:

> As a means of providing depth to the narrative, the strips featured the use of contemporaneous texts such as letters to and from home, photographs, postcards, songs, etc., with both the commentary and dialogue often interspersed with jargon and nicknames that had to be repeatedly explained within caption boxes to the readers who were unaccustomed to First World War-related terminology. (166)

Wurtz concurs with this estimation of the work, suggesting that "*Charley's War* draws upon previous literary responses to the Great War and employs a multifaceted narrative structure and distinctive artistic style as it explores the possibilities of comic form to occupy multiple places in the spectrum between detail and abstraction" (206).

Representations of photos, in particular, allow for character development, since each one "suggests fully-developed characters, each with their own past, each holding candid memories of their own familial histories" (Hughes Jachimiak 166). But more than that, photos point to the process of constructing memory as a way to combat "postmemory"—defined by Hirsch as something which "characterizes the experience of those who grow up dominated by narratives that preceded their birth, whose own belated stories are evacuated by the stories of the previous generation shaped by traumatic events that can be neither understood nor recreated" (qtd. in Hughes Jachimiak 166–67).

Though they are drawn, and hence fictional, the photos in this comic serve to point readers back to their own similar experiences with photos of fathers or grandfathers who might have served in the war, not to fixate on those people or memories but to move beyond their pastness as a way to understand the war by creating new memories through visually experiencing the war via the strip. Hence the critic can claim that "[w]ithin the context of the reimaginings of the First World War that have taken place since the 1970s, *Charley's War* can be recognized as a communally-experienced constructed site of memory. The readers of the comic were part of a continuum of postwar generations of readers bound by shared texts and shared narratives" (171). Emery describes them by saying that by 1981, "letters in praise of *Charley's War* were regularly published in *Battle*. Many of them were from veterans of the Great War, acknowledging the strip's excellence after being shown it by grandsons and great-grandsons" (np).

What appears at first glance to be a simple, and somewhat strained, device—the inclusion of Charley's letters home, which routinely ignore the truth about the war as he is currently experiencing it—is read as a clever tool for erasing the gap between home and the Front by Hughes Jachimiak (168). Wurtz makes an attempt also, saying that the letters are variously indicative of the inadequacy of language to "represent the unrepresentable," a device that "undercut[s] any sense of narrative integrity," a way of focusing not on the Great War but on Charley's war, and a sign that "Charley's lack of intelligence limits his ability to think about the war or to discuss it in any depth" (210). Indeed, Charley's naiveté, which surfaces over and over again in the story, must be dealt with if this strip is to advance its agenda to make a meaningful political statement about the war.

Particularly complex and effective is the way the strip combines text and art that highlights and complicates Charley's youthfulness as a tool for critique of the war. On that point, witness the portrayal of the moments before the attack on the Somme. Charley and his mates are gathered around while their General speaks to them. He reassures them that the sustained bombardment will have cut the wire, giving the British easy access to the German trenches, which themselves will have been all but destroyed (32).[68] Yet in the panel before, a text box has asserted, "the wire is not destroyed completely and the deep German dugouts survive!" (32). The character called Ginger says, "S'Truth! Don't he go on, Charley?" and the panel at the top of the facing page has the General pictured head and shoulders only, saying, again, "Not even a rat will have survived our bombardment!" before telling the soldiers how lucky they are to be on their way to a glorious victory (33). The same soldier, one presumes, is pictured—a floating head on a white background— challenging that lie. And the next panel in the three-across has the General, his monocle falling off, pictured head-only as

---

68 Note that I have supplied the page numbers in this volume, which is not paginated.

well, his eyes confused and the head seeming to rotate to a sixty-degree angle, saying "Gad! Who made that facetious remark?" (33).

The dual panel below has a wide shot with faces unrecognizable and one soldier—now, it seems, Charley—saying, "Thanks, Ginger. You're a real chum! You could have landed me right in it!" (33). This interchange points back to one key merit of the text as seen by critic Hughes Jachimiak: Charley's youth and innocence, which is portrayed as a foil to the general type of war comics that display a singular version of rough masculinity to the exclusion of other viewpoints and that, in fact, reflects the generally youthful cast who fought the war (169).

As the text unfolds, Charley's youth and naiveté are deployed in a variety of ways as a strategy to highlight the author's anti-war message by writing against the typical grain of the war story. Charley's everyman status was a purposeful choice on the part of the artist: "The decision to subvert the literary myth that is the war-hero introduces a parallel literary myth of the common man as non-hero that became a common figure in British popular culture after another conflict, the Second World War" (Hughes Jachimiak 169). As Mills himself says, "Charley is a hero, but I made the deliberate choice to make him neither particularly intelligent nor strong; he's just a typical 'Tommy'" (qtd. in Hughes Jachimiak 169).

For example, on the eve of the battle of the Somme, he manages to commandeer a food hamper meant for his commanding officer, Lieutenant Thomas, and the heads of a couple of other nearby regiments, yet this happens, as does much of what transpires for this boy soldier, by happenstance. He is carrying the hamper to the officers' dugout when a German shell lands, knocking him over. He decides that what's in the hamper is "too messed up for posh officers like Lieutenant Snell" and goes into the dugout to apologize (34).

He is chastised for his mistake, but arrives just in time to give his fellow enlisted men a treat. The resulting declaration by a fellow soldier confirms the viewpoint that the strip's artist was trying to create about him: "Cor! You're not so stupid as you look, Charley," says his mate (35).

His commander, Lieutenant Thomas, comes by, and Charley knows he's caught with the goods, since there's no way he and his friends would have delicacies like pâté and caviar. He salutes the officer while saying, "Er…about this partridge, sir…I can explain," but the officer says in an obviously ironic tone, "What partridge, Bourne…I see no partridge. Carry on, men!" (35).

The text next follows Charley, who becomes the reader's eyes and ears, into the battle experience. He is pictured running across what is likely No Man's Land. As he goes, the super-narrator, whose words appear enclosed in square boxes in all parts of this strip, says, "It is only 200 yards from the British to the German lines, but it feels like 2,000 miles!" and Charley's thought bubble reveals him to be thinking, "I'm afraid—but I'm more afraid of showing it. I don't want to let the Lieutenant and the Sarge down!" (40). His focus is hyperlocal once more.

Even when his comrades are pictured with doubts in their minds, Charley persists in his belief in his immediately visible leadership. In the second of three panels arranged vertically on the page, Lieutenant Thomas is charging into a German trench, gun literally blazing. The tracer path of the bullet he fires appears to hit a German right in the face, and he recoils, while behind Thomas, a barely visible Charley, a tiny figure, is again thinking (not saying aloud), "But Lieutenant Thomas has got his head screwed on right! We're going over the wire!" (40). There is no thought or comment about fear now, and no commentary on the gruesomeness of the German's death. But neither is that celebrated. Charley does not see the bigger picture, in other words, but focuses his attention on the tiny matter of his faith in his officer.

As the trench raid continues, someone calls out to Charley, "Bourne! A Hun! Give 'im a Mills bomb!" and Charley does just that, only the grenade hits the German in the helmet and bounces off, because, as Charley says while it flies, "Heck! I forgot to take the pin out!" (41). Whether he is innocent here or just dumb is perhaps a question of which audience is making the determination. All around him, the furious pace of the battle continues as one of Charley's fellow soldiers charges ahead, screaming, "I'm just getting into the mood, so I am, Sergeant dear!" and the Germans, now regrouped, are shown with a flame thrower at work (41).

Once again, Charley's luck is with him. Just as his buddy says, "S'truth! A Jerry liquid fire-thrower. You've had it now, Charley!" the wind changes, and the flame is blown back at the Germans, who are then blown to bits, flying back at the reader as if they were being thrown out of the panel they inhabit (42). Wurtz claims that it is just this type of artistic innovation that makes the strip capable of a sophisticated message. "Images would consistently break through the divides of the panels, lending a further sense of urgency to the dramatics of the narrative, he argues, suggesting also the following:

[W]*ith only a series of pictures on the page, the sequence had to be determined by the reader. The dialogue and captions are clearly aimed at a younger audience, but the complexities of the art and the relationship between the pictures and the words undermine the idea that this is children's literature* (207).

This compelling-sounding argument might also be read simply as a definition of comic or graphic novel form.

Of course there is a relationship between pictures and words. That's the nature of the genre.

Wurtz may be more convincing when he says, "[I]n its simultaneous deployment of several competing narrative structures, *Charley's War* demonstrates the capacity for comic form to represent the violence of the war" (208). Even at the simple level of narrative, the strip portrays this. Charley does take violent action, striking a German with the butt of his rifle as the hand-to-hand combat continues, and he and a few comrades pursue a machine gunner who has continued despite being the only one of his group left. Lieutenant Thomas orders the corporal and three men, including Charley, to clear the machine gun nest out. The corporal is killed while throwing a grenade, leaving Charley, Pop, and Ginger to themselves. They are pictured unsure of what to do—no leadership is visible to them—but Charley happens upon a previously unexploded Mills bomb, throws it, and they capture the man alive. The character Pop, who has lost two boys to gas earlier in the war, charges in and wants to bayonet the man, screaming, "I want vengeance…vengeance for my boys!" (44). But Charley tries to be the voice of reason, pointing out that the man is unarmed. Then, as a desperate next step, he appeals to his own youth: "No, Pop! You can't do it! He's just a kid—like me!" (45).

Miraculously, "As suddenly as it had come, Pop's fit of madness faded," the super-narrator says in a square text box (45). But what's fascinating is that the visuals of Charley and Pop's conversation have Charley drawn as anything but a young man. He has just said he's 16, but the face looks more like mid-20s, or 30. Charley is thus a mix of youth and not-youth ("age" is not the right word here). He is not self-reflective about his youth, because to be such would make him less naïve than he is portrayed as being. Rather, his actions shift between those of the trusting, at times clueless, young person and those of a hardened battle veteran, which is reflected in the art. In those moments when he suddenly grows up, however, he is not aware that this shift happens.

As the scene continues, the German soldier chats with Charley and a couple of his mates, and just when they are sharing a human moment, talking about the parents they have mutually left behind, there appears a panel with no dialogue. It is a close-up of the German, a bullet trace leading to a hole in his forehead and his scream, the inarticulate "AAAAAH!" He has been shot by Lieutenant Snell, the nasty commander of the regiment in the same sector as Charley's. In the panel following, the German is pictured lying dead, a photo of his family in front of him, turned out so the viewer can see it. A thought bubble, Charley's, once again invokes the matter of youth: "Poor blinkin' Jerry! He was only a lad like me!" (46).

The pronouncement betrays childishly simple and unsophisticated thinking, perhaps intensified by the use of exclamation marks, which are frequent in the text and suggest a tone which is not always appropriate to the situation depicted. Possibly, the presumed boy-audience is meant to see their own potential reactions in Charley's, and to stretch beyond this as they recognize the limitations of this point of view. But how is this point driven home?

Previously cited critic Peter Hughes Jachimiak argues that comics like *Charley's War* ought to be read as "sites of (constructed) memory—that is, as culturally-constructed spaces within which both the private and the public, the personal and the collective, meet" (163). They serve to give boys who could not have memory of these events a firsthand feel for them that replaces the memories they have acquired secondhand as postmemory, as was discussed earlier. These memories can then be reflected upon as moral positions are developed that, one presumes, would replicate the anti-war stance stated as the author's intention. One final example will illustrate the case.

As the first day of the Somme ends, Charley surveys the destroyed battlefield contemplatively, and then kneels in front of a wooden pallet, on which he writes. As he does, he thinks, "I ain't very bright, Mick. That sign's the best I can do. But it's somethin' to remember you by, chum" (54).

It would be absurd to say that Mills is suggesting that his audience, which identifies with Charley, think of themselves as not very bright, but the words appeal to the heartfelt nature of Charley's commemoration of his friend. In the final panel on the page, we see the sign, hand-lettered, "Mad Mick held this house he holds it still" with no punctuation and the final "s" on "this" and "holds" turned around backwards, childlike (54). The gesture, and the simplicity of the sign, suggest the one that most kids make the first time they have a "funeral" for a pet mouse or dead bird found in their backyard. Thus Charley's grand day of battle, which has seen him witness tragedy after tragedy, escape death himself, and have to come to grips with the inappropriate shooting of an unarmed enemy who has already surrendered as a POW, reduces to grief for the death of the man most immediate to him.

The super-narrator's declaration below the panel gradually zooms out in historical focus, starting out "Charley's first day of battle is over" and then talking about the number of men killed or wounded (60,000), and finally comparing this to the number of men killed or wounded on D-Day (specified at 4,000). This is best understood by considering the comic's publication context. The strip, which came out from the late 1970s to the early 1980s, was, from the first, placed next to World War II comics in *Battle Action*, as was indicated earlier. Thus the audience would, it seems, be familiar with the D-Day reference. The inclusion of it as a contextualizing move in *Charley's War* thus creates memory in the reader by suggesting that if the familiar actions of D-Day are commemorated, either in comics or history classes or real experience, so must the Somme be, with the simple scale of fifteen times the loss being suggested to any reader astute enough to do some simple mathematics (54).

Were late-1970s readers sufficiently horrified to feel a desire to commemorate the Somme battle? Did they get the point that heroic action is swallowed up in grief and loss, a lesson Charley has learned on July 1st, 1916? Perhaps, but the strip, being the commercial product that it is, does not linger on the point. The super-narrator's text box ends by moving the reader along to the forthcoming issue for sale, with "and the Battle of the Somme has only just begun…" (54).

From here, the story winds through more Somme action before heading towards its end with Charley Bourne turning 17, holding a shaving mirror and saying, "Blimey! Somehow I've survived to be seventeen on the Western Front, Ginger! But when I look at me face…it's like an old man's!" (93). He volunteers to be a runner, the thirteenth. The prior 12 have died (95). And thus the reader is pointed toward the next adventure.

Observing just this one installment in the Charley Bourne war saga indicates at least this much: time passes and the character ages, though his experiences do not mature him the way it seems that they might. The real movement in the story is cyclical, one adventure leading to the next. Yet if events move swiftly when the action is high, they also slow down at times, giving way to background, context, or moral discussion that allows Mills to make his point about the immorality of the war. That he does not have Charley voice these conclusions is perhaps to his credit. It would be easy to use the character as a mouthpiece. It is more difficult to have him remain mired in his own war and locked inside his youthful perspective, and thus to leave it to the reader to figure out how to understand the corrosive effects of the war itself.

In the end, perhaps the best strategy for understanding these alt-texts is to see them for what they are—contributions to a field much larger than they are, their particular part in the memory of the war an important counterpoint to other (dare one say literary?) contributions.

SECTION 3

REINVENTING THE WAR AND THE MODERN MIND

CHAPTER 7

Oh What a Literary War!: Lives re-inscribed

In light of recent state-sponsored violence such as has happened in Argentina, South Africa, and Indochina, theorists have wrestled with the question of how traumatic events of the past are remembered.[69] What has emerged is the notion, borrowed from psychology and memory theory, of "selective forgetting." Memory, in this figuration, is what is left after certain aspects of traumatic experience are forgotten. At times, this process is facilitated by the state out of necessity, such as when state violence is a product of certain of a state's citizens against others (Adelman 388). The hope is that "a communal, selective forgetting [would] allow...a fledgling (and often fragile) new regime to move forward" (388–89). Histories written within this frame, according to Jeremy Adelman, would not distance themselves entirely from past atrocities, but use detailed accounts such as testimonials as a way of marking the place the culture was trying to work away from (389).

Adelman is speaking about the ways in which, as he says it, "Wars occupy a special place in memory making" (387). He takes it as axiomatic that most cultures create their history by

---

69 On Argentina, for instance, see Antonius CGM Robben.

remembering the dead they have lost through violence. His particular concern is to dissect the process of memory when it is coincident with history; hence his question: "But what happens when the living memory of state violence coincides with the heightened quest for public myths for future consumption, when knowledge *from* and knowledge *about* intersect?" (388, italics original). Adelman's statement, "What is known *from* the past is transmitted as memory; what is known *about* the past is called history" presumes that in the former case, witnesses to events exist (388). But what happens in the case such as regards World War I in the present moment, when no witnesses exist?

The "remembering" of the contemporary novelist is not memory of events (or people) themselves, but writing *about* events. Geoff Dyer says, "Constantly reiterated, the claim that we are in danger of forgetting is one of the ways in which the war ensured it would be remembered. Every generation since the Armistice has believed that it will be the last for whom the Great War has any meaning" (18). He goes on to say that "translated into words, the dates 1914–18 have come to mean 'that which is incapable of being forgotten'" (18). The trouble is, as Dyer says in citing Paul Fussell, "[I]t is really hard to shake off the conviction that this war has been written by someone" (97). Fussell made this claim nearly two generations ago, when living memory still existed. Dyer repeated it nearly two decades ago, when there were a handful of survivors. Now, obviously, we are irretrievably past "knowledge *from*."

Long ago, if Fussell and Dyer are right, text, rather than testimony, came to define the war. Neil Oliver advances this idea by claiming, "Even the impact of set pieces of the war itself—First Ypres, the Somme, Passchendaele, Vimy Ridge— is dulled by time and by constant telling and retelling. It can be hard at times to make the players in the drama seem any more real than characters in *The Iliad* or *The Odyssey*" (274).

It would seem, if this is true, that even meaningful versions of knowledge *about* are beyond the possibility of the contemporary novelist. The answer, hit upon in Jill Dawson's *The Great Lover*, CK Stead's *Mansfield*, and Pat Barker's *Regeneration*, is to suture the gap between present and past by portraying the lives of famous historical figures in (contemporary) fiction. Is this a process of creation, recreation, or preservation of memory? Perhaps none of these is precise enough, but that still leaves "re-inscription," with its nuance of both writing (inscribing) and scripting.

CK Stead, in *Mansfield*, inserts the historical person, the New Zealand-born Modernist writer Katherine Mansfield, into a fictional setting dramatizing the years from 1915 to 1918 as Mansfield experienced them. Given that the novel is told from Mansfield's point of view, the war is not something immediate, but distant. Early on, she thinks about it, and the moment she lives in. Viewing two soldiers in a train car, she codes them as "officers carrying with them the mysterious knowledge of what it was like, *really* like 'at the Front'. If she'd been a man she would have wanted to go, to be part of it, to find out, to experience the fear and exhilaration and triumph over self" (16–17, emphasis original). She briefly toys with the idea of asking them what it is like at the Front, and then she wonders if "the Front" is

> … *a fiction, nothing more than a secret society, a club where soldiers went and met with the enemy…and made up stories, all linked together into one big story called 'the Great War', which they brought home and pretended to be reluctant to tell, so friends…had to squeeze hard to get a few drops from the lemon of their secret and unspeakable experience.* (17)

Here she may be read as expressing an impulse similar to Adelman's contrast of memory and history. For Mansfield the character, knowledge *from* is impossible, and knowledge *about* thus becomes a product of her imagination. So, too, this novel, as it takes what Stead claims to be historic facts (about Katherine Mansfield's life) and blends them with fictionalized guesses (about the same) in a process of re-inscribing events.

Mansfield becomes aware as time passes that for her, the war will remain something that provokes fear, but only at a remove. She realizes in bed one night that the war "was going to be…something very large, very terrible…which would give her moments of terror—and then would sail on, leaving her untouched" (46). She tries to keep the war at arm's length (47), but her doubts about what's real come crashing to a halt with the news of her brother's death in a grenade training accident just behind the front lines (69–71). This is described in close narrative detail, but when the news gets to Katherine, it is, naturally, in the form of a telegram, and she understands very little of what went on.

Her response is to devote herself to her brother's memory, so much so that she vows in her diary that she will write about their childhood "and then follow him in death" (81). She pledges in a notebook entry, " 'Nobody knows how often I am with you…I will never be away from you again. You know I can never be Jack's lover again. You have me. You are in my flesh as well as in my soul' " (81, ellipsis original). For a while, her writing does focus on her New Zealand childhood, but even when she turns to broader subjects, she cannot shake her grief. For instance, hearing Bertrand Russell make an impassioned plea for the conflict to end, she thinks, "It was interesting—and then it wasn't. All at once it seemed absurd to her, meaningless when set against the death of her brother and her fears for Freddie" (179).

Freddie is Frederick Goodyear, the other soldier whose experience is realized in *Mansfield*. As a soldier, he feels the need to go to war, doesn't particularly put the war into personal terms, and is both curious as to what it's like and accepting of whatever fate has for him (145). The story reports, "Whatever was waiting for him there, he believed he was ready for it" (186). He takes the whole thing as philosophical proof that there is no God. He even invents an ironic reading of the events: "War was even (you could argue) a lot of people doing their best. That was the biggest irony of all" (187).

For the reader, Goodyear becomes the familiar trope of the Great War combat veteran. His point of view is the one through which the trenches are depicted, as well as the rum ration, artillery fire, and gas, though none of it in more than summary form (197–200). Later, an explosion blows off his leg and leads to his death from gangrene (202). His death costs Katherine their dream of running off together to Scandinavia after the war is over.

But the point is not what happens to these soldiers as much as it is the contrast between the fictional Katherine's way of viewing the conflict writ large and the soldiers'. For her, "'[t]he War' was an abstraction, a puzzle, a nightmare," as she thinks one afternoon while watching a child play (213). Her thoughts are reported to us: "She knew she couldn't write about it—not directly; but perhaps, if she could write about Boy [the child] it would be there" (213). The next day, after working with Sassoon and her husband on a statement against the war, Katherine takes a walk with them: "That walk had had for her a special, resonant kind of dreariness, like living in a moment of 'History' when you would rather have been at a party. There was no escaping the war; it corrupted every-one, even those who opposed it" (214).

Stead here offers his message about historical fiction: because it begins in history, a novel like *Mansfield* might seem that it will erase the difference between knowledge *from* and knowledge *about*. However, suggesting that one could both live in and think abstractly about a moment—where the moment is both itself and part of some future coding called capital-"H" History—is to ask the impossible. The nearest one can get to the details of someone else's lived experience is in summary form. Contrast the narrator's comments about the soldiers' point of view: "In the trenches the men no longer cared about the Cause.... They are loyal, not to the Cause, and only half-heartedly to their nation, but to their comrades, and to the experience of war" (222).

It is tantalizing to see the Mansfield character who comes alive in this novel as a substitute for the lost historical witnesses of the time, but in the end, we are left sharing Katherine's imaginations and wishes that one of the men returning would just open his mouth and tell all but understanding the impossibility of it, something that we regret only if we mistake re-inscribing a life, which is Stead's accomplishment, for writing one, which is now impossible.

"Few sites in the field of literary biography have been so hotly contested as the biography of Rupert Brooke," so begins Hazel Hutchison's essay "The Art of Living Inward: Henry James on Rupert Brooke" (132). Hutchison goes on: "Brooke was held up by many as a national example of patriotism and as the idealization of youth, while others insisted that he was simply a flawed but talented young man" (132). The formulation of Hutchison's claims about the great poet who died in 1915 is most fully realized here:

> So much has been projected onto the memory of this young man that he has become a potent symbol of a particular moment and set of values. Like it or loathe it, he has come to stand for "Englishness"—or at least the particular brand of English nostalgia that was in vogue in the opening stages of the First World War. Many of Brooke's friends and colleagues protested his appropriation as an icon of establishment values. But cultural momentum was at work. The sheer

number of tributes and appreciations written in the weeks
after Brooke's death demonstrates how keen the British were
to find a representative figure on which to focus their grief in
April 1915 and in the months that followed. (132)

Forget the months that followed. Nearly one hundred years
later, in 2009, Jill Dawson pitched her hat into the ring by rec-
reating, or seeming to, a portion of Brooke's life in her novel
The Great Lover. In fact what she does is re-inscribe the poet's
life as a critique of class privilege enfolded into an inquiry into
the nature of Colonialism.

The biography of Rupert Brooke would appear simple on
its face: young man with poetic promise writes verse that is
typical of the early war years, that is, patriotic and sentimental. He is taken up for his fame, but dies early in the conflict
(1915) because of blood poisoning and sunstroke on his way
to Gallipoli. As Hutchison says, this invokes an immediate set
of conflicts regarding his biography and literary reputation,
with most commentators suggesting that the most interesting
thing about his life is what had not yet been, or the question
of what his poetic potential might have led him to had he
lived (138).

No less than Winston Churchill (in an obituary) and Henry
James (in a preface to Brooke's *Letters from America*) weighed
in on Brooke's life in the immediate aftermath of his death. It
was a life that begged construction from the outside, as
Hutchison says: "Brooke's constructed legend is a monument,
partly to his incalculable potential, but also to his personal
ability to elicit strong emotional responses from others. He
remains, like a work of art himself, the focus of many conflict-
ing readings and perspectives, only available through a highly
synthesized construction" (143). It is perhaps this which
draws the interest of Dawson. But the life that she constructs
is anything but the idealized version that was established after

Irish National War Memorial Gardens, Dublin

he died, starting with a memoir edited by his friend Eddie
Marsh. As Hutchison says, "Marsh has been blamed for establishing the myth of Rupert Brooke, but given the restrictions
put on him by [his mother] Mrs. Brooke and the fact that his
memoir didn't emerge until July 1918, long after the myth
had established itself, he can hardly be given all the responsibility" (135). Henry James provided a slight corrective to that,
and that was to "highlight a tension in Brooke's nature
between the charismatic socialite and the troubled inner man"
(Hutchison 138).

Critic and biographer Nicholas Murray, in *The Red Sweet
Wine of Youth: The Brave and Brief Lives of the War Poets*, picks
up this tone: "Rupert Brooke was to become the type of the
young poet sacrificed heroically to war and his death had
profound consequences for the national mood, letting the
sluices discharge more patriotic verse" (46). This, he points
out, was in the period before the Somme, when "the War was
still susceptible of [sic] that kind of exalted presentation" (46).
He then points to Brooke's physical attribute as being

"dashingly handsome," noting that he was someone Yeats called "the most handsome man in England" (qtd. in Murray 46). Paul Fussell claims that "[t]he equation of blondness with special beauty and value helps explain the frantic popularity of Rupert Brooke, whose flagrant good looks seemed an inseparable element of his poetic achievement" (299).

However, Murray also notes another side to Brooke, pointing out that "[h]is amatory and sexual entanglements remained complicated and contradictory until his death and were the cause of a nervous breakdown early in 1912. He seems in particular to have experienced psychological problems to do with revulsion with his own body and its desires" (47). As Dawson constructs her fictional Brooke, she appears to draw on these impulses, also seen in Brooke's letters, that "demonstrate his desire for freedom, both emotional and sexual, for travel, for outdoor life, for wilderness, for new people, and for new experiences" (Hutchison 140).

The Great Lover is entitled after a poem of Brooke's, written in 1914. This piece does not in any way represent his sexual prowess as portrayed in the novel, where the character Brooke is in fact tentative, nervous, and incapable of consummating most of his relationships. As biography, then, the novel could represent the real-life issues that drove Brooke to breakdown, and indeed, Dawson's Brooke at one point has a breakdown and goes away for healing. However, Dawson readily admits that she is not after the truth: "This is a novel. I have made things up…. Of course I made Rupert up, too, and he is 'my' Rupert Brooke, a figure from my imagination" (303). He is not without sourcing, of course, Dawson having used "his poetry, his letters, his travel writing and essays" mixed with "guesswork, the things I know about his life blended with my own dreams of him, and impressions" (303). This method is signaled in the text when one character says to another in a letter, "A biography is a good way to find out things but to my mind, well. It has its limits. After all, a biography is written by a person and a person does not always understand another as well as they might think" (8). She goes on to say that biographies "set too much store by facts and not enough by feelings" (8).

Two thematic lines work in the novel to create Dawson's Brooke, a figure who draws attention away from the historical Brooke's reputation for his poetry as well as his physical charms. Predominating is the class division that separates the Brooke character and Nell, the "maid-of-all-work" (as the text labels her) with whom he carries on a torrid flirtation for the entire course of the plot, a relationship that consists of nothing but a couple of kisses until the very late going, when they spend a night and she becomes pregnant. The other theme is a sort of reverse *Jane Eyre*, or modern updating of that text, if Guyatri Spivak's point about that novel—that it was always about the colonies and how present they are in the "Mother" country—is correct.[70] In fact, rather than hide the "madwoman" in the attic, Dawson puts her on the first page, with the novel opening with a 1982 letter from Arlice Rapoto, a woman from the South Seas, to Nell. Both women have had a Brooke child, though neither has made any claim on him as a father.

The thematic of how class divides is prolonged in this novel, the plot of which in some ways reduces to one long flirtation between two people who, but for their social circumstances, would likely be together. Many, many times in the text, Brooke and Nell's social differences are highlighted. For Brooke, Nell is not so much a person in the early going as a type. "[She] reminds me of a girl I once saw, a working girl…" he muses on one of their first encounters (30).

---

70 See for instance Spivak 249.

He follows up, "Nell...That sumptuous nymph, naiad, the unearthly creature" before going on to think about her body, then adding, "I feel sure she is an extraordinarily intelligent girl," but many times, he cannot credit her with intelligence, as we will see (31, ellipsis original). When he later pictures her visiting her family at home, he says, "[realizing] the marvellous [sic] child was absent...I indulged myself with another brief picture of Nellie there with other buxom maids, picking celery or—what do they do in Fen country?—carrying eels in nets or milk in churns or some such glorious thing" (111). She is not a thinking being to him.

Her wishes are plain. "[H]e and I, for all our different stations, might *share* something," she realizes as she goes over their common experiences of losing a sibling (45, emphasis original). She dismisses the idea: "But this is only a fancy, a thought in my own imagination, after all, and not a hard fact of any kind" (45). But it's not that, as the reader knows, having been inside the head of the Brooke figure, who desires her as much as she does him. Still, he can't get over their divide, but rather reinforces it. She brings him a tray in bed, and he thinks of how she seems to have rejected the idea of learning about the ideas in Moore's *Principia Ethica*, but in fact she had not. He had earlier asked if she had read the book, and she said no. He later says, "You've no interest in books, then, Nell? Or—how would the Webbs put it—in bettering yourself?" (67). She whirls around and responds forcefully to say that she does desire to improve herself, and that she loves books. They proceed to discuss Brooke's Fabian notions about what to do regarding reform of England's Poor Law of 1834, and Brooke waxes on about rights for women, and then notices that he has left her behind. His comment? "The attention span of the British maid is very short," and as he has gotten bored with her, he thinks, "My stock of Subjects to

Take Up with the Servant was exhausted," when they get onto the subject of the women's vote (69). Still, he does not see that he has given her no credit for intelligence, no pardon for not having had time to read the books he has read—many volumes of various sorts are strewn about the room—and no credit for having opinions about subjects on which she has had time to inform herself, such as suffrage.

When he later engages her in discussion of a poem, it seems that he does so only to set her up for mockery. He suggests that a couple of lines are good ones, and when she agrees, says, "Yes! The parlour-maid says the best lines are: 'heartache or tortured liver'.... Nellie, you are a marvel. Oh thank you, darling Nellie. I should have taken you that day in the orchard, shouldn't I, while I had my chance?" (123). There is a pause, and then she slams the door and storms away, her thoughts being, "The cheek of the man! The baldly stated, *to my face*, idea that he could have me any time he wanted, regardless of what my thoughts might be on the matter" (123, emphasis original). The result is a further wedge between them, predicated on his inability to credit her even for control over her life as a sexual being. He does later credit her for her intelligence, but puts it in terms that reflect on himself: "I know that I was not wrong in my estimation of her intelligence" (142).

So why can't they get together? For one thing, because the plot of the novel depends upon this conflict not being resolved. But the social situation is really to blame. As he describes it, "Tradition and Centuries are difficult to undo" (142, capitalization original). He muses on this, realizing that they are destined not to be together: "How could one ever continue a dalliance with the maid when one is watched over at every turn by kindly friends…?" The irony is great: "Easier to have such an adventure with a boy from one's own class than with Nell" (149).

If a vision of his class superiority is what keeps Brooke from recognizing Nell as a person/partner until the late going, then her notion of the sexual mores of the upper classes is what keeps her from seeing him as more than a flirtation, class division working in both directions. She, as his maid, is privy to the details of what stains his sheets, and having witnessed him taking a man into his room and then being responsible to clean up the aftermath, she is convinced that he is interested only in men. This comes, in her mind, as a product of class. She tells her sister Betty, "[F]or the men who go in for it, it is probably a sight more common than we could guess, especially among men who get sent away to school, who spend so much time in each other's pockets, and where doing such things with ladies from their own set is so restricted" (171). Martin Lockerd suggests the milieu that Brooke the person might have come from when he says, "Brooke's adolescent life typifies the conflicted and frustrated sexual desires of the English public school.... His legendary beauty and natural charm made him desirable to members of both sexes, but he was tortured by unrequited and capricious love that led to several breakdowns, anxious affairs, and little sex" (6). This is exactly what Brooke the character experiences. For her part, once she has decided that he is "for men," Nell can't dissuade herself of the notion.

They have by this point shared an electric kiss, but she tells herself after seeing him the next day, "I felt dreadfully sorry for him; sorry for his sickness, too—how much shame and misery it must bring him I could hardly fathom. Truth be told, I struggled to accept that such a *tendency* exists, and I didn't want to know any more about it than had already been forced into my thoughts" (95, emphasis original). But his realization after the encounter is, "I have resolved that Sodomy can only ever be for me a hobby, not a full-time occupation.

I've discovered I'm no true Sodomite" (104). Nell has no idea, though, and can't shake the question.

Much later, she mulls over their encounter at the river, and their kiss, and wonders, "[W]hat sense can I make of it all? I know I wasn't mistaken about the boy Denham in his room. I know that whatever sport he [Brooke] makes of me, it can only ever be that—cruelty and sport" (154). When Brooke proposes to a woman, Nell codes it this way: "Within the range of persons he is *allowed* to fall in love with, this Noel Olivier…would certainly be a reasonable choice" (159, emphasis original). But she thinks of it only as a cover. She tells her sister shortly later, after revealing that they have kissed, "Rupert is–he—He doesn't like girls" (170).

Brooke is often incapable of thinking of Nell as "Nell," or referring to her that way. She is "the maid," and he addresses her as "child" or "girl" or "Nellie." Even in the late going, he doesn't use her name, thinking, "[T]he maid is far too clever" when wondering if he could get away with an affair in his rooms (176). Yet when he says something shocking to her and watches his reaction, he thinks, "She has spark, that girl! Oh yes she is—magnificent!…This one is a corker" (186). They discuss one of his poems, and he thinks, "Why is it that I want to unpeel layer after layer when I'm with Nell? There's such loveliness and wisdom in her. And she has *feeling*, real feeling, without ever being sentimental or squashy" (188, emphasis original). But when she later praises his poem yet can't articulate why, he feels "a cruel pulse of pleasure" (234). This after having tried to convince her of the tragedy and dread that can beset a writer when his work is out in the public eye after having been published, a set of problems that he doesn't recognize are ridiculous next to her real-life issues of making enough money to feed her family (206).

Even when Brooke realizes the risk she takes by being with him outside at night and confesses his shortsightedness on the matter, he dismisses her with, "Thank you, child. You're a very sweet girl" (209). For her part, she stands "on the wrong side of his bedroom door" and wonders how "it always happens: that whatever my heart desires, my mouth fails to utter it" (209). But what was she supposed to say, in a relationship governed by a set of power relations far bigger than she is?

She does take charge after he has returned from a long trip to the South Seas, spending a night with him, but he ruins it by being a know-it-all. Her reaction is swift: "[T]here it is again, my anger with him, for his annoying habit of spoiling everything, of always thinking he knows best" (271). And when he asks her if she will marry her working class boyfriend, she says it depends, but never tells him on what: "Perhaps I hoped he would understand. But of course, nothing between us could ever be simple, or spoken aloud, and he did not understand at all" (271). Only their sexual encounter brings them together, but both know that it is a singular moment, and when she discovers her pregnancy, she naturally can't credit it to Brooke.

The postcolonial also frames this novel, starting with the letters cited above back and forth between the two women Brooke shared intimacy with, Nell and Arlice Rapoto, and ending with this encounter between Brooke and Nell, which Nell summarizes by saying, "I might as well have been from a South Seas island myself for all the likelihood of Rupert understanding me" (271). He leaves the next day, and she has his child nine months later, after marrying Tommy quickly enough that the eventual child can be taken for his. Brooke's summary of the encounter, so much waited for by the reader of this novel, is to say, "I think of Nell again, and her courage, in coming to me in that, and how I wasn't really well, not well

enough to appreciate her" (273). It is consistent with his character to say so, but it again reinforces his class privilege.

As for his colonial privilege, that is already assured, as he
has fathered a child in the South Seas as well. He is aware of
neither, in part because the women maintain their silence, but
also because the war immediately swallows him up. He
returns to Grantchester, and Nell has the following revelation:
"I saw at once how hard it would be for him to acknowledge
me in front of his friends" (295).

The novel ends shortly after Brooke sends Nell a poem, that
which gives Dawson's book its title. The fictional Brooke's
summary is perhaps telling concerning its significance:
"Words are things after all," he says (294). Maybe to him this is
true, but in fact the poem, which is a product of the historical
Brooke, is in no wise true of the character Brooke, even from
its first line: "I have been so great a lover," it begins, but it ends
with a lament: "the best I've known,/Stays here, and changes,
breaks, grows old, is blown/About the winds of the world, and
fades from brains/Of living men, and dies,/Nothing remains"
(299–301). Why? Class, culture, and the colonies, and the jux-
taposition of the work of the poet Rupert Brooke with the
anxieties—partly shared, and partly invented, as Dawson
said—of his fictionalized self makes interesting drama that
reveals tensions in British cultural life, if only through a process of forgetting that allows Dawson to bring to the present
only what she needs to create this mythical version of Brooke.

Pat Barker adopts a similar strategy of selection in her
Regeneration trilogy, an adaptive retelling of the WHR Rivers
story, in which we get a version of the historical anthropologist and psychiatrist (amongst other things) Rivers (not an
entirely accurate one, as I detail in Chapter 8 when talking
about *The Ghost Road*), and we learn of the Sassoon protest
story, also adapted.[71] The conclusion Michèle Barrett offers on

---

71 Barrett, for example, discusses the fictionalized versions of Rivers, Sassoon,
    and Graves in her article (239–40).

Sassoon is representative of critical opinion on the historicity of Barker's characters: "Siegfried Sassoon's fate was to be psychologized by Barker's novel, as he had been in life. The Craiglockhart story in *Regeneration* tells us a great deal about new treatments for shell shock and war psychoses" (240).[72] She further cites Anne Whitehead, who says that Barker portrays her Sassoon as being "on the verge of a psychological breakdown and thus to some extent validates Rivers's treatment of him" (240). Yet Barrett adds that this is not historically accurate: "Neither the writings of W.H.R. Rivers nor any other historical source indicates that Sassoon's protest—the objection of a decorated soldier to the conduct of the war— was the act of a man who was ill" (240–41). Her point is to dislocate the reading of Barker's Rivers as a Freudian and relocate him in an older discursive tradition, that which pits reason against unreason, a category of thinking offered by Foucault (238).

Regeneration itself proceeds along more simple and determinate plot lines than the later two members of the trilogy will do. Several stories of psychological affliction related to the war are told, with Sassoon's being the touchstone that the narrative continually circles back to. Interesting in this context is Fussell's description of the historical figure Sassoon as a producer of memory work: "Of all those for whom remembering the war became something like a life work, Sassoon is the one whose method of recall, selection, and expression seems to derive most directly from the polarities which the war pressed into the recesses of his mind" (101).

This notwithstanding, in *Regeneration*, Barker's most poignant re-inscription surfaces only when one reads past both

---

72 Further discussion of critical opinions regarding Barker's historicity as it applies to Rivers' treatment methods appears in Chapter 8.

Sassoon and Rivers to focus on Billy Prior.[73] Though Prior
never existed as a historical person, Barker's treatment of him
reveals the as yet only vaguely realized presence of a changing
Britain that, after the war, will no longer be able to retrieve the
memory of a stratified culture with a certain set of values—
honor, glory, and so on—because these have been proved to
be impossible to sustain in the face of the machine gun.
Wilfred Owen supplied the best phrase for it in "Dulce et
Decorum Est," calling warmongering based on a false promise
"The old Lie," but it takes a new type of person, one sitting on
the margin between social classes, to dramatize the shift. Billy
Prior serves Barker as this person, a working-class hero like
those in her other fiction, and someone who is the site of what
John Kirk calls "nostalgic memory," albeit somewhat ironi-
cally, since he is an invention.

"'Nostalgic memory' represents a symbolic act of recovery—
of neglected experience, forgotten voices, silent groups," Kirk
explains, adding that "[t]here are forms of nostalgic memory...
which can be *enabling*" by allowing for recollection of the past,
its struggles, and as a way to form identity and community
(605, 606, emphasis original). Barker has said, Kirk reports, that
"'[m]emory is my subject'...writing history/fiction as a desire
for recovery, seeking absence as presence" (qtd. in Kirk 606).
Though fictional, Billy Prior "provides Barker with space to
explore issues of gender, class, and memory. This overall
narrative concern analyzable in Barker's kind of nostalgic
memory links 'now' with 'then,' facilitating an understanding
of history and identity in the present as partly a product of the
past" (607). Kirk summarizes to say: "Barker...is concerned
with giving those written out of bourgeois history's triumphal

---

73 Even more interesting is that as he appears in this novel, memory is a key
   category of his experience but the same is not true, for example, when he turns
   up in *The Ghost Road*.

procession a participating voice," re-inscribing them, in the language I have been using (623). This happens particularly in *Regeneration* via Prior's ability to confound Rivers with knowledge not thought to be possessed by a man of his social station.

In one of their early encounters, Prior stuns the doctor with his knowledge of both psychoanalytic therapy language and the fact that he is reading one of Rivers' own books on anthropology (65). When Prior uses the term "negative trans-ference," Rivers expresses surprise, asking where he had learned the term. Prior's answer? "I can *read*" (65, emphasis original).

This class prejudice is reinforced when Rivers next has a session with Prior, and Prior reminds him that they had ear-lier discussed the different ways that officers and enlisted men react to trauma. One particular set of reactions is for enlisted men to get mutism, while officers stammer. Rivers explains that "it's almost as if for the...laboring classes illness *has* to be physical" (96, ellipsis and emphasis original). Prior's mutism thus marks him as one of them. The trouble is, Prior serves an officer, not a common soldier, and thus sits on a margin that doesn't fit Rivers' diagnostic categories.[74]

They next discuss dreams, with Rivers saying, "officers' dreams tend to be more elaborate" whereas "[enlisted] men's dreams are much more a matter of simple wish fulfillment" (96). Again, Prior is somewhere off the scale, suffering from horrible nightmares. But in discussing the specifics of his dreams, Rivers dislocates Billy from this class-based officers/men binary anyway. Instead, he reminds him, "You don't remember your dreams" (96). But he also gives

---

74 Early in the war, enlisted men were promoted to NCO ranks. This is graphically illustrated by Lewis-Stempel: "When the blood of boy subalterns began to gush over the dull brown soil of Flanders and the chalk flecked earth of the Somme, promotions from the ranks began to accelerate" (59). He does point out that these were not necessarily working-class men, however. DeGroot also discusses the phenomenon of the "temporary gentleman" (298).

his prejudice away when he offers an explanation for the difference in dreams and dreamers: "I suppose it's just a matter of officers having a more complex mental life" (96).

This once again activates Prior's social consciousness. He reminds Rivers of the fact that officers, in his opinion, are a "*gaggle* of noddle-brained half-wits" (97, emphasis original). Prior subsequently asks Rivers, "How do I fit into that?" after which Rivers redirects him to the original complaint: "We-ell, it's interesting that you were mute and that you're one of the very few in the hospital who *doesn't* stammer" (97, emphasis original). They discuss the fact that Rivers does stammer, and as the session goes on, Prior turns the tables on the doctor, taking charge and leading Rivers to ask, only partly ironically, "Is that the end of my appointment for the day, Mr. Prior?" (97). This could be read as his having upended the equation that keeps each of them to his appointed (class-constructed) position.

When Prior turns up that evening, Rivers gives him an off-the-cuff assessment of his condition, saying, "You've recovered almost all your memory *and* you no longer lose your voice" (99, emphasis original). But, one might ask, what does having both memory and a voice mean to this border-dweller? If Prior has recovered his memory, then he has recovered not only his wartime experiences but also the consciousness of who he is, socially (the material fact of this was never lost). How, then, would he be able to function—indeed, to speak— in a social system—that of the trenches—where he sits as a hybrid between types, having to do the work of the officer while having the mind of the foot soldier? It is a question much larger than is related to one person's experience.

Prior says that he wants more—he wants to come back fully—but this will only happen if they delve deeply into his trench experience. He admits that he does in fact remember his nightmares, and Rivers asks if he wants hypnosis to recover the memory that haunts him and causes the dreams. Even here, the relative power of the educated class over the worker is obvious, if we read past the therapist-patient dynamic. Rivers says that people fear therapy because they believe "that they're putting themselves completely in the therapist's power," but he says further, "that isn't true, you remain your-*self* throughout" (101, emphasis original). It's significant that he slips to second-person rather than continuing in third person, as if he registers Billy as both the specific person and the mass of his social class.

Under hypnosis, Prior has his most vivid and horrible memory. As the session ends, the narrator reports, "Rivers watched the play of emotions on Prior's face as he fitted the recovered memory into his past" (104). What he has seen was a horrible shell attack that destroyed the bodies of two men, leaving an eye amongst the duckboards for Prior to pick up (103). Doctor and patient then discuss not the memory itself, but the fact that Prior has remembered it. He remarks that the memory is not as bad as he thought it would be, and gives an example of a British officer who led his men in a circle at night and accidentally attacked a British wiring party, killing several and losing a number of his men in the attack. Prior had thought that his lost memory would resurface as something like that. Now that he knows that his worst memory doesn't reach that level of dreadfulness, he marks the end of his analysis: "I couldn't see what else I'd need to forget," and he shortly adds, "I just wanted to understand why it happened" because "I don't think of myself as the kind of person who breaks down" (105).

Perhaps this indicates his class confusion. Officers, whose education is certainly superior and who, Rivers says at one point in the text, have "greater mental complexity" than others (this from the mouth of Billy, who reminds him that he has said it, though he gets the quote just a bit wrong [133 cf. 96]), are figured as the upholders of British upper-class values, the type, one might say, who don't break down. But Prior has broken down, marking him as a member, in this way of thinking, of an inferior class. The fact that his memory is recoverable, and recovered, indicates that his type of man stands as an interrogator of the assumptions of class privilege represented by Dr. Rivers, a bridge between classes, a new type of man who will continue to be the locus of challenge to classist assumptions because he has access to complex sets of memories.

Rivers assures Prior that things will be different than before the war, ultimately landing on the point that class distinction is not going to be as strong: "[T]hings'll be freer after the war. If only because hundreds of thousands of young men have been thrown into contact with the working classes in a way they've never been before. That has to have some impact" (135).

Perhaps this indicates a world in which Billy Prior is inscribed into history. But even here, Rivers reinforces the class prejudice he would seem to be denying by naming the opposition that will have been closed as being one which divides "young men"—individuals—and "the working classes"—faceless, indistinguishable masses. And in any case, the representative figure of nostalgic memory, Prior, will be dead near the end of part three of Barker's trilogy, dashing Rivers' prediction of social change in the years following the war. That is not yet in view as *Regeneration*'s narrative closes, but it demands Barker's—and our—full attention in the latter two parts of her masterpiece trilogy.

CHAPTER 8

The Great War and the Modern Psyche: Fussell's vision reborn

Near the beginning of *The Great War and Modern Memory*, Paul Fussell claims "that there seems to be one dominating form of modern understanding; that it is essentially ironic; and that it originates largely in the application of mind and memory to the events of the Great War" (38). This forms the motif for his book and locates interest in the psychological aftermath of the war that informs our thinking about the 1914–18 period even to the present.

Vera Brittain, writing in 1950, reminds us that the now-familiar Freudian mode of understanding human consciousness became established only after the war. "The modern jargon of popular psychology[—]'reaction', 'repression', 'anxiety neurosis', 'combat fatigue', 'battle-hysteria'—had not then [during the war] become the current coinage of speech…," she rightly claims (183). "But I saw enough cases of what was then called 'shell-shock' to realize the intimate relationship between body and mind, and subsequently to understand the modern psychotherapists' insistence that more people are ill because they are miserable, than miserable because they are ill" (183). She then offers an example of a man who was unable to speak when brought into the hospital where she was nursing in 1917 near the front lines. He was treated as a paralysis case, she says, though doctors could not find any physical problems to explain his condition. He was then sent along for further care, hopefully, she indicates, to "a specialist better acquainted with the strange vagaries of the human mind than the army doctors at Etaples in 1917" (183–84).

In offering these opinions and this instance of the wounded man, Brittain puts into relief the two worlds that the Great War straddled. Conventionally, these were that of the hopeful (for the First World) 19th century and the dreadful 20th century, and the hinge between them was technology, beautiful in the 19th century, horrible in the 20th. In fact, she elucidates the contrast, indicating, "[W]e all had experienced the tremendous revolution—one of the greatest in history—which carried the nineteenth century into the twentieth. It became my intention to attempt to estimate [in *Testament of Youth*] the apocalyptic quality of these changes which transformed forever the world into which my contemporaries and I were born" (194). She further describes this change by calling the time of the war "a vast age of transition…details [of] which changed as each disastrous, tragic, and dramatic epoch merged into another" (195). Perhaps echoing Virginia Woolf's famous proclamation about December 1910 being a time when human character changed, Brittain says, "Mankind was never the same again after 1914 any more than it was ever the same again after the Crucifixion" (197).

While the war went on, Brittain's point of view was already forming that this moment marked a divide. She cites a letter she wrote to her brother in 1917 in which she said, "I think that 'Before' and 'After' this war will make the same kind of division in human history as 'BC' and 'AD'" and indicates after looking back at her words that while at the time, "this seemed an extravagant and even absurd assessment,…after half a century it does not seem to me that I was so far wrong in my estimate…" (196). What she says about the coming of Christianity could equally apply to the coming of Freudian psychology: "The transition from the pagan to the Christian world meant a vast spiritual change affecting all human lives from the first century onward; it challenged existing values irrespective of whether those challenged understood the issues involved" (196).

George Mosse makes the argument that the war was imbricated in the cultural/literary movements of the day, pointing out that the Futurists, German Expressionists, and Cubists all shared a vision that had as its core "the new speed of time and the simultaneity of experience" that grew out of the technological inventions showcased in the early 20th century (55). These included the automobile, cinema, and telecommunications devices including the telephone and telegraph, which collectively "seemed to revolutionize time itself" such that "[a] single reality or an absolute space no longer seemed to exist, and instead many men and women confronted a 'chaos of experience'" (54). Mosse further says that there is no question the war "played a crucial role in the memory of people" in the interwar period, imparting a sense of "mental confusion and universal chaos" (182). The latter description might in fact be one that someone unfamiliar with Modernist fiction could use to describe works like those of Woolf, Joyce, or, to a lesser degree, DH Lawrence. Jay Winter claims that "[e]ven a glance at the vast literature surrounding the well-known cadences of TS Eliot's 'The Wasteland' [sic] and WB Yeats' 'The Second Coming' remind us that apocalyptic images were inextricably part of literary responses to the Great War and its aftermath" (200). Yet while

Modernism was coexistent with the war and the period following, and while the war did work its way into Modernist literature, it did not form the core of that literature, nor has Modernist form survived in the sort of abundance that Brittain's portrait of the moment might have predicted it would. But much later, a handful of novels reprise this grand shift toward emphasis on the psyche. In this group are Barker's *The Eye in the Door* and *The Ghost Road* and Urquhart's *The Underpainter*, all of which explore the topic of shell shock and its treatment using a Freudian framework.[75]

There is, however, a caution to be taken. These novels cannot be taken as accurately representing the 1920s, because, as Barrett argues, "[P]sychotherapy...has been overemphasized as a factor in the historical and literary interpretation of shell shock" (238). Focusing particularly on Barker, she says that the *Regeneration* trilogy, "has contributed to a Freudianization of shell shock" (238). She points out that the obituaries published after Rivers' death in 1922 mention him as an anthropologist and reviser of Freud's approach more so than a healer of victims of shell shock (245–46). She claims that the idea of Rivers as Freudian psychotherapist primarily owes its existence to Barker (246). She elucidates as follows:

> WHR Rivers was an important figure for his engagement with Freud's ideas. He regarded Freud's discovery of the unconscious as a major development, and as a framework for therapy. But he did not accept the definitional place attributed by Freud to infantile sexual experience in causing neurotic or psychotic mental states. The historical Rivers thought that soldiers' mental traumas could be caused by their adult experience of the war as opposed to childhood experiences. (246)

She adds, "[Rivers] used the idea of repression to analyze and treat these men, but it was only very loosely a Freudian

---

75 The condition was originally called, especially by medical personnel, "war neurosis," as Michèle Barrett points out (237).

approach" (246). If Rivers is to be credited with anything respecting Freud, it is that his "appropriation of some aspects of Freud's model helped to overcome prejudice against Freud, who was a more marginal figure in wartime Britain" (246).

Karolyn Steffens echoes this, pulling no punches with her first sentence: "Pat Barker continually invokes contemporary conceptions of trauma, largely stemming from a cultural context in which Freudian psychoanalysis and post traumatic stress disorder have saturated the popular imagination" (36). The emphasis decidedly falls on "contemporary," the argument following saying that Barker writes more about our conception of the wartime therapeutic praxis of psychoanalysis than what was the case at the time. As Audoin-Rouzeau and Becker say, "Psychological suffering, after 1914–18, was unexpressed...first of all due to a lack of appropriate words" (176). Steffens adds, "Although frequently praised for her historical accuracy, Barker and the *Regeneration* trilogy are fully immersed in our contemporary trauma culture," the invention of which came, in Steffens' figuration, largely with the publication of Cathy Caruth's *Unclaimed Experience* in 1996 (37). That "Barker's trilogy could not have been written without contemporary trauma discourse is the result of the pervasive cultural understanding of Freudian discourse in the late twentieth century" (Steffens 37–38). Steffens cites Mark Rawlinson as providing a gloss on the trilogy: "Caruth's definition of trauma as the narrative of belated experience 'would also be a good description of the trilogy, which could in this context be considered a form of belated vicarious experience'" (qtd. in Steffens 38).

Steffens makes the case that collapsing together Freud, Barker, and trauma theorist Caruth allows for the argument that "Barker successfully acts as an agent of

20th Light Division Memorial, Langemark, Belgium

collective remembrance by employing psychoanalysis, intertextuality, and the cultural history of shell shock" (38). Steffens urges instead that we see the novels as putting "the trauma discourse of the late twentieth century in conversation with WHR Rivers's specific psychoanalytic method," calling for an analysis that examines the trilogy "in relation to Rivers's specific adaptations to Freud's talking cure and dream interpretation" (38).

Steffens points out a further problem with Barker's use of historical sources when she shows that the session where Rivers analyzes Anderson in *Regeneration* is "a rewriting of one of Rivers's actual case studies" from his volume *Conflict and Dreams* (41). Steffens outlines three ways in which the clinician Rivers differed from Freud, making the point that critics tend to collapse the former onto the latter, a misreading of the historical Rivers' methodology (44). Barker, rather than sticking to a historical point of view, "adapts Rivers's case studies in order to actually expand their significance and broader relevance for the Freudian talking cure. In her adaptations, she does not subvert Rivers' theories, but rather extends them even further than Rivers does himself" (51).

The emphasis on Rivers as Freudian therapist, as it turns out, is blatantly a misreading of his life/work. Barrett, whose work was introduced above, makes the point directly: "A retrospective Freudianization of shell shock in Barker's trilogy is partly achieved through casting Rivers as a figure whose military psychiatry appears to dominate his life and work, which was far from being the case," a point made through reading his obituaries, from 1922 (246). There, he is credited primarily as an anthropologist, and Barrett claims that "[t]he Rivers who exists in the mind of literary critics, in the wake of Barker's trilogy, is Mrs. Hopkinson's [who wrote a letter to the newspaper noting his work with shell shock victims] rather than *The Times*'s" (246).

So if Barker is historically inaccurate, what does her "Freudianization" of Rivers, and by extension, of the contemporary World War I canon, indicate? Introducing an interview with Barker, *Contemporary Literature* says of her trilogy, "It articulated many of the current concerns with national myths and public memory in Britain in the 1990s, particularly surrounding the First World War" (Brannigan, "Interview" 368). John Brannigan, in his critical book *Pat Barker*, says that "when [Barker] has set novels in the past, in the *Regeneration* trilogy for example, she has often been exploring the implications of the past for the present" (3). Read Barker as representing the desire of people in our day (assuming that her novels, published in the early 1990s, are still revelatory of the contemporary moment) to use a familiar therapeutic model to deal with a trauma that still bothers them as a holdover from the war that ended 100 years ago, and you might say that she is not simply (reductively) reading the war era as if it were only or best understandable from the mindset of the present.

Rather, she is showing that the impulse to deal with the war still lingers in the collective contemporary psyche. If that is what she accomplishes, then the point is neither that she has mistaken her own point of view for one that seamlessly applies to the world of the 1920s (Steffens' claim), nor that the war itself is being pulled into a contemporary framework, but that the past and the present as it regards the war must be collapsed together to achieve this hoped-for closure.

If we think we know Freud better than we do, or if the method that we now call "Freudian" is in fact pastiche, then let the work of correction begin (and that is Steffens' project). But whatever Barker's motivation, or however imprecise her method, the facts that she writes the war as she does and that people read and responded to her work with accolades (Man Booker Prize) betray a lingering doubt in the culture that the war is really over as far as collective memory is concerned. This is an argument that could also be extended to the texts of other writers, including, as will be shown below, to Urquhart's *The Underpainter*.

Barrett points out that within the first fifty pages of *Regeneration*, Freud is invoked four times (237). *The Eye in the Door* is almost equally redolent of mentions of the good doctor. At one point, jokingly, Billy Prior says in response to Rivers' suggestion that he would remedy a fantasy for men with sweaty feet with carbolic soap, "Really? A leap ahead of Dr Freud there, I think" (72). Later on, when Rivers is talking with Manning, who is in treatment because of the effects of his fears of being outed as gay, he takes a metanarrative approach: "'Are you familiar with the strict Freudian view of war neurosis'? he asked. Manning, he knew, had read a certain amount of Freud" (158). Read that as, "her audience, Barker knew, had read a certain amount of Freud," and you have pretty succinctly the argument offered above.

The plot of *The Eye in the Door* revolves around a series of marginally interconnected happenings, never fully resolving the question of whether the jailed Beattie Roper, who has been convicted of participating in a plot to kill the Prime Minister, will be released. It is hinted that she will, her conviction having come on a betrayal of one man by another when the latter was having a dissociative episode. But the point is less plot than portrayal of the psychological struggles of three men, and their therapist: Billy Prior, the dissociative one; Charles Manning, a closeted homosexual; and Siegfried Sassoon, whose case takes up a great deal of narrative in the first novel of this trilogy, *Regeneration*. Each is plagued with troubling dreams, and their doctor, WHR Rivers, also ends up having nightmares and performing self-analysis as well as inviting his patients to participate in his self-diagnosis. Barker's picture of these traumas, rooted in her interpretation of Freud's similar preoccupation, could be read as signaling the unhealed psychological remnants of the war lingering in the contemporary mind.

The first scene in *The Eye in the Door* is not over when Manning says to another character, "It *is* neurasthenia, isn't it?" (15, emphasis original), and says that Rivers "took one look at me and decided I was neurasthenic" (17). Manning reports being "in quite a state when I came out of the hospital," and relays the story of suddenly smashing a vase against the wall in the middle of a party (17). Later on the night when he tells this to Billy Prior, Manning walks out into London, and he has an episode where he cowers in the street as if a raid is going on. It feels "[l]ike being naked, high up on a ledge, somewhere, in full light, with beneath him only jeering voices and millions of eyes," the narrative indicates (26).

Even where Freud is not invoked specifically, the therapy-language that fills particularly the chapters featuring Rivers' interior monologue is recognizably pop-Freudian. Take for example Rivers' thoughts about Prior: "It was almost as if the experience—whatever it was—had triggered an attempt at dissociation of personality" (141). In typical Freudian fashion, this experience, we learn as events unfold, was in fact two. One reflected Prior's childhood, and the other was a tragedy in the trenches.

When Rivers is writing a report on military training, he indicates that for soldiers to best deal with the trauma of war, they should allow their imaginations to "play around the trials and dangers of warfare" (213). The alternative is to "carry out a prolonged system of repression by which morbid energy may be stored so as to form a kind of dump ready to explode on the occurrence of some mental shock or bodily illness" (216). Pretty much doctrinaire Freudianism to a (contemporary) audience well-schooled in what Barrett points out was a new and not entirely accepted notion—the discovery of the unconscious (Barrett 246).

Rivers gets so involved with his patients that he dreams what they dream. In one instance when this happens, he wakes up and stares into the darkness, "faintly amused that his identification with his patients should have reached the point where he dreamt *their* dreams rather than his own" (244, emphasis original). He becomes a sort of amalgam of doctor and patient through his clinical work. Having a nightmare, he awakens and concludes, "The dream was about dissociation," which is the diagnosis he ends up focusing on with Manning, Sassoon, and Prior and which I take to be the key to understanding the thematic relevance of this novel (164).

Manning becomes a patient when the "anxiety attacks he'd suffered ever since his return from France had become more severe, partly as a result of his obsession with the Pemberton Billing affair," which was a trial at which various people were outed as homosexual (151). He sees Rivers, who describes the general process which has led to the trial using quite perfect Freudian language: "[S]adistic impulses are aroused that would normally be repressed, and that also causes anxiety" (156). Manning's trouble, it turns out, stemmed from dreams that recurred in the wake of an experience of seeing a soldier under his command sink into the Flanders mud and disappear. He ended up shooting the man, for the good of the others, and now lives with what he describes as "a waking dream" in which he sees a grasping hand and hears a voice asking "Where's Scudder?" which was the soldier's name (173, 167, 168). The experience "out there," to Manning, didn't allow him to process the horror of things. "When I was out there, I could be in blood up to the elbow, it didn't bother me. It's almost as if instead of normal feelings being cut off, there aren't any divisions left at all. Everything washes into everything else. I don't know if that makes sense" (171). Rivers says that it does, but in saying so, he contradicts his opinion rendered in other cases, that of Sassoon and Prior, which suggests that dissociation—the ability to be two persons—is a survival mechanism, albeit problematic when trying to integrate into civilian life.

Sassoon provides the best proof of this. His story, much more fully rendered in *Regeneration*, is dragged into *The Eye in the Door* in the late going. His take on the war is that, "I survive out there by being two people, sometimes I manage to be both of them in the same evening" (229). Things started to fall apart when he could no longer dissociate: "I'd always coped with the situation by blocking out the killing side, cutting it off, and then suddenly one's brought face to face with the fact that, no, actually there's only one person there and that person is a potential killer of Huns" (231). Rivers, in his mulling over what Sassoon has said, takes it as a given that "most of us survive by cultivating internal divisions" (233). He shortly elaborates, "Siegfried had always coped with the war by being two people: the anti-war poet and pacifist; the bloodthirsty, efficient company commander. The dissociation couldn't be called pathological, since experience gained in one state was available to the other" (233). Billy Prior is a different case, however. It was "[a]lmost as if his mind had created a warrior double, a creature formed out of Flanders clay" (245). The trouble was, "he had brought it home with him" (245).

Prior's dissociative personality is the most powerfully portrayed element of the novel, and it takes up the good part of Barker's attention. Fully half a dozen times, if not more, his mental state is on display, beginning when he has a waking dream about being back in a childhood scene which ends in a nightmare (55–58). He is analyzed by Rivers, who recognizes with a shock that there are two Priors—the patient, whom he had seen earlier at Craiglockhart, and the public Prior, who was "formidable" (76).

His next scene occurs at night, at a cattle pen where Prior is to meet a character called Mac. The scene becomes both surreal and mixed up with dreams and memories from the past, and while he does meet and have a conversation with Mac, the scene ends with him falling into a children's trench but mixing it up for the real thing. This then gives way to his thinking that he is his own (abusive) father, and then (apparently) reintegrating into his own person, having sex with a woman who had nursed him as a child (117-18).

Shortly after this, he loses three hours in the middle of the day, his "fugue," as Rivers will later name it (134), the result of reading the name of a friend on a casualty list (123). The narrative tells us, "[H]e was aware, somewhere on the fringes of his consciousness, that it was not 'a little disturbance.'

Cross of Sacrifice, Lindenhoek Chalet Military Cemetery, Belgium

Something catastrophic had happened" (123). Later, when a man named Spragge follows Prior and his girlfriend, Sarah, on a boat (Spragge is connected with the Beattie Roper episode), Prior fights him, but afterwards has no recollection of doing so (190).

Finally, he visits Rivers as his other self, this person claiming, "I was born two years ago. In a shell-hole in France. I have no father" (240). By this time, the cruelty of Prior's father to his mother is well documented in the text. To anyone familiar with popular narratives of personal trauma, the psychic dissociation of Prior and other-Prior is easily understandable. Rivers' consciousness describes it by saying, "Prior had created a state whose freedom from fear and pain was persistent, encapsulated, inaccessible to normal consciousness" (245). He continues to have bad dreams, now mostly about his childhood, rather than the war, a fact that Rivers sees as progress (252).

Prior realizes that in the role of his dissociated other, he had betrayed Mac, though he does not remember this.

The cost was both to Mac and to Beattie Roper, who each remains in prison, Roper for the aforementioned plot, and Mac as someone who will not do his war duty. Though he is never quite satisfied that he understands why he betrayed Mac, Prior does understand that thinking through the past is his mind's way of trying to admit and get beyond his betrayal of his childhood friends and helpers (255). Summing up his feelings about what he has done, Prior thinks, "What had happened was altogether darker, more complex" than simply saying that he did his duty as a soldier in bringing Mac in (266). And this realization effectively ends the plot of this novel, which veers off to Sassoon before briefly having Manning and Prior meet once more to discuss moving on with life.

As it winds towards its end, the novel reinforces the power of the war itself in creating identity. Prior concludes, "[I]f you asked anybody who'd fought in France whether he thought he was the same person he'd been before the war...*all of them* would say no. It was merely a matter of degree. And one did feel at times very powerfully that the only loyalties that actually mattered were loyalties forged there. Picard clay was a powerful glue" (255, emphasis original).

Ultimately, the question for all of these analysands is the one that Barker's novel forces the contemporary audience to reckon with as well: whether it is healthy to be dis-integrated in personality. To be two people is a survival mechanism, but at the same time, it comes with danger. For Prior, it means that he is able to perform acts that he doesn't recall, including betraying a friend and thus participating in the incrimination of Beattie Roper. Rivers sums up with a seeming contradiction, thinking of Sassoon: "Perhaps, contrary to what was usually supposed, duality was the stable state; the attempt at integration, dangerous" (235). The same statement could apply to contemporary culture still fixated on a 100-year-old war.

Like *The Eye in the Door, The Ghost Road* extends the Freudianization of Rivers' method, dealing with his analyses of several cases in scenes sprinkled through the book, though there is no single overt reference to Freud. The language used is unmistakably Barker-adapted Freud, however, as in the following example, taken from a scene where Rivers is contemplating his childhood. There was a picture of his uncle, Will, who had survived the horrors of having a leg cut off during an earlier war. Rivers has apparently suppressed the memory of it, but after a conversation with his sister he starts to recall it, and to analyze himself in relation to it: "Had he also deliberately suppressed the visual image of it, making it impossible for himself to see it in his mind's eye?" (95). Prior has apparently participated in an earlier conversation on the matter, for Rivers now recalls that he, "told that Rivers attributed his almost total lack of visual memory to an event in his childhood that he had succeeded in forgetting, has said brutally, 'You were raped or beaten,'" and Rivers has to agree with the idea, though not with the notion that the experience had been as severe as Prior proposes (95). But as Rivers contemplates the image, he asks, "Was this *the* suppressed memory? He didn't know" (96, emphasis original). The notion that early repressed trauma creates adult personality is unquestioned, by either Rivers or Prior.

The picture, of his uncle having the stump of his leg cauterized by hot tar, now appears to him in singular detail: "not the blood, not the knife, but that resolutely clenched mouth"—the silent mouth, which he now deals with on an everyday basis in his practice with shell-shocked World War I soldiers (96). His job, he thinks, is to say to the men, "Go on… cry. It's all right to grieve. Breakdown's nothing to be ashamed of—the pressures were intolerable" (96). This, as critics like Shaddock have pointed out, speaks to the task of Rivers the curer of shell shock. His task is to get them to speak,

but also "stop crying. Get up on your feet. Walk," and thus
return to the war (96). It is a tension based in class-bound,
culture-bound ideals that he ultimately comes to recognize as
false. As John Lewis-Stempel explains, "Only understood in
retrospect is that officers who literally 'put on a brave face'
suppressed emotions, and the effect was to suppress their
mental defenses over time" (292). Shaddock says that the
dying cry of the character Hallet, which is interpreted as
saying, "it's not worth it," speaks to Rivers, becoming
"a visceral howl against the codes of British masculinity, the
glorious warrior ethic, that perpetuates the war" (670).

Focusing on this theme allows one to forgive *The Ghost
Road* for plot lines that tend to be open and undetermined,
even to the end of the text. The last we see of Dr. Rivers, he
is dealing with the dying Hallet, afterwards slumping at
the nurses' station, nearly asleep on the job, a vision of the
Melanesian Njiru's voice coming to him (Barker 276)[76]. We
part from Billy Prior as he dies after having been wounded in
battle (273). Even Barker's slide toward the symbolic—as for
example in Rivers' vision: "A long moment, and then the
brown face, with its streaks of lime, faded into the light of
the daytime ward" (276). This vision—which appears to be
a double of Prior's death, reported just before: "He gazed at his
reflection in the water, which broke and reformed and
broke again as bullets hit the surface and then, gradually, as
the numbness spread, he ceased to see it"—does not create
closure (273).

Brannigan points out that in many of Barker's works the
key motif is "dereliction—physical, economic, social,
emotional, and psychological" (3). This leads Barker to depict
the trauma experienced by those "living close to the margins
of physical and economic survival," such as her soldier

---

76 Large intercut sections in this novel concern Rivers' earlier trip to Melanesia,
   where he worked with Njiru on anthropological research.

characters (3). His claim to follow is crucial: "Barker's novels contain scenes of recovered memory, displaced memory, relived or anamnestic memory, and in each case there is a larger political and historical conflict being played out in the memory crises of particular individuals" (4). The "inability of shell-shock victims to distinguish the remembered from the real...for example, serves to bring into critical focus the European narratives of modernity and rationality which underpin the war" (4). Or, as Margaret Higgonet describes the time, it was "a period of crisis at the threshold of modernism, when forms broke up" (vi).

Thus *The Ghost Road* features memory, but not as the closed loop of thinking about the past. Rather, the memories the key characters ruminate on lead forward, creating narratives that remain unresolved, just as the plotlines in the novel are open when the last page is turned. Barker has not left this matter unremarked upon. Billy Prior, back at the Front, writes in his notebook, reflecting as he does so on the act of writing: "I think it's a way of claiming immunity. First-person narrators can't die, so as long as we keep telling the story of our own lives we're safe. Ha bloody fucking ha" (115).

Largely speaking, and especially if we read *The Ghost Road* as displaying Rivers' Freudian psychotherapeutic method, that's what the doctor's job is as well—to make up (or recover) stories that help men make sense of what they have not been able to speak out. As Prior describes it in his narration while near the Front waiting be called back to battle, "He'd thought of them [war souvenirs from his first deployment] often at Craiglockhart as Rivers probed his mind for buried memories of his last few weeks in France. Souvenirs, my God. When the mind will happily wipe itself clean in the effort to forget" (145). Talking, for Billy Prior, cannot exist at the level of narrative memory outside of the smallest frame of reference. This is why words like "honour" and "courage" lead to "vomit

Cross of Sacrifice, Oxford (Botley) Cemetery, England

vomit vomit" and the powerful words are now the little ones, like "us, them, we, they, here, there" (257).

In reducing language to its essentials, Prior has become like the childhood Rivers, who had been slapped by his father for crying at the barber shop, an incident that in retrospect probably was a reflection of his horror at the picture of his uncle having his leg cut off. Rivers asks, "[W]hat had it meant—Trafalgar, the Napoleonic wars—to a four year-old for whom a summer's day was endless? Nothing, it could have meant nothing" (95). Like Prior, he had no way to contextualize the experience, no story to tell himself to make things feel right. Instead, he has only the visceral reaction that the soldier has, a bodily memory as much as a textualized one. As Jennifer Shaddock says, "[W]ar neurosis was a psychic compromise between the British masculine ideals of duty, honor, and patriotism and the individual's instinct to survive" (662). We could take that as indicating the opposition between values, which rely on narrative to construct and pass them on, and experience, which tests them. Whatever the case, for both Prior and Rivers, stories will always be told, but not of grand battles and great victories. Rather, as Prior says, "Only the names meant anything. Mons, Loos, the Somme, Arras, Verdun, Ypres," and only to those who have experienced action in the places corresponding to those names (257).

Conventionally, a war novel ends with the death of its protagonist, and in *The Ghost Road* we have the working-class figure Billy Prior meeting his end.[77] But take Prior's earlier narration as a gloss on both his death and the final scene with Rivers envisioning Njiru: "Ghosts everywhere. Even the living were only ghosts in the making. You learned to ration your commitment to them. This moment in this tent already had the quality of *remembered* experience" (46, emphasis original). The novel itself thus can be figured as a site where memory about the war and desire for healing from its long-forgotten wounds meet and as a reflection on the cultural conditions that demanded and received it along with its mates in the *Regeneration* trilogy. Taken together, they betray a contemporary cultural longing for story as a strategy to make sense of past trauma.

The opposite is true of Urquhart's *The Underpainter*, because its protagonist, the American painter Austin Fraser, has no traumatic memories, because he missed the war, and thus no way to code trauma. He begins with a declaration: "Even though there is nothing in me that wants to court the past, it fills my mind, enters my painting. The *tock, tock* of my cane striking ice is like the noise that beads make as they click together on a string. It is the sound of memory at work, creating a necklace of narrative" (9). Yet he resists memory because he has never managed to create lasting relationships, not even with his girlfriend/model Sara or his best friend in Canada, where he spends his summers, George Kearns, and as time goes by and the war comes and goes, memory becomes precisely what divides Fraser from his Canadian friends. His lack

---

77 See Barrett's discussion of working-class Billy Prior (247).

of war memories, because he did not participate, combines with the absence of any facility in understanding their shell shock to render the divide between them unbridgeable and to indicate why, in Canada (not to say other former British Empire countries), war stories still need to be told.[78]

The friendship of the two young men is broken early, with George heading off to the Great War, his expectations simple: "I expect I'll be killed in the war anyway" (87). He is not killed, but returns from the war with shell shock, as does his post-war companion, Augusta. Her trauma is less visible than George's, which has physical manifestations. She is troubled, however, by the fact that she has mercy-killed her friend, Maggie, via overuse of anesthetic after Maggie is brought to her operating theater with grave and horrifying wounds (238). One can only imagine what Rivers might have done to help her deal with this trauma.

After both she and George are many years home following the war's conclusion, they receive a visit from Austin, accompanied by George's former lover, Vivian. George declares when they meet, "Everything about me has changed completely," to which Vivian says, "Not in my view, you haven't" (278). But the truth is that aside from a tremor, he suffers from internal afflictions that the Americans have no capacity to understand. Austin realizes that "[George] is hiding something terrible...something he isn't able to remove from the expression on his face" (281). Yet the trouble is that Austin, being the reader's eyes, has no category into which he can slot the difference, the Freudian discourse so familiar now not apparently having filtered into his mind, even as late as 1937.

Austin has a conversation with Augusta in which she tells the American about the light in France during the war, and about what it was like in the military hospital dealing with all

---

78 My argument sets aside the motif of painting and questions relating to art and canonicity that are featured in a significant portion in the text.

of the dying. But at one point, Austin reports, "She stopped speaking [...] and looked at me, remembering, I suppose, that I had experienced neither battles nor casualties" (290). She endeavors to explain, saying, "It is astonishing to me...how a world—a complete social system—can be constructed and then dismantled, just like that" (294). She tells him how Maggie had been killed, and how she herself had returned from the war unable to remember the events. She had learned, she says, how to "anesthetize herself, to put herself into a great darkness, a dreamless [dissociative?] sleep. Her return to the world...was like a return from diethyl ether, but more gradual, more prolonged" (296).

As he listens, Austin is acutely aware that he is the American displaced in Canada, observing shell shock from a distance, because he lives in a disengaged world of art that does not seem to respond to the modern truth that the war in Europe has happened, even though it has been over for nearly two decades when these scenes take place. She tells him of being in a shell shock hospital back home, and of her reawakening, which had at first been joyous, but then turned dark as she remembered that her brother, Fred, was dead, and that she had killed Maggie (298). Her declaration wakes Austin up a little bit: "What were any of us to do with the rest of our lives anyway? After all that. We were only in our early twenties and our lives were finished. And yet here we are, George and me, right in the middle of the aftermath. What makes it just continue and continue?" (299). Austin's narration tells us, "I had no answer for this," and of course he doesn't, being a nonparticipant for whom the war is now just a part of time past (299).

And yet despite being away, somewhere else, somewhere lost—a walking fragment of the 19th century who feels somehow like he can remain on that island—the American, forced to confront the war trauma of the Canadian, has to confront also the onrushing 20th century, with its Freudian shock. This happens when he learns the desperation to which George had sunk during the war. He was a pigeon dispatcher, but during the battle of Passchendaele, the birds were so confused and the noise so loud that they could not fly. "It was then," Austin's narrative voice reports, "that George knew that language in all its forms was becoming irrelevant, that nothing in the mayhem around him could or should be documented" (301). This feeling is at least partly explained by the way Randall Stevenson explains Great War poetry, which could no longer rely on familiar language but came to depend instead on "accumulated fragments" to convey the misery the writers observed (167). "Successions of barely connected images, unsentimentally recorded, evoke the ruined landscape of the trenches—and the uneasiness of its observer," he writes (Stevenson 175).

When Austin goes upstairs in the morning to find both George and Augusta dead from morphine overdoses, he also finds George's porcelain collection shattered. It is a final message to his American friend, who had never appreciated the beauty of the collection, and it says precisely what George wished to communicate, "[T]hat I had never understood, that I was responsible" (312). His language is not that of the psychotherapist, though the events are a direct reaction to the psychological trauma stemming from what had happened in the war. But at least he can credit the war for these events, recognizing that the relationship of George and Augusta is rooted in "their shared war, their shared recovery, their knowledge of this for all the years after" (308).

A contemporary Canadian friend of George and Augusta's observing this aftermath might easily say that their shell shock had never been cured, despite their release from hospital.

Austin Fraser doesn't have that language at his disposal, and his tendency to distance himself from others doesn't allow him to penetrate further than to repeat what he has been told. Augusta had earlier said to him, "[D]o you know what George would say to me? He would say that there was no place in such a beautiful world for unhappiness such as ours" (304). Later, when Austin walks down the street on a bright, sunny morning, he expresses his desire: "I wanted to believe in a new, clean light, wanted to believe that it would banish forever the dark rooms behind George's China Hall" (325).[79] But it is how he ends the declaration that betrays his lack of understanding of the power and tragedy of shell shock, and by extension of the events of the war. He says simply this: "The examined past" (325). Even a hint of analysis, taking the word both in the common sense and to mean treatment, is something he has no interest in.

This sends out a signal to the contemporary reader educated by a novelist like Barker to expect a Freudian approach to the aftereffects of the Great War: Austin Fraser's reaction is oddly foreign, a signal of his Americanness. This, in turn, points past Austin the character to the contemporary canon of fiction written in the US, which is decidedly bereft (though not entirely so) of Great War fiction.

That this occurs to the reader also points in the other direction, signifying that for someone with a British/Commonwealth cultural heritage, the Great War is still coded as a site of psychological trauma that demands telling. That the language to do so is provided by the wealth of contemporary fiction about the war is what allows people to wrestle with the grief it has left as a legacy.

---

79 The store where George sold his artistic China pieces and behind and above which he lived.

When All That's Left
Is Imagination:
The grammar of remembering

The belated revival of the Great War as traced through the fiction collected and analyzed here is no mere extravagance. This literature, incredible in its variety of form, scope, and reach, should be read as a sign that World War I is not lost to time despite these texts existing at a moment when individual memory of the war has been erased. Nobody who remembers the war as a combatant currently remains alive. Only a handful of people exist who have any memory of the time period itself. Hence any memory that exists outside of theirs is collective, in the sense that it is assembled out of the memories of others.

This term, collective memory, suggests the ways in which historical events are preserved down the generations, a process which is inevitably social. As Fabian says, "[A]s a cognitive faculty memory can only be attributed to individual minds (or brains); in that sense collectivities cannot remember," which is why "[a]s a social practice, memory is a communicative practice; all narrated memory is in that sense collective" (93).[80]

---

80 Here he uses the same term as Assmann to mean something slightly shifted. Assmann would see communicative memory as something more immediate and the accretion of it at the cultural level as cultural or collective memory. See the discussion in Chapter 4.

Since nobody has cognition of events not experienced, all that is left about the war down into the present is collective memory in the form of story.[81]

Naturally, when an ethnographer talks about story, he or she is not necessarily meaning finely wrought story in the sense that fiction is that. It might be unformed tales or stream-of-consciousness narrative that is being referred to. However, if we are talking about the act of writing about the war in the form of fiction, what is in mind are stories that fall into the category Fabian describes when defining collective memory: that which is "in need of being preserved, cared for, protected against an outside" (94). The collective, the group, places value on its stories. They are not simply "public memory," or memory which is known outside the individual. That type of memory might even be promoted through things like commemorations without being shared (94). In contrast, collective memory is shared, and hence valued. This, too, points to desire.

The impulse to remember what can't, in fact, be recalled other than at secondhand motivates writers to embrace the Great War as both a cultural heritage and a burden, something readers can learn from and that they almost inexplicably are drawn back to, but also something that, in the present, is always the product not of its own reality but of later reinvention of it. If events of 100 years ago shape the collective mind today, then such memories must not be in a form that begins in fact and then moves to fiction, but in a form that begins in fiction and then works its way into minds and lives as fact because collectively remembered. Memory in this way plays tricks with time.

---

81 Collective memory as a concept, in an interesting coincidence with our interest in the Great War, is a term coined in the 1920s by Maurice Halbwachs (Rigney 616). His focus was "small-scale communities like the family or the parish, though later expansions of his idea put collective memory into the context of the nation" (617).

Tyne Cot Cemetery, Belgium

So does the Great War itself. Winter eloquently explains that the 20th century was lived looking backwards at the war, a fact reflected in literature and art. The reason for this was "the universality of grief and mourning in Europe from 1914" (223). People had a public life of mourning, but they also dealt with grief privately.[82] In one sense, the continued fixation on the Great War shows that, while contemporary people have no *particular* grief, the grief they feel is not the less real for that. While a person may not lament the loss of a remembered grandfather, those who live with the war's legacy still deal with "the timeless questions about the truncation of millions of lives, about promise unfulfilled, about the evanescence of hope" (Winter 224). They (or we) are survivors at a distance, but they (or we) still mourn. Or perhaps better, they refuse to let go out of fear that, when mourning is over, forgetting will have begun. Winter describes the process of bereavement as a series of stages, suggesting that the "process

---

82 Audoin-Rouzeau and Becker have three excellent chapters on this in *14–18: Understanding the Great War*. See Section III, "Mourning."

of separation from the dead…[is] of forgetting as much as remembering" (224).

Consider the claims of Smethurst and Craps in their article on Pat Barker's *The Ghost Road*: "The…centenary of the First World War will no doubt bring with it a reshuffling and reconsideration of the way that this particular war is memorialized in a variety of cultural contexts" (142). Then, pointing out that the last soldier, Claude Choules, died in May 2011, they say, "[T]his confluence of memories will necessarily take place through the circulation of existing primary or secondary texts, lending an extra urgency to the task of critically re-examining canonical representations of the war, [and] mapping their continuing contributions to twenty-first–century identity construction" (142). True as far as it goes, but there's something more.

Julian Barnes, speaking through the fictional narrator of his novel *The Sense of An Ending*, says this: "[W]hat you end up remembering isn't always the same as what you have witnessed" (3). Describing a scene in a history class where the teacher is challenging a student to come up with a reason why one might say that Henry VIII's reign was full of unrest, Barnes has character Finn say, "But there is one line of thought according to which all you can truly say of any historical event—even the outbreak of the First World War, for example—is that 'something happened,'" the point being that as the past recedes into history, it grows vague to the point of shadowy outlines (5). Of course, the (positivist) historian can't abide the idea, and even the teacher in Barnes' novel responds to the claim by saying, "Well, that would put me out of a job, wouldn't it?" (6).

The point comes up again sometime later when the class debates the causes of the war. Most want an either-or answer:

it was Princip's fault, or it was the fault of unstoppable historical forces. But one answer that is given seems more true to the
way that history is really remembered, and that is as follows:
"[T]hat everything was down to chance, that the world existed
in a state of perpetual chaos, and only some primitive storytelling instinct, itself doubtless a hangover from religion, ret-
rospectively implied meaning on what might or might not
have happened" (12). The point, notice, is not what might or
might not have happened. That is taken as lost. The idea,
rather, is to look at the stories themselves, sort out their contradictions, understand their rationale, and live with the fact
that we will never know, but that what can be studied is what
we think we know.

Later still, the narrator reflects on what he knows about
memory from the point of view of an older person. "History,"
he says, "isn't the lies of the victors…. It's more the memories
of the survivors, most of whom are neither victorious nor
defeated" (61). Even within one lifetime and concerning one's
own life, there can be little certainty. Tony says, "[A]s the
witnesses to your life diminish, there is less corroboration,
and therefore less certainty, as to what you are or have
been" (66). But the irony is that ancient history, Greece and
Rome and so forth, seems more certain. At least, Tony claims,
it is "the history that's been more or less agreed upon" (67).
What he doesn't say, of course, is that this is only the case
because the point of view of the historian has been accepted
uncritically as an accurate space from which to interpret what
sources there are. But he gets closer to the truth when he talks
about his own history: "[T]he history that happens
underneath our noses ought to be the clearest, and yet it's
the most deliquescent. We live in time, it bounds us and
defines us, and time is supposed to measure history, isn't it?
But if we can't understand time…what chance do we have

with history—even our own small, personal, largely undocumented piece of it?" (66).

We have no chance only if we believe in the idea that we have to make sense of history, to untangle it, see it from a broad perspective, when in fact, if it's right under our noses, as he says, our point of view can't help but be partial. We have only fragments, viewed from a singular perspective. But as time passes, and especially when we're dealing with events that we did not experience, we gain something—a longer view. If the result is a loss—the loss that comes with, as Tony says, agreeing on what happened—then the benefit is that we may also tell and retell (invented) stories without fearing that we damage "truth."

Fabian claims, "Remembering, especially in the hortative sense of commemoration, that is, something that is to be done, performed, or fulfilled, calls for stories to be told," and if his point ended there, we would have a useful formula for valorizing contemporary Great War fiction as memory (99–100).

British Grave Markers, Tyne Cot Cemetery

The Cenotaph, Whitehall, London

However, he goes on to say, as discussed in an earlier chapter, "Yet stories…are lies" (100). His notion, speaking as an anthropologist, is to emphasize that "we should not lose sight of the truth and rationality aspects of memory" (100). This sounds like his focus is on an outmoded notion based in positivism, but his concept is anything but as he goes on to say that we should remember that academic and popular thought are not, in fact, diametrically opposed, but rather two aspects of the same dialectic process (100).

What does that say for fiction? Perhaps that in a moment when story-as-remembrance is historically out of reach and fact-as-remembrance is suspect, story-as-fact is all we have. Fiction, remembrances of the war created by others who themselves did not live through what they describe, remains our inheritance. What we make of it is what matters, not whether we can attach it somehow to, or reduce it to, verifiable "facts."

As we get further from the war, we inevitably get further from memory of one sort. Kabir helps by introducing the idea of "postmemory," which I previously cited as described by Marianne Hirsch. Postmemory is that which "characterizes the experience of those who grow up dominated by narratives that preceded their birth, whose own belated stories are displaced by stories of the previous generation, shaped by traumatic events that they can neither understand nor create…" (qtd. in Kabir 180). She goes on: "[It is] a space of remembrance, more broadly available through cultural and public, and not merely individual and personal, acts of remembrance, identification and projection" (qtd. in Kabir 180). This, then, might be the clue that can allow us to build a bridge back one hundred years to the war. Confronted with our own forgetting, we must loop backwards, Kipling's chosen quotation for the Stone of Remembrance—"Their name liveth for

Tyne Cot Cemetery, Belgium

evermore"—perhaps functioning as a warning more than
a prediction. We worry that if not for what we do, in this generation, their names won't live, but become like some dead
language of the past, a relic, not a tool of communication. So
we act, becoming part of the "voluntary witnesses to the event,
a volunteer 'army' of witnesses who choose, like the original
volunteers of 1914–17, to make ourselves part of a mass movement" (Williams *Media, Memory* 267). Thus we "keep faith
with 'spectral images' of the past, to the point of keeping
faith 'with us who die' as John McCrae first called on us to
do" (267). But does that equal remembering?

The person and memory of Harry Patch allow me to inter-
rogate this. Patch lived through and remembered the war, and
in his later life, he talked about it.[83] His recollections were
recorded with video and audio records, and they survive in
the form of written accounts of him as a person and of his
memories. I have read the books about and by him. Thus
while I do not remember the war, I remember what Harry

---

83 Though for decades he wouldn't, as he explains in his book *The Last Fighting
Tommy*, co-written with Richard van Emden (199).

Patch remembered about the war. In 2012, I visited his grave, a monument like many others commemorating his life and listing the date of his death. While I was there, I commemorated his life, though I had never met him. All of these actions were attempts to close an uncloseable distance, not between him and me, but between Harry Patch's experiences of the war and my own lack of the same. In some measure, perhaps symbolic, I inherit Patch's memories because our lives overlapped, I have read his words, and I have visited his grave.

In the aftermath of the war and through the first part of the 21st century, "people had to live with the shadow of war. The dead were there, in one way or another, living among the living. In their public ceremonies on Armistice Day and in their private thoughts and dreams, the survivors had to live with the fallen," Winter says (144). We don't share this burden, in one sense, because while the graves are still there, our memories cannot be firsthand, because we are not survivors. We came after. But then why, when we are not surrounded by the dead in the same way people who knew them and lost them were, do we continue to mourn them, if, as I have been arguing, that's what we are doing by writing about them?

The value of this collective memory is not that it assures individual recollection, which is now impossible. "We will never forget" thus cannot be said in earnest by anyone alive today. Rather, it might be more accurate to say, "We will never forget to remember" *pace* Fabian, or, to extend it in my own direction, "We may not remember, but we will not forget that we must remember the act of forgetting." Memory becomes what Fabian describes when he says, "Memory…is communicated and shared more widely than individual recollections of events. It acquires its collective functions largely through modes of representation sanctioned by literature and other media, and while it may evoke painful and disturbing experiences it usually has a positive, soothing effect" (111).

There is a key function assigned to stories, in the form of novels.

> [They] *prepar[e]* *the ground for a belief in a general human-*
> *ity by generating empathy with other people's existence*
> *through immersion in fictional stories.…* [S]*hared stories at*
> *a local and national level are effective by capturing people's*
> *attention and imagination through the immersive depiction*
> *of singular individuals and their experiences across time.*
> (Rigney 621)

The emphasis is on how novels can create bonds between people, say, in different places in Europe without making recourse to traditional nationalistic means of forming identity. However, for my purposes, the claim could as easily suggest that novels can bind people of British and other Commonwealth heritage together (or perhaps, in the case of the Irish, drive them away) as they make reference to a shared past. What happens is a kind of triangulation where, say, a fictional British soldier is "immersively depicted," to borrow and adapt the term Rigney offers, and experienced by a young person from London and an older person from Toronto. Both become able to understand their shared heritage in memory of the Great War as they observe the character and understand his values and experiences. "Given the nature of artistic production, this 'thickening' of the relations between individuals across great distances is a largely unplanned and noninstitutionalized process," Rigney says (622).

It is said well here:

> *Memory is an interpretive process. It is not a simple re-pre-*
> *senting of events as they unfolded, but rather a complex pro-*
> *cess of highlighting and erasing. Cultural memories can be*
> *preserved only through articulation, and repeated acts of*
> *narration leave traces on the memory itself. How it has been*
> *articulated in the past becomes part of how it is remembered*
> *in the present.* (Turner and Falgout 122)

Stone of Remembrance, Lindenhoek Chalet Military Cemetery, Belgium

The novels I look at here are involved in this process of change, and even as they shift the past, they preserve it in a living and tangible way in the present and thus ensure that this past will exist for the future.

Thus when later writers contribute more story, the scale that we judge them on is not, necessarily, how accurate they are, but on what they're doing and why, and the simple answer to the "why" question might be hiding in the etymology of the word "memory" itself. "The English word *remember* is derived from the Latin word *memorari*, and *memorari* shares a core of meaning with *narrare*, the source of the English word *narrate*" (Turner and Falgout 105, italics original). Stories, thus, may be validated as memory. In fact, for our sakes, they better be, because they are all we have left that is a product of the present.

Think about that. All we have left that is tangible, changing, exciting, and alive with respect to the Great War are the stories that people *now* create. It's a strange idea, but seeing what is now created as having value, not the same as "real" or firsthand memories, but because it too exists on a plane of meaning that does not demand verification or authentication but can simply exist to tell the truth for itself, gives these latter-day, second-hand, after-thoughts the same gravity as the narratives created by the war's participants, or even firsthand memory of the events of the war themselves.[84]

Perhaps Smethurst and Craps are right, and the continued presence and production of these novels points to "fulfillment of a wish for a racially defined British national unity in the face of increasingly fractured postcolonial identities" (143). If so, "remembrance of the First World War can grant nostalgic access to a time before the influx of formerly subjugated peoples into Britain forced the colonizers into an unwelcome confrontation with the Other whom the centre/periphery divide had previously kept at bay" (143). But I prefer to see the situation less reductively, or at least, not as signaling only the racism that may rest at the core of contemporary Britain or British identity construction as a legacy of Empire. Rather, it would seem that we could view the situation as a product of the complex interaction of trauma, sorrow, commemoration, a felt need to remember, memory itself, both latent and observable, and other factors (which may, of course, include postcolonial anxiety) all of which add up to the continuing presence of the Great War at the core of the contemporary psyche of British, Canadian, and other citizens of the English-speaking countries mostly closely connected together during the conflict.

Or perhaps Boyne's narrator in *The Absolutist*, already discussed at length here, is correct, and the grammar of the past-in-present is always and only conditional, not in the sense of what might have been, but what has been made in the absence of the thing-in-itself. When discussing the need to remember,

---

84 As Turner and Falgout point out more than once, verification or authentication is the preferred mode of knowing in the West, cf. 105.

Geoff Dyer says that writer Timothy Findley "acknowledges that the most vivid feature of the Great War is that *it took place in the past*" (83, emphasis original). That sounds obvious, but then he explains that in novels that talk about the time before the war, there is always this sense of it already having happened. The Great War has always been problematic as a function of time.

Dyer describes a couple having tea at Thiepval as presented in the novel *Birdsong* by saying, "The future presses on the lovers like the dead weight of a geographical strata. The Great War took place in the past—even when it lay in the future" (84). Then he adds his zinger: "To us, it *always* took place in the past" (84). That sounds like a simple statement of fact, so let's adjust the grammar a little: "To us, the Great War *has always taken* place in the past," we could say, and the idea would be to suggest via use of the perfect tense that it is not simply a fixed event of the past, but an event of the past that is constantly being surveyed in the present. It not only happened, therefore; it is happening, now, through

Stone of Remembrance, Edinburgh

what we read and write. Because it was traumatic, it carries into the present the character of trauma. That is, it always outpaces the mind's capacity to comprehend it. Another formulation might work as a gloss. Visiting a war cemetery, Dyer concludes as follows: "The war, it begins to seem, had been fought in order that it might be remembered, that it might live up to its memory" (15). Past, the presentness of the event, and future are inseparable in the grammar of memory concerning the Great War.

It shouldn't surprise us that the war is remembered. But nor should it trouble us that the memory of it takes on new forms with each new generation. Fiction written after the fact can be said to be commemoration. It is not the dead thing that a monument is (that is not to say not meaningful). Rather, it lives in a way that the words of Christ suggest in the statement, "Do this in remembrance of me." The idea is to remember not as a static monument, but bodily—in a recreation of His acts, in actions. Reading a war novel is not being in the

Gravestone of Harry Patch, Somerset, England

trenches, nor is writing one. But the novel can remind us of what it was like there, or, to go back to the matter of grammar, invoke the feeling of *having been* there.

The day when novels about the Great War cease to be written is the moment when we pass inevitably from commemoration to monument. That time, it can be safely said from the present historical position, is yet in the future. Perhaps, it will never come at all.

Works Cited

Adelman, Jeremy. "Remembering in Latin America." *Journal of Interdisciplinary History*, vol. 39, no. 3, Winter 2009, pp. 387–98.

Assmann, Jan and John Czaplicka. "Collective Memory and Cultural Identity." *New German Critique*, vol. 65, Spring-Summer 1995, pp. 125–33.

Audoin-Rouzeau, Stéphane and Annette Becker. *14–18: Understanding the Great War*. Trans. by Catherine Temerson. Hill and Wang-Farrar, Straus, and Giroux, 2002.

Bakhtin, M. M. "Discourse in the Novel." *The Dialogic Imagination: Four Essays*. Ed. by Michael Holquist. Trans. by Caryl Emerson and Michael Holquist. U of Texas P, 1981, pp. 259–422.

———*Rabelais and His World*. Trans. by Helene Iswolsky. Indiana UP, 1984.

Barker, Pat. *The Eye in the Door* (1993). Plume-Penguin, 1995.

———. *The Ghost Road* (1995). Plume-Penguin, 1996.

———. *Life Class* (2007). Anchor, 2008.

———. *Regeneration* (1991). Plume-Penguin, 1993.

———. *Toby's Room* (2012). Anchor-Random, 2013.

Barnes, Julian. *The Sense of an Ending* (2011). Vintage International-Random, 2012.

Barrett, Michèle. "Pat Barker's *Regeneration* Trilogy and the Freudianization of Shell Shock." *Contemporary Literature*, vol. 53, no. 2, 2012, pp. 237–260.

Barry, Sebastian. *A Long Long Way*. Viking-Penguin, 2005.

Berliner, David. "The Abuses of Memory: Reflections on the Memory Boom in Anthropology." *Anthropological Quarterly*, vol. 78, no. 1, Winter 2005, pp. 197–211.

Bishop, Alan and Mark Bostridge, eds. *Letters from a Lost Generation: First World War Letters of Vera Brittain and Four Friends*. Abacus-Little Brown, 1999.

Boag, Simon. "Freudian Repression, the Common View, and Pathological Science." *Review of General Psychology 2006*, vol. 10, no. 1, 2006, pp. 74–80.

Boyd, William. *An Ice-Cream War* (1983). Vintage-Random, 1999.

Boyden, Joseph. *Three Day Road: A Novel* (2005). Orion-Phoenix, 2006.

Boyne, John. *The Absolutist.* Other, 2011.

Brannigan, John. "An Interview with Pat Barker." *Contemporary Literature* vol. 46, no. 3, 2005, pp. 366-92.

———. *Pat Barker.* Contemporary British Novelists-Manchester UP, 2005.

Brittain, Vera. *Because You Died: Poetry and Prose of the First World War and After* (2008). Ed and Intro. by Mark Bostridge. Virago, 2010.

Burton, Pierre. *Vimy.* McClelland & Stewart, 1986.

Carleton, Sean. "Drawn to Change: Comics and Critical Consciousness." *Labour: Le Travail,* vol. 73, Spring 2004, pp. 150–77.

Christopolou, Zacharoula. "The Literature and Memory of World War I. Remarque, Aldington and Myrivilis: Fictionalizing the Great War." *James A. Rawley Graduate Conference in the Humanities* (8 Apr. 2006), Paper 9, pp. 1–14. www.digitalcommons.unl.edu.

Corrigan, Gordon. *Mud, Blood and Poppycock: Britain and the First World War.* Cassell, 2004.

Cruz, Consuelo. "Identity and Persuasion: How Nations Remember Their Pasts and Make Their Futures." *World Politics,* vol. 52, no. 3, 2000, pp. 275–312.

Cumyn, Alan. *The Sojourn* (2003): Emblem-McClelland & Stewart, 2004.

Dawson, Jill. *The Great Lover: A Novel.* Harper-Perennial, 2009.

DeGroot, Gerard J. *Blighty: British Society in the Era of the Great War.* Longman, 1996.

Donaldson, Allan. *Maclean.* Vagrant-Nimbus, 2005.

Dyer, Geoff. *The Missing of the Somme.* Hamish Hamilton, 1994.

Eigenbrod, Renate. "A Necessary Inclusion: Native Literature in Native Studies." *Studies in American Indian Literatures,* vol. 22, no. 1, Spring 2010, pp. 1–19.

Elton, Ben. *The First Casualty* (2005). Black Swan, 2006.

Emery, Neil. "Into Battle: A Chronology of Charley's War," in Mills, Pat. *Charley's War: 2 June 1916–1 August 1916 (2004).* Illustrated by Joe Colquhoun. Titan, 2004: np.

Fabian, Johannes. *Memory Against Culture: Arguments and Reminders.* Duke UP, 2007.

Farrell, JG. *Troubles* (1970). Phoenix-Orion, 1993.

Feo, Katherine. "Invisibility: Memory, Masks and Masculinities in the Great War." *Journal of Design History,* vol. 20, no. 1, 2007, pp. 17–27.

Findley, Timothy. "Everything I Tell You Is the Truth: Except the Lies." *Journal of Canadian Studies*, vol. 31, no. 2, 1996, pp. 154–65.

———. *The Wars* (1977). Penguin, 1986.

Fisher, Susan. "Hear, Overhear, Observe, Remember: A Dialogue with Frances Itani." *Canadian Literature*, no. 183, Winter 2004, pp. 40–56.

———. "War of Words." *Canadian Literature*, no. 173, Summer 2002, pp. 198–204. EP1–12.

Flannery, Eoin. "Irish Cultural Studies and Postcolonial Theory." *Postcolonial Text*, vol. 3, no. 3, 2007, pp. 1-9.

Flothow, Dorothea. "Popular Children's Literature and the Memory of the First World War, 1919-39. *The Lion and the Unicorn*, vol. 31, no. 2, Apr. 2007, pp. 147–61.

Foreman, Michael. *War Game* (1993): Pavilion, 1997.

Freud, Sigmund. "Mourning and Melancholia (1917)." *The Standard Edition of the Complete Psychological Worlds of Sigmund Freud, Volume XIV (1914–1916): On the History of the Psycho-Analytic Movement, Papers on Metapsychology and Other Works: 237–58*. http://www.english.upenn.edu/~cavitch/pdf-library/Freud MourningAndMelancholia.pdf.

Fussell, Paul. *The Great War and Modern Memory* (1975). Oxford UP: 2013.

Gordon, Neta. *Catching the Torch: Contemporary Canadian Literary Responses to World War 1*. Wilfred Laurier UP, 2014.

Greenberg, Jonathan D. "Generations of Memory: Remembering Partition in India/Pakistan and Israel/Palestine." *Comparative Studies of South Asia, Africa and the Middle East*, vol. 25, no. 1, 2005, pp. 89–110.

Gubar, Marah. "On Not Defining Children's Literature." *PMLA*, vol. 126, no. 1, Jan. 2011, pp. 209–16.

Hanson, Neil. *The Unknown Soldier: The Story of the Missing of the Great War* (2005). Corgi, 2007.

Härting, Heike and Smaro Kamboureli. "Introduction: Discourses of Security, Peacekeeping Narratives, and the Cultural Imagination in Canada." *University of Toronto Quarterly*, vol. 78, no. 2, Spring 2009, pp. 659–86.

Hartnett, Sonya. *The Silver Donkey* (2004). Illustrated by Don Powers. Candlewick, 2007.

Hastings, Tom. "'Their Fathers Did It to Them': Findley's Appeal to the Great War Myth of a Generational Conflict in *The Wars*." *Essays on Canadian Writing*, no. 64, Summer 1998, pp. 85–103. EP1–22.

Herron, Tom. "Dead Men Talking: Frank McGuinness's *Observe the Sons of Ulster Marching towards the Somme*." *Éire-Ireland*, vol. 39, nos. 1–2, 2004, pp. 136–62.

Higonnet, Margaret R. "War Toys: Breaking and Remaking in Great War Narratives." *The Lion and the Unicorn*, vol. 31, no. 2, Apr. 2007, pp. 116–31.

Hill, Jacqueline. "Art Imitating War: *Observe the Sons of Ulster Marching towards the Somme* and Its Place in History." *Études-Irlandaisis*, vol. 34, no. 1, 2009, pp. 37–52. EP1–14.

Hochschild, Adam. *To End All Wars: How the First World War Divided Britain*. MacMillan, 2011.

Hodgins, Jack. *Broken Ground* (1998). Douglas Gibson-McClelland & Stewart, 1999.

Holmes, Richard. *Tommy: The British Soldier on the Western Front 1914–18*. HarperPerennial, 2005.

Hughes Jachimiak, Peter. "'Woolly Bears and Toffee Apples': History, Memory, and Masculinity in *Charley's War*." *The Lion and the Unicorn*, vol. 31, no. 2, 2007, pp. 162–75.

Hutchison, Hazel. "The Art of Living Inward: Henry James on Rupert Brooke." *The Henry James Review*, vol. 29, no. 2, Spring 2008, pp. 132–43.

Huyssen, Andreas. "Present Pasts: Media, Politics, Amnesia." *Public Culture*, vol. 12, no. 1, 2000, pp. 21–38.

Itani, Frances. *Deafening* (2003). Phyllis Bruce–HarperPerennial, 2004.

Kabir, Ananya Jahanara. "Gender, Memory, Trauma: Women's Novels on the Partition of India." *Comparative Studies of South Asia, Africa and the Middle East*, vol. 25, no. 1, 2005, pp. 177–90.

Kant, Immanuel. *The Critique of Judgement* (1892), 2E. Translated by JH Bernard. http://oll.libertyfund.org/titles/kant-the-critique-of-judgement.

Kendall, Tim, ed. *Poetry of the First World War: An Anthology*. Oxford UP, 2013.

Kiberd, Declan. "Frank McGuinness and the Sons of Ulster." *The Yearbook of English Studies Vol. 35: Irish Writing Since 1950*, 2005, pp. 279–97.

Kirk, John. "Recovered Perspectives: Gender, Class, and Memory in Pat Barker's Writing." *Contemporary Literature*, vol. 40, no. 4, Winter 1999, 603–26.

Labio, Catherine. "What's in a Name? The Academic Study of Comics and the 'Graphic Novel.'" *Cinema Journal*, vol. 50, no. 3, Spring 2011, pp. 122–26.

Lanegran, Kimberly. "Truth Commissions, Human Rights Trials, and the Politics of Memory." *Comparative Studies of South Asia, Africa and the Middle East*, vol. 25, no. 1, 2005, pp. 111–21.

Lawrence, Iain. *Lord of the Nutcracker Men*. Dell Laurel-Leaf-Random House Children's, 2001.

Lawson, Tom. " 'The Free-Masonry of Sorrow'?: English National Identities and the Memorialization of the Great War in Britain, 1919-31." *History & Memory*, vol. 20, no. 1, Spring–Summer 2008, pp. 89–120.

Le Naour, Jean-Yves. *The Living Unknown Soldier: A Story of Grief and the Great War* (2004). Trans. Penny Allen. Arrow, 2006.

Lewis-Stempel, John. *Six Weeks: The Short and Gallant Life of the British Officer in the First World War* (2010). Orion, 2011.

Lloyd, David. "The Indigent Sublime: Specters of Irish Hunger." *Representation*, no. 92, Autumn 2005, pp. 152-85.

Lockerd, Martin. "Into Cleanness Leaping: Brooke, Eliot, and the Decadent Body." *Journal of Modern Literature*, vol. 36, no. 3, Spring 2013, pp. 1–13.

Loughran, Tracey. "Shell Shock, Trauma, and the First World War: The Making of a Diagnosis and Its Histories." *Journal of the History of Medicine and Allied Sciences*, vol. 67, no. 1, Jan. 2012, pp. 94-119.

MacCallum-Stewart, Esther. " 'If They Ask Us Why We Died': Children's Literature and the First World War 1970-2005." *The Lion and the Unicorn*, vol. 31, no. 2, Apr. 2007, pp. 176–88.

Mann, Susan, Ed. and Intro. *The War Diary of Clare Gass 1915–1918*. McGill UP, 2000.

Martin, Elaine. "Graphic Novels or Novel Graphics? The Evolution of an Iconoclastic Genre." *Comparatist*, vol. 35, May 2011, pp. 170–81.

McCall, Sophie. "Intimate Enemies: Weetigo, Weesageechak, and the Politics of Reconciliation in Tomson Highway's *Kiss of the Fur Queen* and Joseph Boyden's *Three Day Road*." *Studies in American Indian Literatures*, vol. 25, no. 3, Fall 2013, pp. 57–85.

McDonald, Donna M. "Not Silent, Invisible: Literature's Chance Encounters with Deaf Heroes and Heroines." *American Annals of the Deaf*, vol. 154, no. 5, Winter 2010, pp. 463–70.

McGuinness, Frank. *Observe the Sons of Ulster Marching towards the Somme*. Faber & Faber, 1986.

"*Maisie Dobbs* (book review)." *Kirkus Reviews*, 15 May 2003, p. 713.

Mills, Pat. *Charley's War: 2 June 1916-1 August 1916.* Illustrated by Joe Colquhoun. Titan, 2004.

Minogue, Sally and Andrew Palmer. "Women and Dead Babies in Modern English Fiction." *Journal of Modern Literature*, vol. 29, no. 3, 2006, pp. 103–25. EP1–30.

Morpurgo, Michael. *Private Peaceful* (2003). Scholastic, 2006.

Moseley, Merritt. "Revaluation: J.G. Farrell's *Troubles*." *Sewanee Review*, vol. 119, no. 3, Summer 2011, pp. 489–93.

Mosse, George L. *Fallen Soldiers: Reshaping the Memory of the World Wars.* Oxford UP, 1990.

Murray, Nicholas. *The Red Sweet Wine of Youth: The Brave and Brief Lives of the War Poets.* Little Brown, 2010.

Nel, Philip. "The Fall and Rise of Children's Literature." *American Art*, vol. 22, no. 1, Spring 2008, pp. 23–27.

New, WH. "Review Essay: Ice Crystals." *Journal of Modern Literature*, vol. 23, nos. 3–4, 2000, pp. 565–73.

Nicolson, Juliet. *The Great Silence: 1918-1920 Living in the Shadow of the Great War.* McArthur, 2009.

Norton-Taylor, Richard. "Executed Soldiers to Be Given Pardons." *The Guardian*, 15 Aug. 2006. Online. www.theguardian.com. 13 July 2014.

O'Malley, Seamus. "Amnesia and Recovery of the Great War in Plays by McGuinness and Barry." *New Hibernia Review*, vol. 16, no. 4, Winter 2012, 110–26.

Oliver, Neil. *Not Forgotten.* Hodder & Stoughton, 2006.

Ormiston, Rosalind. *First World War Posters.* Foreword by Gary Sheffield. Flame Tree, 2013.

Palmateer Penee, Donna. "Imagined Innocence, Endlessly Mourned: Postcolonial Nationalism and Cultural Expression in Timothy Findley's *The Wars*." *ESC: English Studies in Canada*, vol. 32, nos. 2-3, 2008, pp. 89–113. EP1–26.

Panaou, Petros and Frixos Michaelides. "Dave McKean's Art: Transcending Limitations of the Graphic Novel Genre." *Bookbird: A Journal of International Children's Literature*, vol. 49, no. 4, Oct. 2011, pp. 62–67.

Parker, Peter. *The Last Veteran: Harry Patch and the Legacy of War.* Fourth Estate, 2010.

Patch, Harry with Richard van Emden. *The Last Fighting Tommy: The Life of Harry Patch, the Oldest Surviving Veteran of the Trenches* (2007). Bloomsbury, 2008.

Pegler, Martin. *Sniping in the Great War.* Pen & Sword Military: 2008.

Persico, Joseph E. *Eleventh Month, Eleventh Day, Eleventh Hour: Armistice Day, 1918 World War I and Its Violent Climax* (2004). Random, 2005.

Phelan, Tom. *The Canal Bridge.* Lilliput, 2005.

Rigney, Ann. "Transforming Memory and the European Project." *New Literary History*, vol. 43, no. 4, Autumn 2012, pp. 607–28.

Robben, Antonius CGM. "How Traumatized Societies Remember." *Cultural Critique*, vol. 59, Winter 2005, pp. 120–64.

Royle, Trevor. *The Flowers of the Forest: Scotland and the First World War.* Birlinn, 2007.

Ruben, Joey. "A Writer Takes Off at 90." *Publishers Weekly*, Jan. 29, 2007, p. 53.

Sassoon, Siegfried. "Repression of War Experience" *Never Such Innocence: Poems of the First World War.* Ed. Martin Stephen. Everyman-Dent, 1993: 302–03.

Saunders, Rebecca and Kamran Aghaie "Introduction: Mourning and Memory." *Comparative Studies of South Asia, Africa and the Middle East*, vol. 25, no. 1, 2005, pp. 16–29.

Shaddock, Jennifer. "Dreams of Melanesia: Masculinity and the Exorcism of War in Pat Barker's *The Ghost Road.*" *MFS Modern Fiction Studies*, vol. 52, no. 3, 2006, pp. 656-74.

Shechter, Andi. "Out of the Genre Ghetto: New Approaches, Standalones, and Smaller Publishers Redefine Mystery." *Library Journal*, 1 Apr. 2004, pp. 36-39.

Smethurst, Toby and Stef Craps. "Phantasms of War and Empire in Pat Barker's *The Ghost Road.*" *ariel: A Review of International English Literature*, vol. 44, nos. 2–3, Apr.–July 2013, pp. 141–67.

Spivak, Guyatri Chakravorty. "Three Women's Texts and a Critique of Imperialism." *Critical Inquiry*, vol. 12, no. 1, Autumn 1985, pp. 243–61.

Stamp, Gavin. *The Memorial to the Missing of the Somme.* Profile, 2007.

Stead, CK. *Mansfield: A Novel.* Vintage, 2004.

Stedman, ML. *The Light Between Oceans: A Novel* (2012). Scribner, 2013.

Steffens, Karolyn. "Communicating Trauma: Pat Barker's *Regeneration* Trilogy and W.H.R. Rivers's Psychoanalytic Method." *Journal of Modern Literature*, vol. 37, no. 3, 2014, pp. 36–55.

Stevenson, Randall. *Literature and the Great War 1914-1918.* Oxford UP, 2013.

Strachan, Hew. *The First World War*. Penguin, 2004.

Sullivan, Joan. *In the Field*. Breakwater, 2012.

Tabachnick, Stephen E. "The Graphic Novel and the Age of Transition: A Survey and Analysis." *English Literature in Transition, 1880–1920*, vol. 53, no. 1, 2010, pp. 3–28.

Talbot, Robert J. "'It Would Be Best to Leave Us Alone': First Nations Responses to the Canadian War Effort, 1914-18." *Journal of Canadian Studies/Revue d'etudes canadiennes*, vol. 45, no. 1, Winter 2011, pp. 90–120.

Thermaenius, Pehr. *The Christmas Match*. Uniform, 2014.

Thompson, Eric. "Canadian Fiction of the Great War" *The War Novel*, pp. 81–96. http://cinema2.arts.ubc.ca/units/canlit/pdfs/articles/canlit91-War(Thompson).pdf.

Trumpener, Katie. "Memories Carved in Granite: Great War Memorials and Everyday Life." *PMLA*, vol. 115, no. 5, Oct. 2000, pp. 1096–1103.

Turner, James West and Suzanne Falgout. "Time Traces: Cultural Memory and World War II in Pohnpei." *The Contemporary Pacific*, vol. 14, no. 1, 2002, pp. 101–31.

Urquhart, Jane. *The Stone Carvers* (2001). Emblem-McClelland & Stewart, 2002.

———. *The Underpainter* (1997). McClelland & Stewart, 1998.

van Emden, Richard. *The Quick and the Dead: Fallen Soldiers and Their Families in the Great War*. Bloomsbury, 2011.

Vance, Jonathan F. *Death So Noble: Memory, Meaning, and the First World War*. UBCP, 1997.

Vandaele, Jeroen. "Humor Mechanisms in Film Comedy: Incongruity and Superiority." *Poetics Today*, vol. 23, no. 2, 2002, pp. 221–49.

Weaver, Jace. "More Light Than Heat: The Current State of Native American Studies." *American Indian Quarterly*, vol. 31, no. 2, 2007, pp. 233–55.

Weintraub, Stanley. *Silent Night: The Story of the World War I Christmas Truce* (2001). Plume-Penguin, 2002.

Whitehead, Anne. "Open to Suggestion: Hypnosis and History in Pat Barker's *Regeneration*." *MFS Modern Fiction Studies*, vol. 44, no. 3, 1998, pp. 674–94.

Williams, Chris. "Slashing the Hun with Cartoons." *BBC History Magazine*, Dec. 2016, pp. 43-46.

Williams, David. "A Force of Interruption: The Photography of History in Timothy Findley's *The Wars*." *Canadian Literature*, no. 194, Autumn 2007, pp. 54–73. EP1–25.

———. *Media, Memory, and the First World War*. McGill-Queen's UP, 2009.

Williams, Jennifer H. "The Canon and the Cutting Edge: Teaching the Graphic Novel." *Pedagogy*, vol. 12, no. 1, 2009, pp. 193–99.

Winspear, Jacqueline. *Birds of a Feather: A Novel* (2004). Penguin, 2005.

———. *Maisie Dobbs: A Novel* (2003). Penguin, 2004.

Winter, Jay. *Sites of Memory, Sites of Mourning: The Great War in European Cultural History*. Cambridge UP, 1995.

Wurtz, James F. "Representing the Great War: Violence, Memory, and Comic Form." *Pacific Coast Philology*, vol. 44, no. 2, 2009, 205–15.

Wyile, Herb. "Jane Urquhart: Confessions of a Historical Geographer." *Essays on Canadian Writing*, no. 81, Winter 2004, 58–83.

Zunshine, Lisa. "What to Expect When You Pick up a Graphic Novel." *SubStance*, vol. 40, no. 1, 2011, pp. 114–34.

Note: Where a document was unavailable in original format but was consulted in a digital edition, pages were assigned EP ("electronic pagination") numbers beginning at "1" for reference purposes.

Index

Brian Kennedy is Montreal-born and raised, and now teaches British and postcolonial literature as well as writing courses at Pasadena City College, California. He has a PhD in contemporary British literature, and his previous publications include essays on Virginia Woolf, Henry James, and Graham Greene, an edited book on California issues, and books and academic articles on hockey and Canadian culture. He has held a research fellowship at Saint Mary's University, Halifax; given presentations at the Bakhtin Centre at the University of Sheffield, England; and lectured on literature at colleges in Mumbai, India. His work has been translated into Russian, Spanish, Portuguese, and Dutch.